ML 1WK

UNIVERSITY OF STRATHCLYDE

D0414661

Thatcher and Thatcherism

Thatcherism produced dramatic changes in most aspects of public life, both in Britain and abroad. *Thatcher and Thatcherism* surveys the origins and impact of Thatcherism as a cultural construct and an economic creed. Centring on the career of Margaret Thatcher, the author argues that Thatcherism was a bold experiment in ideologically driven government that failed to meet its objectives while nevertheless decisively shifting the political landscape of Britain.

Thatcher and Thatcherism includes discussion of:

- privatisation and the fate of the trade unions;
- Britain's slow economic decline versus Thatcher's delusions of British grandeur;
- the legacy of the Falklands and of Britain's approach to Europe;
- education, the civil service and crime;
- the poll tax fiasco;
- Thatcher's legacy and its impact on both the Major and Blair governments.

This second edition has been substantially revised and expanded. Eric J. Evans draws on the latest political memoirs and archives from the Thatcher Foundation to shed new light on her career, prime ministership and fall. Also included is a new chapter which evaluates the continuing influence of Thatcher after her removal from power in 1990. It discusses the extent to which the 'New Labour project' represents a continuation of Thatcherite centralism by other means. The second edition also includes a critical discussion of the election results since 1979 and a chronology of key events.

Eric J. Evans is Professor of Social History and Head of Department at the University of Lancaster. His many books include *William Pitt the Younger* (1999), *Sir Robert Peel* (1991), *The Great Reform Act of 1832* (2nd edition, 1994) and *The Forging of the Modern State, Early Industrial Britain, 1783–1870* (3rd edition, 2001).

The Making of the Contemporary World

Series Editors: Eric J. Evans and Ruth Henig

The Making of the Contemporary World series provides challenging interpretations of contemporary issues and debates within strongly defined historical frameworks. The range of the series is global, with each volume drawing together material from a range of disciplines – including economics, politics and sociology. The books in this series present compact, indispensable introductions for students studying the modern world.

Thatcher and Thatcherism

Second edition

Eric J. Evans

Routledge
Taylor & Francis Group

LONDON AND NEW YORK

First published 1997
by Routledge
11 New Fetter Lane, London EC4P 4EE

Simultaneously published in the USA and Canada
by Routledge
29 West 35th Street, New York, NY 10001

Second edition published 2004 by Routledge

Routledge is an imprint of the Taylor & Francis Group

© 1997, 2004 Eric J. Evans

Typeset in Times by Prepress Projects Ltd, Perth, Scotland
Printed and bound in Great Britain by TJ International Ltd, Padstow, Cornwall

British Library Cataloguing in Publication Data
A catalogue record for this book is available from the British Library

Library of Congress Cataloging in Publication Data
Evans, Eric J., 1945–
   Thatcher and Thatcherism/Eric J. Evans.–2nd ed.
      p. cm. – (The making of the contemporary world)
Includes bibliographicical references (p.) and index.
1. Thatcher, Margaret. 2. Conservatism–Great Britain–History–20th century.
3. Great Britain–Politics and government–1979–1997. 4. Conservative Party
(Great Britain) 5. World politics–1945–1989. I. Title. II. Series
   DA591.T47 E94 2004
   941.085′8′092–dc22

ISBN   0–415–27012–X (hbk)
       0–415–27013–8 (pbk)

Contents

Acknowledgements

The production of this book has been greatly facilitated by the help of many who have shared their insights with me both in private conversation and by more formal comment. I would particularly like to acknowledge the contributions of three. My co-editor, Ruth Henig, has generously shared with me her much more hands-on knowledge of the contemporary political world. Mike Goldsmith, of Salford University, gave up a considerable amount of time to making detailed suggestions for improving the manuscript, not least by sharing with me his immense knowledge of local government scholarship. Heather McCallum's enthusiasm for what was at the time of the first edition the new *Making of the Contemporary World* was vital. She combined unfailing cheerfulness and enthusiasm with the shrewdest appraisals of what was possible within the context of the Series. Her astute judgement had a considerable influence on the structure and shape, if not the argument, of the book. This new edition is, of course, considerably expanded and this has given me the opportunity not only to update but also to expand my ideas. I hope that Heather will be gratified to know that the basic principles underpinning the volume remain in place six years on.

All of the above, and many others, have saved me from much error. For that which remains, I am entirely responsible.

Eric Evans
Lancaster, October, 2003

Preface

Six years have passed since the first edition of this book was published. They coincide with the first six years of what is sometimes called the 'New Labour project' under the premiership of Tony Blair. In October 2002, Margaret Thatcher announced that, on medical advice, she would take no further part in public life. This revised, and considerably expanded, second edition judges the significance of both of these developments. For the first time, it is possible to make a judgement about the extent of Thatcher's influence not only in office but 'in the wings' after she fell from power. What was the final chapter in the first edition has been divided into two to enable more extended coverage of the extent of Thatcher's influence after 1990. This includes evaluation of the extent to which Blair has governed on Thatcherite principles. Elsewhere, I have treated Thatcher's foreign policy in more detail. I have made some changes to every chapter and have, of course, brought the Guide to further reading up to date. Thatcher is of scarcely less interest to publishers in 2003 than she was in 1997, and much of value has appeared in the last six years.

As a historian whose writings have mostly covered an earlier period of British history, I have been fascinated by the tendency for emphases and judgements about a contemporary figure to alter over a short space of time. This is, in many respects, a different book from the one I wrote in 1997. My overall assessment of Thatcher has perhaps not altered much, but my judgement about her longer-term significance certainly has. She was, without doubt, the most influential Prime Minister of the second half of the twentieth century. She irrevocably altered the political landscape of the United Kingdom (UK) and also altered – for good or ill – the reputation of the UK beyond these shores. Returning to her career confirms at least one judgement about the nature of political influence. Outsiders with talent, determination and energy are always likely to make more important, and more lasting, changes to the landscape than those who emerge from within a political élite. They are inclined to make more difference, and few political leaders have mattered more than Margaret Thatcher.

Eric Evans
Lancaster, August 2003

Chronology

1925	Margaret Thatcher is born, as Margaret Roberts, the daughter of a grocery retailer, in Grantham (Lincolnshire).
1935–43	Attends Kesteven and Grantham Girls' Grammar School.
1943–7	Attends Oxford University, reading for a degree in Natural Sciences, specialising in chemistry.
1947–51	Works as a research chemist and begins part-time study as a lawyer.
1950	Fights the constituency of Dartford (Kent) for the Conservatives.
1951	Fails in the general election to win Dartford at the second attempt although the Conservatives win power from Labour. Marries Dennis Thatcher.
1953	Gives birth to twins: Mark and Carol.
1954	Having qualified as a lawyer, is called to the Bar by Lincoln's Inn, takes her bar finals and begins working as a tax lawyer.
1959	Elected as Conservative MP for Finchley when the Conservatives, under Harold Macmillan, win the general election with an increased majority.
1961–4	Takes up her first government post as Parliamentary Secretary in the Ministry of Pensions and National Insurance.
1964–70	Holds a succession of front-bench posts while the Conservatives are in opposition under the leadership of Alec Douglas-Home and Edward Heath.
1967	Becomes a member of the Shadow Cabinet.
1970	Becomes Secretary of State for Education and Science when the Conservatives win the general election, a post that she holds throughout the Heath government (1970–4).
1974	Briefly becomes shadow spokesperson on the environment and on Treasury matters. The Conservatives lose two general elections under Heath.

1975   Challenges Heath for the party leadership and wins (February) on the second ballot. Becomes Leader of the Opposition and the first woman leader of a major political party in the UK.

1975–9 Is Leader of the Opposition during a period when Labour either has a very small majority or, from 1978, is kept in office only with the support of the Liberal Party. During the winter of 1978–9, the so-called 'Winter of Discontent', there is a rash of strikes and growing fears about trade union power works against Labour.

1979   Labour loses a confidence vote in the House of Commons, which precipitates a general election, held in May. The Conservatives win with an overall majority of forty-three. Thatcher becomes Prime Minister. The change in economic policy is signalled by a reduction in the rate of income tax and a substantial increase in the rate of value added tax (VAT). Thatcher begins to implement stringent deflationary economic policies, which lead to sharp rises in unemployment amid a general recession. The Conservatives also win sixty of the seventy-eight seats in elections for the first European Parliament. The Lancaster House Conference agrees to free elections in Southern Rhodesia (Zimbabwe), leading to that country's independence. Conservative legislation restricts trade union rights to picketing and attacks the 'closed shop'. Changes in immigration regulations remove the automatic right of the husbands or fiancés of those settled in the UK to join them.

1980   Geoffrey Howe's budget reveals the deflationary 'medium-term financial strategy'. Rioting in Bristol (April). Unemployment exceeds 2 million.

1981   Rioting in Brixton (April), Liverpool and Manchester (July). The Scarman Inquiry criticises levels of poverty in inner cities and calls for more sensitive policing. The British Nationality Act creates three categories of British citizen.

1982   Unemployment exceeds 3 million. The Falklands War takes place in May and June after Argentinians invade and occupy the Islands (April). In June, Argentine forces surrender after British forces capture Port Stanley.

1983   The Conservatives win the general election with an overall majority of 144 (June). Thatcher is elected a Fellow of the Royal Society. The United States invades the Commonwealth island of Grenada without consulting the UK. US cruise missiles are sited at Greenham Common (November).

1984   The National Union of Mineworkers (NUM) strike begins (March). At Fontainebleau, the EC budget rebate to Britain is settled (June) and a permanent British contribution to EC funds settled. An Irish Republican Army (IRA) bomb explodes in the Grand Hotel, Brighton, during the Conservative Party conference (October). Thatcher narrowly escapes injury. The sale of British Telecom (November) is the first of the major 'privatisations' of public utilities and other companies, which continue into the 1990s. An agreement is signed between China and the UK, which sees Hong Kong revert to Chinese control from 1997. The second European elections see the Conservatives win forty-five seats to Labour's thirty-two.

1985   The NUM strike ends in victory for the employers – and the government. Riots in Brixton and Handsworth (September). The Anglo-Irish Agreement is signed by Thatcher and the Irish Prime Minister, Garret Fitzgerald. The Irish Republic government is given a limited say in the affairs of Northern Ireland. Security liaison between Britain and Ireland improves. Thatcher refuses to support Commonwealth proposals for further sanctions against South Africa. The Local Government Act abolishes the Greater London Council and metropolitan councils, whose functions are transferred to smaller district councils.

1986   A crisis over the Westland helicopter company leads to the resignations of Michael Heseltine and Leon Brittan from the Cabinet (January). The Single European Act is signed (February). The Northern Ireland Assembly is dissolved (June). A print workers' strike is defeated by papers owned by Rupert Murdoch. Thatcher allows US warplanes to fly from Britain to attack targets in Libya.

1987   The Conservatives win the general election with an overall majority of 102 (June). Unemployment levels fall below 3 million (June). The government announces that a new Community Charge (poll tax) will be introduced in Scotland in 1989 and in England and Wales in 1990. A stock exchange crash (Black Monday) sees £50 million wiped off share values (October).

1988   The Immigration Act tightens controls over immigration. The top rate of income tax is reduced to 40 per cent and a further fall in the standard rate is introduced. Thatcher gives a speech in Bruges opposing moves towards greater European unity

(September). General Certificate of Secondary Education (GCSE) examinations replace separate GCE Ordinary Level and Certificate of Secondary Education (CSE) examinations. The Education Reform Act introduces the national curriculum to be followed in all state schools. MPs vote to allow the televising of parliamentary debates. The Employment Act gives workers the right to ignore the result of a union ballot in favour of strike action. A US Boeing is blown up by Libyan terrorists over Lockerbie, Scotland (December).

1989   More than 3 million residents of Hong Kong holding British passports are refused the right to residency in the United Kingdom. Britain rejects the European Social Charter (May). Thatcher becomes the longest serving Prime Minister of the twentieth century, beating the nine years of Winston Churchill. The Third European elections see considerable Conservative losses: the Conservatives win thirty-two seats, Labour forty-five. Interest rates reach 15 per cent. Cruise missiles are removed from Greenham Common (August). After disputes between the Chancellor of the Exchequer, Nigel Lawson, and Thatcher's economics adviser, Alan Walters, both resign (September/October). John Major becomes Chancellor of the Exchequer. Anthony Mayer challenges Thatcher for the leadership of the Conservative Party (December).

1990   Anti-poll tax riots in London (March). The Employment Act makes it unlawful to refuse to employ people not in a trade union. Thatcher is awarded the Order of Merit. National Health Service legislation introduces market mechanisms, via 'purchasers and providers'. Britain joins the European Monetary System (EMS) at an exchange rate of 2.95 deutschmarks, which many commentators consider far too high (October). Geoffrey Howe resigns from government and makes a damaging resignation speech in the Commons (November). Heseltine announces a challenge to Thatcher's leadership (November). Thatcher fails to get an overall majority in the first leadership ballot and withdraws from the second after Cabinet ministers tell her that she is unlikely to win. Her prime ministership ends (November).

1992   Thatcher leaves the Commons at the dissolution of parliament before the general election, having represented Finchley for the Conservatives continuously since 1959. Takes her seat in the House of Lords as Baroness Thatcher of Kesteven.

1 The 1970s

Explanations and origins

INTRODUCTION

Margaret Thatcher is an extraordinary phenomenon. She is the only woman Prime Minister in British history. She was Prime Minister from May 1979 to November 1990, and eleven and a half years was a comfortably longer stint than anyone else achieved in the twentieth century. She also held the office for a longer continuous period than anyone for more than a century and a half – in fact, since Lord Liverpool's fifteen-year tenure was prematurely halted by a stroke in 1827. She won three successive general elections, the last two with landslide majorities. No other party leader in the last century won more than two, and then with smaller majorities overall. Although it is still too early to be sure, the claims of Thatcher's supporters that she changed the course of British history cannot be lightly dismissed as either heroine worship or grandiose posturing. At the very least, she cast a long – opponents would say baleful – shadow across the two main political parties into the twenty-first century. Controversial and partisan as she was, she also changed the mind-set of the nation.

Change as moral crusade was the leitmotif of her career. As early as 1977, when asked by the right-wing journalist Patrick Cosgrave, who was then acting as one of her special advisers, what she had changed, she replied, simply, 'Everything'.[1] When she was preparing her first Queen's Speech in 1979, a speech which many of her detractors say she would like to have given in person, it was uppermost in her thinking: 'If the opportunity to set a radical new course is not taken', she wrote in her memoirs, 'it will almost certainly never recur . . . . I was determined to send out a clear signal of change'.[2]

Certainly, she shook the country up. Certainly, too, she exercised the most profound effect on the structure and social composition of the Conservative Party, which she led for nearly sixteen years, from

February 1975 to November 1990. Her influence on the Labour Party was scarcely less substantial. 'New Labour', it might be argued, was the logical response to Thatcherite hegemony in the 1980s. Thatcher also profoundly altered the nature and orientation of the governmental machine. She required a fundamental reappraisal of the role and loyalties of the civil service, which, like most professional structures, she was determined to turn upside down.

Once she had found her feet, she addressed both the nation and international political leaders in hectoring tones. Straightforward, simplified and frequently moralistic, messages were conveyed with insistent, repetitive clarity. Thatcher transformed, by ignoring, the nuanced subtleties of international diplomacy. She became more readily recognised worldwide than any figure in British public life, except perhaps the most prominent, or notorious, members of the royal family. Her leadership, policies and personality alike, excited stronger passions, for and against, than those of any other twentieth-century Prime Minister, with the possible exception of Lloyd George.

IDEAS?

Thatcher was the only twentieth-century Prime Minister to become eponymous. The use of the term 'Thatcherism' might be taken to imply a more or less coherent body of thought or ideology, much as well-established terms such as 'Liberalism', 'Marxism' or, indeed, 'Conservatism' do. Thatcherism is markedly different from any of these. It offers no new insights and, although profoundly ideological on one level, it is better seen as a series of non-negotiable precepts than as a consistent body of thought.

Most modern commentators share the present writer's view that Thatcherism does not represent a coherent ideology. Jim Bulpitt sees Thatcherism continuing a traditional Conservative preoccupation with 'statecraft' – by which is meant winning elections and retaining control of high politics. The then editor of the *Daily Telegraph*, in a sympathetic valedictory piece written the day after Thatcher announced her resignation in November 1990, asserted that 'Thatcherism . . . is not really an economic doctrine at all. It is a powerful collection of beliefs about the capacities of human beings in political society'. Sheila Letwin, another Thatcher sympathiser, sees individualism as the key attribute. Her view is that, since people naturally follow what they perceive as their own interests, Thatcher was merely drawing upon basic human motivation, rendering it a political programme relevant to the circumstances of the late 1970s and 1980s.[3]

Those who see Thatcherism as an ideology fall into two categories. Tory 'wets', like Gilmour and Prior (see below, pp. 15 and 20–1), accused her of slavish adherence to monetarism when traditional Conservatism was rooted in pragmatism, flexibility, compromise and common sense.[4] Marxists (see Chapter 10), who rarely think other than ideologically anyway, tend to see Thatcherism as an ideological campaign, in the interests of the capitalist rich and powerful, to create new forms of political and cultural domination over the underprivileged.[5]

Debates about ideology, often politically motivated and intellectually sterile, should not be allowed to deny Thatcherism its visceral power. Thatcher had no difficulty identifying what she was *against*: state interference with individual freedom; state initiatives that encourage an ethos of 'dependency'; woolly consensuality; high levels of taxation; the propensity of both organised labour and entrenched professional interests to distort market forces; and a reluctance to be 'pushed around', either personally or as a nation-state. In one sense, being 'against' all of these implies that their obvious antitheses will guide policy: individual rights; private enterprise within a free market; firm, perhaps authoritarian, leadership; low levels of personal taxation; union and vested interest bashing; simple patriotism.

Thatcherism embodies a series of interconnected political attitudes rather than a coherent body of thought. Few of these attitudes are new. Free trade ideology developed out of Adam Smith's distinctive contribution to the eighteenth-century European Enlightenment and reached its apogee in the Liberalism of William Gladstone, who fought – and lost – a general election in 1874 on the policy of abolishing income tax. Disraeli and Salisbury in the last third of the nineteenth century both exploited patriotism, through the burgeoning British Empire, as an effective vote winner for the Conservatives in the first age of mass politics. Attacks on the grasping, exploiting professions were the small change of eighteenth-century satire, while trade unions were widely tolerated in Victorian society only when their members – mostly a highly skilled minority of the labouring population – used collective activity in the furtherance of capitalist objectives rather than as a challenge to the dominant ideology of the age.

The importance of Thatcherism, therefore, lay not in the novelty of its ideas but in the context of their operation in the late 1970s and 1980s. Two facts stand out. First, she actually believed in, and drew strength from, a set of precepts which most sophisticated politicians in the 1970s – not least those in her own party – found almost unbelievably crude and shallow. Second, she retained throughout her career the unshakeable conviction that the domestic virtues she had absorbed from a dominating father in a lower middle-class, non-conformist home – hard work, taking personal responsibility, prudence, thrift, plain dealing and an over-riding concern to see that the books balanced – could be transferred into the public sphere as guiding precepts for government. In a television interview broadcast in January 1983, she asserted that her views were 'born of the conviction which I learned in a small town from a father who had a conviction approach'.[6]

We should not exaggerate either the ordinariness of Thatcher's origins or the extent to which their political philosophies intertwined. Her public recollections of her father seem to have been conveniently selective. On one point, though, all would agree. Alfred Roberts moved up in the world on the basis of talent and hard work. From a modest beginning in the archetypal 'corner shop' just after the end of the First World War, he invested his small profits in the purchase of adjacent properties in the mid-1920s. He went into local politics at about the same time, opposing the Labour Party and, particularly, the co-operative retail movement. He became an alderman in 1943 and, as Mayor of Grantham in 1945–6, had indubitably arrived as a big man in that small town. 'Alderman Roberts' remained a figure of some substance there until his death.[7] Drawing on both his Methodist background (he was a local preacher) and his involvement in Grantham affairs, Thatcher's father was very much more communitarian in outlook than she was. Officially an independent, he had Conservative leanings if anything, but was a Conservative of the 'one-nation' type. He possessed the successful shopkeeper's interest in, and knowledge of, his customers, and he was careful to involve himself in a wide range of the town's main social and political activities. He does not appear to have made the same kinds of often censorious moral distinctions between social groups that his daughter was prone to do, and his 'convictions' had little to do with conflict and the need to win victories over 'inferior' ideologies. Alderman Roberts had his enemies and he knew who his political opponents were, but he was no 'conviction politician', as his daughter implied.

The reasons for Margaret Thatcher's political success are complex and will be examined in detail later in the book, where the role of luck will be evaluated. However, it is clear that she possessed political skills of a very high order. She extracted maximum benefit from the fact that she was not an orthodox political 'insider' at a time when 'insider politics' were coming under increasingly hostile scrutiny. She could engage with the aspirations of the lower middle classes because she had been brought up as one of them, and she developed a genius for presenting her own attitudes, values and beliefs as if they were beacons of common sense. At least from the early 1970s, she viewed established politics – mired and ensnared by misbegotten notions of consensus and the enfeebling apparatus of state provision – much as early nineteenth-century radicals viewed the political system before the Reform Act of 1832: as 'Old Corruption'. She offered a battered and disillusioned electorate a new beginning based on old truths. She presented herself as a 'conviction politician' who would roll back the frontiers of the state. As she told the House of Commons in 1983, hers was a vision of 'long-term economic growth' based on the creation of an 'enterprise culture'.[8]

EARLY CAREER

The 'newness' of Thatcherism was personal and political, not ideological. She was not an original thinker. Furthermore, little in her career before the early 1970s suggested that she was in any way an exceptional, still less a mould-breaking, politician. She served her constituents in the north London suburb of East Finchley capably but unremarkably from her first election in the Conservative landslide of 1959. She rose steadily, and loyally, in the party hierarchy under the leadership of Edward Heath from 1965 to 1970. By the time of his rather unexpected victory at the election of 1970, she was sufficiently senior to be promoted to the middle-ranking post of Secretary of State for Education. Here, although she reversed Labour policy by halting the drive towards compulsory comprehensive schooling, she nevertheless assented to the creation of more comprehensive schools than any Education Secretary before or since. Although she already enjoyed a good argument, she revealed little of her later propensity for shaking received departmental orthodoxies and humiliating civil servants and junior ministers who disagreed with her. She was a rather conventional secretary of state by the standards of the time. Ironically, in view of her later reputation as the scourge of 'big government', her conventional view of a minister's duties encompassed a strenuous and successful fight against the severe expenditure cuts that were a feature of the first two years of Heath's government. She attracted widespread publicity only for withdrawing free school milk from children over the age of seven. Although the easy slogan 'Margaret Thatcher, milk snatcher' was regularly heard, the policy was not an example of robust radicalism. Rather, it reflected the dominant perception that the health value of free school milk was a declining asset when most families were enjoying rising living standards and a much more varied diet.

It could not be said, therefore, that Thatcher had established herself by the early 1970s as a dynamic new force in British political life. Rather the reverse. She was cautious, competent and gave the outward impression of wanting to fit in. But politics is a volatile and uncertain business in which luck plays a quite outrageous part. Had the Conservatives won fewer popular votes but four more seats than Labour in the February 1974 general election, rather than the other way round, then it is likely that the Thatcher phenomenon would not have been unleashed upon the world. Criticism of Heath's government had become increasingly forceful within the Conservative Party after the collapse of a brief economic boom engineered by his Chancellor of the Exchequer, Anthony Barber. This was followed by the imposition of wage controls, industrial unrest and, in response to the latter, the imposition of a power-saving three-day week. Heath gambled that he could break a damaging miners' strike by appealing to the country on the cry of 'Who governs Britain?'. The gamble almost paid off; the election could have gone either way. Indeed, in terms of votes cast and seats won, it did. The Conservatives won almost 200,000 more votes than Labour but four fewer seats. For a few days afterwards, an electoral pact with the Liberals, which would have kept Heath in Downing Street, seemed possible. However, he lost office in March 1974 and failed to win it back in October when the Labour Prime Minister, Harold Wilson, called another election to secure an overall majority, which he only just achieved. Nevertheless, the Conservative share of the popular vote dropped from 37.9 per cent in February to 35.9 per cent – the only occasions it had been below 40 per cent since 1945.[9] Indeed, the party's share in October 1974 was the lowest in the century until the John Major debacle of 1997 (see Chapter 11).[10]

THE CONSERVATIVE LEADERSHIP

Heath had therefore lost two desperately close elections within eight months. Had he won either, he would have retained, or regained, the premiership. Margaret Thatcher would, in all probability, have remained a tolerably loyal and efficient, if unimaginative, Cabinet minister hoping for further promotion by working with the political grain of Heathite Conservatism rather than against it. By the time Heath would have retired, or resigned, five years or more later, other challengers would most likely have made their mark. The Conservative Party is, however, notoriously intolerant of electoral defeat, and Heath's departure after the second election of 1974 was inevitable. What was *not* inevitable was Thatcher's succession. During the last months of the Heath administration, it is true, she had become increasingly disenchanted with the way in which yet another post-war government elected with high promise seemed unable to break out of the cycle of economic boom followed by slump, unable to control the power of the unions, unable to halt

Britain's apparently inexorable economic decline. The rapid, and largely unforeseen, rise in oil prices in 1973–4 served to heighten the sense of crisis. It was now much easier to argue that only a radical new approach would do.

Thatcher allied herself with the radicals on the right of the Tory Party. She was not, however, their intellectual leader. Sir Keith Joseph fulfilled that role, and even he had inherited it from the now hopelessly marginalised Enoch Powell, probably the twentieth-century politician with the largest brain and the smallest amount of common sense. Joseph articulated a coherent critique of what was known as 'consensus politics' and advocated most of the economic policies that later became known as distinctively Thatcherite. He called for a smaller role for the state, steep cuts in taxation and greater incentives for businesses to chase markets. As they won profits, they would create new jobs in industry, thus helping to reverse the years of economic decline. Successful competition within a free market was a much more effective means of securing full employment than the essentially defensive, spoiling tactics of an overpowerful and arrogant trade union movement. At a speech in Preston in September 1974, Joseph argued that a priori government commitment to full employment was cruelly mistaken. The state could not guarantee jobs. It could only pay for them on borrowed, or printed, money. In the longer term, such a policy would destroy the very objective it sought.[11]

This frontal assault on the central tenet of Keynesianism – the dominant economic belief of both Labour and Conservative governments since 1945 that governments could 'manage' demand in order to secure full employment – proved immensely influential. Above all, following the theories of the so-called Chicago school of anti-Keynesian economists, F. A. Hayek and Milton Friedman, Joseph called for strict control of the money supply.[12] Put crudely, Joseph and the right-wing economists who had influenced him believed that successive governments had paid for welfare provision by printing money. The consequence was inflation, the rate of which had been increasing sharply and which now threatened to spiral out of control. After some years of fluctuation between 5 and 10 per cent, it rose to 24 per cent in 1974.[13] Inflation ate away at the value of people's savings, demoralised and literally devalued a lifetime of effort. It was also likely to lead to political instability and social conflict, even in mature democracies. For monetarists, therefore, inflation was the prime target.

Although Keith Joseph was the most senior, and probably the intellectually best equipped, advocate of policies that were becoming increasingly influential within the Conservative Party, he had considerable weaknesses as a potential leader. Like many who are excited by ideas, he tended to spend more time on reflection than on action. He did not always distinguish well between small print and large. The civil servants with whom he worked, most of whom admired him enormously, could nevertheless be driven to distraction both by the delays taken in reaching even straightforward decisions and by the retrospective hand-wringing that followed complex ones. Perhaps fatally for his leadership prospects, he did not always distinguish effectively between the logical conclusion of a closely reasoned argument and the need to make such conclusions politically attractive or expedient. He suffered enormous political damage during a speech about social policy in the Birmingham constituency of Edgbaston a week after the October election of 1974 when he suggested that those feckless and disorganised folk in the lowest social classes, whose high birth rates were a disproportionate charge on the social services budget, should be directed to practise contraception. Partly because of this gaffe, but mostly because he was clear-headed enough to realise his own political limitations, he stood aside when the challenge to Edward Heath's leadership was launched in November 1974.

Into the breach stepped Margaret Thatcher. She would not have stood against Joseph but was now the only Cabinet minister prepared to oppose the Conservative leader. Her performance in the first leadership ballot by Tory MPs vindicated her decision. She won 130 votes to Heath's 119, a more than respectable performance for a candidate who was relatively untried; it was, nevertheless, short of the 15 per cent lead required for a knockout victory. However, a combination of Heath's stubbornness and the misplaced loyalty shown to him by William Whitelaw, the standard-bearer of the centre-left, played into Thatcher's hand. Much of her support came from MPs who wanted Heath out far more than they wanted her in. Wits at the time called it the 'Peasants' Revolt', knowing that most of those who voted for her had been back-benchers vexed by Heath's high-handed ways and bemused by the shock of losing two elections in a year. In no sense did their votes represent a commitment to monetarist policies or, come to that, to the views of the ordinary delegates to Conservative Party conferences. Had Whitelaw, a classic example of the principled Tory gent, pressed his own claims earlier, there is little doubt that the centre of the party would have rallied to him. As it was, his moment passed. Margaret Thatcher won almost twice as many votes as Whitelaw in the second ballot, gaining an eighteen-vote majority over both him and the three other contenders. For the first time – but certainly not the last – Thatcher benefited from taking a clear stand against the established élite of her own party. The Tory Party faithful had gained a leader who understood their motivation and prejudices.

CONTEXT

The immediate context of Thatcher's great experiment in government needs more exposition. Three closely linked factors can usefully be identified. The first revolves around Britain's growing economic troubles during the period of the so-called Keynesian consensus, roughly from 1945 to 1973. This period saw both unprecedented social advance – characterised by effective welfare provision, better housing, sharply rising living standards and successive consumer booms – and accelerating relative economic decline. For right-wing thinkers, the social successes were, if not illusory, then certainly unsustainable. In the period 1950–70 they had been funded by economic output, which had increased by approximately two-thirds. The problem was that other nations' output had been increasing much faster. Britain had, therefore been slipping down a succession of league tables. During the decade 1962–72, for example, France sustained an annual growth rate of 4.7 per cent, while Britain could manage only 2.2 per cent. In the period 1969–73, the annual rate of gross domestic product (GDP) per employee for European Economic Community (EEC) countries was 4.63 per cent, while in Britain it was 2.79 per cent. This represented a substantial improvement on the position in the late 1950s, although still a relative decline. Whereas Britain had been ninth in the international league table of GDP per head, it had fallen to fifteenth in 1971 and would fall further – to eighteenth – by 1976.[14] Right-wing theorists tend to look particularly hard at a culture that permits restrictive labour practices to flourish. They were, therefore, fiercely critical of the powerful role exercised by British trade unions, particularly during periods of Labour government. Statistics showing that labour productivity in the United States ran approximately 50 per cent higher than that in Britain, while West Germany productivity was more than one-quarter higher,[15] suggested to economists and right-wing politicians alike that trade unions should receive particular attention in the developing critique. The circumstances surrounding the fall of Heath's government – the only Tory administration during what was to prove to be a fifteen-year period dominated by Labour – gave extra force to the argument.

The second relevant factor is the crisis of confidence caused by the end of the long post-war boom in the late 1960s. By the early 1970s, international agreements on fixed exchange rates were breaking down, creating a volatile economic climate, which was substantially worsened by the oil crisis of 1973–4. Britain, like many countries following Keynesian prescriptions, attempted to sustain domestic demand in order to keep unemployment levels low. Even so, by 1971, the number of people out of work reached almost a million, roughly three times the average levels of the 1950s and 1960s. Keynesian anti-unemployment policies could be pursued only at the risk of building up inflationary pressures. These were exacerbated during periods of economic growth when British consumers developed an understandable, but economically distressing, preference for overseas manufactures – particularly Japanese cars and electronics. Adverse balance of payments figures mounted alarmingly. A trade deficit of £110 million in 1965 had reached £1,673 million by 1975.[16] At the end of 1973, the quadrupling of oil prices, which brought a short period of growth to a shuddering halt, threatened to put inflation into orbit. In Britain, it reached a peak of 26.9 per cent in August 1975.[17] The value of the pound continued to plummet on international markets. Formally devalued in 1967, it lost a further 30 per cent of its value between 1971 and 1975.

The symbolic nadir of Britain's decline was the revelation in 1971 that Rolls Royce, for so long the talisman of the nation's manufacturing excellence, was bankrupt. It was saved from going under, but only at the cost of creating a government-owned company that ate up huge amounts of taxpayers' money. By the middle of the 1970s, the tide seemed to have turned decisively in favour of monetarism. Keynesianism now appeared to be a busted flush: a one-way street to hyperinflation and political instability. Restrictions on money supply and tight restrictions on government expenditure appeared to be the only roads back to economic virtue and governability.

The third contextual factor requires a brief look at the economic policies of the Wilson and Callaghan Labour governments, which staggered on, first with a tiny parliamentary majority and later by virtue of a pact with the Liberal Party, from 1974 to 1979. The electorate had invested limited confidence in Labour in 1974, probably on the basis that only a party that had close links with the trade unions could save the country from ungovernability at a time of profound economic strain. Labour attempted to respond. A 'Social Contract' was cobbled together whereby the governing party agreed to discuss with union leaders, almost on a basis of equality, the major questions of the day. In return for this the unions agreed to recognise an obligation wider – more patriotic even – than their members' pay packets. For a time, the Contract delivered. Both inflation and pay demands became more moderate in the years 1976–8. From the mid-1970s, significant amounts of North Sea oil and gas were beginning to become available. In 1978, North Sea oil produced more than one-half of the country's energy needs. The prospects both of energy self-sufficiency and perhaps even of permanent economic recovery began to brighten.

Labour's experiment with consensus, however, went hand in hand with policies for meeting continuing short-term crises. One such appeared during 1976 and it had profound consequences. Labour's Chancellor of the Exchequer, Denis Healey, proposed to deal with yet another run on the pound by a strict set of economic measures: stringent reductions in expenditure, wage restraint and moves towards a balanced budget. These, of course, were the key tenets of monetarist economic policy. It is worth stressing that the first post-war moves towards deflation and sound money came not from Thatcher or her new-right gurus, but from a Labour government. Callaghan told the Labour Party conference directly in 1976: 'You cannot spend your way out of recession' – but neither he nor Healey was a free agent.[18] The Bank of England's reserves were so depleted, and the currency so depreciated, that the government felt an international loan necessary to stave off the prospect of currency collapse or even bankruptcy. The International Monetary Fund's loan of $3.9 million naturally came with further deflationary strings attached in the form of additional expenditure cuts. Although in part externally imposed, and therefore divisive internally, monetarist economic policies were alive and well within the Treasury and the upper echelons of the Labour Party in the years 1976–8. Monetarism in Britain pre-dated the Thatcher government.

Naturally, the Tories exploited Labour discomfiture and disunity. Much was made of a Labour government needing to go cap in hand to international bankers. A key feature of Opposition speeches in the years 1976–9 was loss of sovereignty and a weakening of the authority of government. Thatcher was also keen to stress the importance of Britain's full commitment to the North Atlantic Treaty Organisation (NATO) and, particularly, to the alliance with the United States. To this extent, she was stressing traditional Tory commitment to a strong Britain linked to its powerful 'natural' ally. She seems not to have considered the extent to which Americans any longer saw Britain as at all 'special'. In economic terms, Thatcher naturally stressed her belief in new-right, deflationary policies. However, since Denis Healey was busy putting many of these into place anyway, the general theme was that Labour was acting under duress. Only the Tories could be trusted to continue with policies of prudence and sound money.[19]

Two factors brought the Callaghan government down. The first is the one most usually stressed. The internal contradictions of maintaining a deflationary policy in a party whose paymaster was the trade unions proved too much during the winter of 1978–9, the so-called 'winter of discontent' that followed the unions' rejection of yet another pay restraint, this time a 5 per cent limit. The Social Contract, which the

Conservatives had always claimed to be an illusion, finally fell apart. The rash of strikes brought back to the centre of debate claims about 'ungovernability' and the need for firm action. Popular hostility to unions 'holding the nation to ransom' was gleefully stoked by a generally anti-Labour press. The second factor in Labour's demise has received less attention, at least in England. However, it was the party's failure to carry through its proposals for devolution in Scotland and Wales that alienated the minority parties and which left Callaghan vulnerable to a vote of no confidence, which he eventually lost by a single vote on 28 March 1979.[20] 'We shall take our case to the country', Callaghan defiantly told the Commons when the result was announced. Privately, he was far from confident that the coming general election was winnable.

2 Election and depression, 1979–81

THE SIGNIFICANCE OF 1979

Good fortune contributed at least as much to Margaret Thatcher's becoming Prime Minister in 1979 as it had to her winning of the Conservative leadership four years earlier. Not surprisingly, this crucial element was given little emphasis by Thatcher herself. Her clear, but simplified and determinist, explanation of the victory allowed for luck only in terms of how sensibly the public would react to a demonstrably superior Tory message:

> The Government's defeat in the confidence debate symbolized a larger defeat for the Left. It had lost the public's confidence as well as Parliament's. The 'winter of discontent', the ideological divisions in the Government, its inability to control its allies in the trade union movement, an impalpable sense that socialists everywhere had run out of steam . . . . The Tory Party, by contrast, had used its period in Opposition to elaborate a new approach to reviving the British economy and nation. Not only had we worked out a full programme for government, we had also taken apprenticeships in advertising and learnt how to put a complex and sophisticated case in direct and simple language. We had, finally, been arguing that case for the best part of four years, so our agenda would, with luck, strike people as familiar common sense rather than as a wild radical project.[1]

That Thatcher's explanation contains considerable truth is not to be doubted, but how 'new' was the Tory approach and how consistently, and insistently, had it been put across since Thatcher became leader? Thatcher, quite rightly, laid great stress on the electoral consequences of the winter of discontent. She might have had to put her 'complex and sophisticated case' across in less favourable circumstances. With the International Monetary Fund's 1976 stringencies fading from the memory, and an election to win, the Chancellor of the Exchequer's spring budget of 1978 had been reflationary. One author has called it 'Healey's last Keynesian fling'.[2] Healey was providing the Prime Minister with the normal platform for electoral recovery, while the party attempted to re-establish some semblance of unity behind a realistic pay policy.

Although Healey's budget can be seen in retrospect as storing up trouble by encouraging expectations that the government could not meet, in the short term his financial manipulations opened up a window of electoral opportunity. Despite the traumas of the past three years and unemployment at nearly 1.4 million – in post-war terms, damagingly high – signs were appearing by the summer that the government was beginning to regain popularity. Callaghan, who had made something of a speciality of commonsensical television 'fireside chats', booked himself an appearance in early September. The general expectation was that, in the course of one of his standard-issue avuncularities, the Prime Minister would announce a general election to be held the following month. Unsure how robust Labour's partial political recovery would prove to be during the rough and tumble of an election campaign, however, he confided that there would be no immediate election. Perhaps a leader who had held a longer lease on power (Callaghan had been Prime Minister only since the spring of 1976 and loved the job, particularly his weekly audience with the Queen) would have taken the risk. As it was, during the winter that followed, the fates, the Scottish nationalists and, above all, the unions combined to bring crashing down that rickety edifice that was Labour's election chances. The loss of a confidence motion in the Commons (see Chapter 1) also deprived Callaghan of the most valuable perk available to a Prime Minister: the ability to choose an election date to maximise his party's chances of victory. Thatcher *might* have won in October 1978; she could hardly have lost in May 1979.

How united were the Tories? Thatcher and her advisers, notably Keith Joseph and the economist Alfred Sherman, had indeed long planned her 'new approach' for reviving the economy. A new right-wing Centre for Policy Studies had been set up in 1974 to challenge financial and other orthodoxies. It was, however, far from clear that her party was willing to swallow their bitter medicine of savage deflation and free market determination of wages that the right advocated with increasing stridency during the years of opposition. The Shadow Employment Secretary, James Prior, certainly was not. *The Right Approach to the Economy*, published in October 1977 as the basis of the party's programme for the next election, demonstrated clearly enough the battle that was being waged for the soul of the party. Crucially, the question of whether it believed in incomes policy was fudged in generalities about consultation with both employers and unions.

Thatcher had beaten Heath for the leadership in 1975, but this did not mean that she could do as she wished. Nearly all of her initial Shadow Cabinet had voted for Heath. Even after she had dismissed six Heathites, replacing them with more congenial right-wingers such as John Biffen and Angus Maude, most of the Shadow Cabinet remained in the centre, or centre-left, of the party. Some – such as Prior, Maudling and Hailsham – were too senior to sack. Many had inherited wealth and had been brought up to old-style traditions of service. They distrusted ideology, believing it to be inimical both to the proper practice and to the electoral prospects of Conservatism. Their most elegant writer, Ian Gilmour, had been delivering a waspish and snobbish, if coded, warning about the dangers of leadership by the defensive lower middle classes as early as 1975:

> We cannot really believe that this is the moment for the party of Baldwin and Churchill, of Macmillan and Butler, of the Industrial Charter and the social advances of the 1950s to retreat behind the privet hedge into a world of narrow class interests and selfish concerns.[3]

In 1977, Gilmour published *Inside Right*, a developed statement of his centre-leftist philosophy of Conservatism. Replete with historical and theological allusions, it savaged Thatcherite economics, denouncing 'the *sans culottes* of the monetarist revolution'. Gilmour also cheekily attempted to distance the Conservative Party from any contamination with ideology: 'British Conservatism is not an "-ism". It is . . . not a system of ideas. It is not an ideology or a doctrine'.[4] The leader had, indeed, marked him down for the tumbril but she could not afford to sharpen the guillotine just yet. After all, she had still to pass her own acid test: winning a general election. She knew perfectly well, as she told the television interviewer and ex-Labour MP Brian Walden, that the still entrenched party élite would allow her only one chance at that.[5] As the election approached, Edward Heath made a speech to the party conference of 1978 in which he advocated the continuance of pay policy under an incoming Conservative government. In her reply, Thatcher made clear her own strong preference for free collective bargaining. As so often, she spoke directly to the minds of the party faithful, who cheered her to the rafters. She knew, however, that many Shadow Cabinet colleagues remained unconvinced and were unsure whether she could sell her message to the electorate. The winter of discontent changed the political landscape dramatically, making it much easier for Thatcher to argue that her view must prevail. Conciliation, accommodation and consensus had all been tried, yet the winter's rash of damaging strikes, particularly in the public sector, demonstrated their futility.

The Conservative Manifesto, which had been planned almost one year earlier, underwent minor revisions largely to exploit the public's anti-union mood. It promised to tackle the problem of secondary picketing, whereby those not directly involved in a strike turned up, often in threateningly large numbers, to 'offer support' to their fellow workers. The manifesto also contained a pledge to help more people buy their own homes. Overall, however, it looked little different from the 1970 manifesto on which Edward Heath had won. Pledges to improve education and health services found a prominent place, as did support for the police and a commitment to strengthen Britain's defence systems. The Tory manifesto of 1979 offered some evidence of Margaret Thatcher's distinctive sense of mission. It promised to rebuild the economy and offer fresh hope to 'a divided and disillusioned people'.[6] Specific statements about economic policy, however, were rare. For example, no mention was made of privatisation, which was to be the central plank of Thatcherite economic policy during the 1980s.

During the campaign, also, Thatcher reined in her natural combativeness. She took lessons in speech delivery and presentation from the Tory Director of Publicity, Gordon Reece; she lowered her voice, learned to speak more slowly and generally softened her image. The effect was certainly less strident, but also eerily synthetic. Party managers nevertheless claimed to detect increased voter appeal and Reece would gain a knighthood for his skills in image manipulation. As the campaign proceeded, Thatcher deployed a fine range of political skills. She presented herself as someone passionate for change in order to rebuild Britain's morale yet not as someone likely to veer off in wild or uncharted directions. In April and early May 1979, she frequently relied upon that caution and canniness that is an important, but understressed, part of her political make-up. Knowing that the Labour Party and its union supporters had all but lost the election before it started, she avoided risk.

Callaghan attempted to exploit one of the very few advantages that Labour possessed in 1979 – his greater personal popularity than Thatcher. He dropped into his practised, indeed threadbare, routine as the experienced uncle who had seen it all and who was solid, unflappable and secure. He could be trusted both to see it through and to see Britain right. Old voters must have been reminded of Stanley Baldwin, the long-serving, pipe-smoking Conservative Prime Minister of the 1920s and 1930s. One newspaper cartoon summed up Callaghan's image brilliantly: 'If you want a Conservative Prime Minister, I'm your man'. Baldwin, however, never had to face a winter of discontent and when faced with his own challenge from the unions – in the General Strike of 1926 – he defeated it. The Callaghan image was in any case duplicitous. The outgoing Prime Minister was never as nice as he seemed; he could be testy, overbearing and manipulative. In any event, Thatcher had an effective riposte for Callaghan's promotion of consensus as the way forward. In one of the few examples in which that notoriously humourless lady used irony wittingly and with success, she told an interviewer who charged her with divisiveness:

> The Old Testament prophets did not say 'Brothers I want a consensus'. They said: 'This is my faith, this is what I passionately believe. If you believe it too, then come with me.'[7]

The Tories' election advertising was also superior to Labour's. Saatchi and Saatchi, in charge of this aspect of the campaign, produced one spectacularly effective poster. It depicted a dole queue snaking into the distance and it carried the caption 'Labour isn't working'. It was perfectly true that deflationary policies had driven unemployment comfortably over the million mark. Naturally, the Tories concealed the fact that they planned to see it rise much higher still.

Thatcher's victory was decisive, but not overwhelming. The Conservatives won 339 seats to Labour's 269 and had an overall majority of forty-three seats. They won just short of 43.9 per cent of the popular vote, the lowest proportion in modern times for a party winning a clear overall majority. The swing away from the Labour government, however, was larger than had been experienced at any election since 1945. Who had voted for Thatcher, and for what, in practice, had they voted?

First, considerably more had voted against Labour than had voted positively for the Conservatives. Nevertheless, negative votes produce positive outcomes, and some striking new patterns emerged in May 1979. Labour's long-term position had been jeopardised by a decline in the number of manual workers in the electorate. Twice as many manual workers normally voted Labour as voted Conservative, but they now constituted only 56 per cent of the electorate. When Wilson won narrowly in 1964, they had accounted for 63 per cent. Worse, as Ivor Crewe's detailed study showed, they were beginning to turn against the trade unions – alienated, no doubt, by the shenanigans of the winter of 1978–9.[8] In contrast, Tory policies stressing wider home ownership proved very popular, particularly among the upper working classes of southern England.

Electoral geography, it can now be seen, was of much greater significance than short-term swings or the precise numbers of seats won. Historically, the Conservative Party has always been stronger in England than in the other countries of the United Kingdom. It has also performed better in the rural areas and small towns of England than in its industrial heartlands.[9] Within England, however, it has usually been able to show a reasonable spread of support. The 1979 election showed a significant change. Swings to the Conservatives were much less pronounced in the north of England than in the south. Compared with 1955, when the Tory lead over Labour in terms of seats was very similar to 1979, Thatcher's Conservative Party won thirty-four more seats in the south and Midlands, twenty fewer in the north of England and fourteen fewer in Scotland. Thatcher was winning where the economy was relatively strong and losing where it was contracting. Clearly, her message of effort, thrift and individual self-reliance struck a chord where economic opportunity was likely to reward these virtues and not, indeed spectacularly not, where jobs were in much shorter supply. As Peter Jenkins put it:

> Labour was becoming the party of decline, the Conservative Party the party of growth. Slowly the political culture of the south was moving northwards ... colonising the Midlands, ghettoising Labour's strength in the inner cities and the urban centres of manufacturing decline.[10]

This chasm would widen over the next decade, and this is one of the main reasons why Thatcher's period in office proved to be one of such bitterness. Whereas in the 1870s Benjamin Disraeli worked with considerable success to make the Conservatives regularly electable by stressing its 'one-nation' appeal, almost exactly a century later Margaret Thatcher's first electoral success showed that the Conservatives could win power by appealing to the better-off. Notwithstanding the regulation soothing, mendacious platitudes on the steps of No. 10 Downing Street the day after an election – and Thatcher was brazen enough to quote St Francis of Assisi there on the afternoon of 4 May 1979: 'Where there is discord, may we bring harmony' – the message appeared to be that the British people had elected a government that believed in the virtues of competition but which now needed only to appeal to that competition's winners in order to hold power. Nothing symbolised the end of the cross-party consensus more starkly.

THE COURAGE OF HER CONVICTIONS?

Winning general elections is one thing, using the power they bestow to effect change is quite another. In Thatcher's view, although Harold Wilson and Edward Heath had achieved the former, they had spectacularly failed in the latter. Thatcher was determined not to repeat their mistakes. It was her rooted conviction that the biggest mistake they had made was in trying to preserve a played-out consensus. She was also aware that the profound economic destabilisation of the 1970s had affected most Western democracies. Everywhere, so it seemed, high-taxing, big-government administrations were in trouble. Thatcher had some justification for believing that the great experiment she now intended to launch could become part of a change that would affect the whole of the developed world.

Great thoughts are, however, often belittled by practicalities. Thatcher the free market visionary yielded place in important respects to Thatcher the hard-headed politician. Large pay rises were immediately granted to the police and armed forces. After all, a visionary government might need to defend itself and, in any case, Thatcher knew well enough how well the redemption of this election pledge would play with her natural constituents. A second pledge, however, was much more tactical and much more costly. The Conservatives had agreed during the election campaign to honour any recommendations that might be made by Hugh Clegg to rectify pay anomalies that had opened up in recent years between workers in the public and private sectors. The general tendency during the 1970s had been for workers with muscle to bludgeon and threaten their way to large pay awards and for those without to lag behind. Callaghan had appointed Clegg, an academic but an old Labour man and sympathetic to the unions, to reintroduce elements of fairness into the process. Instinct told Thatcher that this type of redistributive activity conflicted with her vision of Conservatism; political reality, however, told her that it would lose the support of too many floating voters who were not members of powerful unions to renege on Uncle Jim's promise of largesse. Through 1979 and 1980, the bills for public-sector pay awards kept piling up and, with them, inflation. After one year in office, inflation stood at 22 per cent, more than double what it had been in the last days of Labour. A government pledged to rebirth and renewal by squeezing inflation out of the system had not got off to a good start.

It was because the government knew of inflationary pressures building up that the first budget of the new Chancellor, Geoffrey Howe, actually raised taxes. This was done, however, in ways of which most Conservatives approved since Howe initiated a radical shift from direct to indirect taxation. The top rate of income tax was, therefore, reduced from 83 per cent to 60 per cent to give wealth creators what was deemed the necessary incentive to chase markets and engender elusive economic growth; at the same time, the standard rate went down from 33 per cent to 30 per cent. The key indirect tax, VAT, was almost doubled – from 8 per cent to 15 per cent. Although VAT did not apply to food and some other necessities, taxes on consumption nearly always hit the poor hardest as they must spend a larger proportion of their income on the basics. Thatcher knew well enough how controversial the measure would be. She later explained that a government could only get away with it 'at the beginning of a parliament, when our mandate was fresh'.[11] Her overriding concern, however, was to use this structural shift 'to boost incentives'. Interest rates were also raised to 14 per cent, and would reach 17 per cent by the end of the year. Most who reflected on its implications concluded that the budget helped the rich at the expense of the poor.

Year 1 of the Thatcher revolution also saw other moves towards the achievement of economic freedom, notably the abolition of restrictions on the import and export of capital. Although overseas investment was very attractive for the wealthy, its effects were more than counterbalanced by foreigners' desire to buy North Sea oil, the most important new energy resource of the time. James Prior, rather to his surprise confirmed as Secretary of State for Employment, had introduced a new bill to outlaw secondary picketing and restrict the operation of the so-called 'closed shop'. It became the Employment Act (1980) and was roundly criticised by right-wingers, who wanted much more aggressive measures – such as compulsory ballots before strikes could legally be held and the abolition of sympathetic strikes. In coded messages during television interviews and through carefully placed leaks from her private office, Thatcher contrived to convey the impression that she shared their frustrations.[12]

In year 2, the gloves came off. Thatcher learned fast how government works and felt ever more sure of her ground. This security was at least matched by her furious frustration that more had not been achieved during what Keith Joseph called 'the lost year'.[13] The solution was an unprecedentedly fierce attack on public spending. What was mysteriously called the 'medium-term financial strategy' (MTFS) was revealed during the 1980 budget. This set targets to control the growth in the supply of money. Financial journalists had to master new pieces of jargon, M0 through to M3, as various means of calculating the amount of money in circulation. No one could satisfactorily explain how you measured money supply, why one measure should be favoured over any other or, indeed, whether any measure actually meant very much. Even its main implementor, Nigel Lawson, then a junior minister at the Treasury, soon admitted that 'too much hope was invested in the whole idea and . . . too much . . . claimed for it at the outset'.[14] Monetarism, as implemented, appeared the ultimate triumph of ideology over common sense. It made Ian Gilmour's flesh creep.

While the quality newspapers spread esoteric monetarist references lavishly, and sometimes uncomprehendingly, over their financial pages, the thinking behind it was brutally simple: restrict the supply of money and reduce government borrowing needs and you squeeze inflation out of the system. As inflation was, by 1980, identified as the most potent dragon to be slain, any measures to achieve this, including raising taxes and cutting public spending, could be represented as the lances of St George. In simple terms, Howe and Thatcher were prepared to create an economic slump in order to kill inflation and resurrect the simple notion of 'proper money' for the benefit of the British people.

Howe's 1980 budget, the direction of which was confirmed by its successor the following year, achieved its deflationary ambitions with spectacularly gruesome effect. In 1980–1, manufacturing production fell by 14 per cent, gross national product (GNP) actually contracted by 3.2 per cent and unemployment rose to 2.7 million. Adult unemployment rose more rapidly in 1980 than in any single year since 1930, when the world absorbed the consequences of the Wall Street Crash.[15] Britain lost approximately 25 per cent of its manufacturing production capacity in 1979–81, making the nation ever more dependent upon the provision of services. Had North Sea oil and gas supplies not increased by more than 70 per cent during this very period, it is hard to see how the government could have avoided bankruptcy. The Thatcher inheritance depended critically on North Sea oil.

Silver linings could be glimpsed by those intrepid enough to search for them amid the encircling gloom. It was some comfort that the productivity of those who remained in work during this period increased sharply. This was a key element in the government's drive towards greater international competitiveness. Inflation also began to come down; by the spring of 1982, it was back in single figures. However, this had little to do with monetarism, at least directly. The value of the pound sterling in international markets had appreciated so much in a suddenly oil-rich nation that manufacturers were finding it ever more difficult to sell abroad. The price of imports, which those British who could afford them were still avid to consume, was commensurately low, while the huge rise in unemployment was reducing workers' bargaining power and reducing the rate of wage rises.

As ever with the Thatcherite experiment, the effects of the slump were felt unequally across the country. Old manufacturing areas were hardest hit; those that specialised in services, and particularly financial services, got off more lightly. Inequality began to be institutionalised. Meanwhile, despite the government's best endeavours, public expenditure continued obstinately to rise. It reached 44.5 per cent of gross domestic product (GDP) in 1982. An important reason for its growth was the huge increase in unemployment benefit payments. Taxes were also still rising. The overall burden of taxes, direct and indirect, was calculated at 34 per cent of GDP in 1978–9; by 1982–3, this had risen to almost 40 per cent.

The effects of what Denis Healey wryly termed 'sado-monetarism' caused convulsions both within the Conservative Party during 1981 and outside. A number of riots took place in the inner-city areas of London, Liverpool, Manchester and Bristol. The rarity of such events in twentieth-century Britain was another factor that both alarmed the Tory Party and affronted public opinion, which was more inclined to blame hopelessness and despair born of government policy than it was the intrinsic lawlessness and violence of working-class British youth. Thatcher herself saw matters differently. 'Here' she recalled in her memoirs, 'was the long awaited evidence [for our opponents to argue] that our economic policy was causing social breakdown and violence'. All of this, however, 'rather overlooked the fact that riots, football hooliganism and crime generally had been on the increase since the 1960s, most of the time under the very economic policies that our critics were urging us to adopt'. When she visited the riot area of Toxteth in Liverpool in July 1981, she noted that its housing conditions were not the worst in the city. 'Young people . . . had plenty of constructive things to do if they wanted. Indeed, I asked myself how people could live in such surroundings without trying to clear up the mess and improve their surroundings. What was clearly lacking was a sense of pride and personal responsibility' – and, no doubt, the stern voice of Alderman Roberts to put the fear of God into them.[16]

In January 1981, Margaret Thatcher undertook her first Cabinet reshuffle, promoting promising right-wingers such as John Nott and Leon Brittan and either demoting or sacking wits, 'wets' and centre-left intellectuals such as Norman St John Stevas and Ian Gilmour. Her changes were characteristically cautious, however. Many survivors, for example James Prior, Francis Pym and Michael Heseltine, remained entirely unconvinced about the direction of government policy. What was still a non-monetarist Cabinet was, however, kept largely in the dark concerning economic policy. As Pym later complained: 'The 1981 budget was rigidly deflationary and thus highly controversial at a time of deep recession, yet the strategy behind it was never discussed in Cabinet and was only revealed to the full Cabinet on budget day itself'.[17] Thatcher preferred to formulate policy with Treasury ministers whom she trusted and with economic advisers such as Alfred Sherman and a new appointee, Alan Walters. The Cabinet let her get away with it. Conviction politicians tend to be intolerant of long-winded debate, and Thatcher was a utilitarian, radical about constitutional convention: if it did not provide the support she wanted, then she was quite happy to marginalise it.

Later in the year, James Prior, who seemed incapable of resigning from the government on principle, although he continued to snipe at it covertly, was pushed out to Northern Ireland and as far from Thatcher's sight as could be decently arranged. David Howell, whose tenure at the Department of Energy had long seemed a contradiction in terms, moved to Transport. Prior's replacement at Employment was Norman Tebbit, a self-made man with a sharp brain who preferred robust, if sometimes unreflective, conviction to anguished intellectual pretension and abuse to wit. He was the one of the first of the younger group of able Thatcherites to be promoted to Cabinet office because he was of the truth faith. Along with Nigel Lawson, who replaced Howell at the same time, he was the newcomer to make the greatest impact. His promotion boded ill for the trade unions just as it symbolised Thatcher's long-delayed feeling that she was at last in control of her government team.

In late 1981 and early 1982, we can now see, Thatcher was at her most formidable, although in considerable adversity. She had acquired all the experience necessary to exercise powerful leadership. She could clearly see what fevered speculation in the press about the implications of miserable opinion poll findings and spectacular by-election losses all too readily obscured, that inflation was coming down while productivity was going up. There need be no election for more than two years. Meanwhile, she could face down opposition in the Commons. After all, the Labour Party had considerably greater troubles than the Conservatives. They had lost some of their brightest and best political leaders to the newly formed Social Democratic Party. Worse, they had saddled themselves, in an age when image, appearance and presentation was beginning to matter much more than content, argument or debate, with an inveterately scruffy socialist bibliophile as a leader. Surely Michael Foot was unelectable? Certainly, at Prime Minister's question time Thatcher preferred facing Michael Foot across the despatch box rather than the equally intelligent, and much more brutally effective, Denis Healey. So, although she entered the new year with the lowest approval ratings of any Prime Minister since opinion polling began, she was confident of her position despite mounting speculation that a fearful Conservative Party would replace her as leader before the next election. As she also knew, things in politics have a habit of turning up to transform the scene utterly; 1982 would prove to be the year in which Thatcher discovered popularity to go along with her increasingly formidable sense of destiny.

3 Thatcher triumphant, 1982–8

MRS THATCHER'S CONSTITUENCY

These years saw Margaret Thatcher in her pomp. She achieved absolute dominance within the Conservative Party, which she proceeded to transform (see Chapter 4). Her Cabinet reshuffles in this period were designed to consolidate that dominance. Only those she believed to be true believers of her version of politics were promoted to the highest offices, certainly those concerned with the economy. It is said that the key criterion for promotion from the ranks of the back-benchers was the answer to the simple question: 'Is he one of us?'. The gendered question was doubtlessly unintentional, but significant nonetheless. The first woman Prime Minister did little to advance the political cause of women. Minimal progress was made during the 1980s. Thatcher did appoint Emma Nicholson, a posh and plummy-voiced left-winger who later defected to the Liberals, as vice-chairman of the party, charged with advancing the cause of women. Actual advances oscillated between snail-like and imperceptible. Thatcher opposed Nicholson's suggestion that women should be taxed independently. At the 1983 general election, women Conservative MPs numbered thirteen. In 1987, only forty-six of the 633 Conservative candidates (7.3 per cent) were women. This paltry proportion – considerably lower than Labour's (14.6 per cent) and that of the Liberal/SDP alliance (16.6 per cent) – was nevertheless larger than ever before. However, only seventeen female Conservative candidates were actually elected. Thus, only 4.5 per cent of the parliamentary party that supported Thatcher's last government were women.[1] Nicholson was bitter: 'Had the Conservative Party really wanted it, the pattern could have been changed. The Conservative Party is . . . an army led from the top'.[2]

Thatcher achieved two successive spectacular election victories. In 1983, the Conservatives won 397 seats to Labour's 209; Labour's share of the popular vote (at 27.6 per cent) was only 2 per cent higher than that of the newly formed Alliance Party (an amalgam of defectors from Labour in 1981 – the Social Democrats – and the Liberals). Although Labour, under a new leader, Neil Kinnock, fought a much better campaign in 1987 and succeeded in seeing off the challenge from the Alliance, the party's recovery against the Conservatives was hardly noticeable. The Conservatives won 376 seats to Labour's 229, and maintained their share of the popular vote at 42.3 per cent.[3] The 1987 election, however, also confirmed the growing trend towards two nations (see Chapter 2). The Conservatives won 227 (87 per cent) of the 260 seats in the south and Midlands, with 52 per cent of the popular vote. In Scotland, Wales and much of the industrial north, Thatcher's policies were resoundingly rejected by the electorate.

The system, however, allowed the Prime Minister to ignore these discordant regional messages. Hers were more than merely large election victories. Since 1945, no party had sustained its majority over three successive general elections. The victories gave Thatcher unprecedented authority, which she clearly intended to use to achieve her vision of change. She was in no doubt about the significance of the sledgehammer blows to Britain's political left that 1983 and 1987 represented. As she wrote, with characteristic trenchancy, about 1983: '[it was] the single most devastating defeat ever inflicted upon democratic Socialism in Britain'.[4]

Why were the Tories so successful? The so-called 'Falklands factor' played a huge part in the government's recovery of popularity in 1982–3 (see Chapter 8). Many voters supported the Conservatives in 1983 because they saw in Thatcher a powerful leader who had stood up for Britain against a foreign power. The Conservatives had no compunction about unfurling the patriotic flag. It is worth remembering, however, that the tide of popular opinion was beginning to turn with the economic recovery under way at the beginning of 1982, before the war began. In 1987, the economy – enthusiastically stoked by Nigel Lawson – was roaring away, living standards were increasing rapidly and the great Stock Exchange crash of October was still four months off. The electorate voted for the promise of continued prosperity. The Conservative slogan was simple, mendacious and powerful: 'Britain's Great Again. Don't Let Labour Wreck it'.[5]

Other factors also played a part. The election was fought on redrawn boundaries, which gave a small, but not insignificant, advantage to the Tories. As commentators have also pointed out, the Conservatives had the enormous good fortune to be faced by a divided opposition. Labour's appalling disarray in 1980–1 led to both splits and deep unpopularity.

The Alliance had enough popular support to come a good second in well over 100 constituencies, but in a first past the post system this is of no value. Winning one-quarter of the popular vote will, if that vote is equally spread, secure less than 4 per cent of the seats while handing the largest party a fair number of seats they would have been unlikely to win in a straight fight. This happened in 1983. The Tory share of the popular vote under Thatcher never exceeded 43 per cent – a substantially smaller proportion than Churchill and Macmillan achieved in the 1950s. Yet this produced two landslides, largely because the anti-Tory vote was so evenly split. There is no doubt that the quirks of the British electoral system favoured the Tories and it is no surprise that Thatcher should be so vehement in her defence of its simple virtue of providing secure majority governments – not least for her!

Fastidious commentators queried the legitimacy of pushing through radical and divisive policies supported by little over two-fifths of those who voted and not much more than one-third of the electorate as a whole. Thatcher brushed them aside. She won on the existing rules and could also point out that the Tory lead over their main opponents in both 1983 and 1987 was huge. The populist in her knew perfectly well that the electorate is uninterested in the arcana of constitutional argument, proportional representation and the rest. Such considerations could safely be left to academics, political scientists and the Liberal Alliance. The intelligentsia would, of course, scribble away – but not in the kind of newspapers that Thatcher's new supporters read (see Chapter 6). Thatcher was rightly confident that she was much better at making simple, but powerful, appeals to popular opinion than they were. Furthermore, if her opponents chose to split, that was their affair. The Conservative Party would happily harvest the benefits.

There are, however, some more positive points about support for Margaret Thatcher, which her opponents make grudgingly, if at all. She appealed to important sections of the electorate that had never voted Tory in such large numbers before. The skilled working classes – bloodlessly called the 'C2s' by the Census Office – stood out. In 1987, for example, Thatcher's appeal to their self-interest and their aspirations to self-improvement gave her an 18 per cent lead over Labour among manual workers in the booming south-east of England. Those working-class council house tenants who had recently bought their homes under Conservative policy also proved grateful, and loyal. In the 1987 election, 40 per cent of council house *owners* voted Conservative, virtually the same as the Tories' global share of the vote; only 25 per cent of council house *tenants* did. Labour's traditional constituency, the working class, was in any case eroding both in numbers and in loyalty. Social and economic changes that Thatcherism helped to promote had seen manual workers shrink to less than one-half of the labour force by the late 1980s. The new jobs were predominantly service sector and middle class – historically Conservative territory. In 1983, only 38 per cent of manual workers and 39 per cent of trade unionists voted Labour.

By contrast, the unskilled, when they bothered to vote at all – which they did less often than the better off – still voted Labour. As Peter Jenkins put it, there was a real danger that Labour was becoming the party less of the working class than 'of the underclass'.[6] Thatcher also gave the working classes, especially in the south and the Midlands, powerful negative reasons for voting Conservative. Opinion poll surveys in the early 1980s among what proved to be the 'new' Thatcher voters revealed how averse many of them were to the power and restrictive practices of trade unions and how amenable to the argument that the state had excessive power over people's lives. Their views had changed after a few more years of vigorous Thatcherism, but the prosperity most were enjoying in 1987 kept enough of them loyal.

For some, voting Labour doubtlessly represented a denial of legitimate hopes of economic improvement. It is interesting also that by the end of the 1980s opinion polls were beginning to understate Conservative support and overstate Labour's. This is difficult to explain but may have something to do with the difference between openly *declaring* that one supported a party that appealed pretty nakedly to self-interest and actually *doing* so in a secret ballot.

The pronounced, and ever increasing, regional imbalance in support for the parties also worked in the Conservatives' favour. Labour could count on strong, indeed by 1987 increasing, support in the north of England, Wales and Scotland, but these were areas of economic decline (a decline accelerated by the application of Thatcherite, monetarist policies). Voters were migrating from them towards the more prosperous south and the Midlands. As this happened, so the redistribution of parliamentary seats also favoured the Conservatives. Paradoxically, however, it also helped to save Labour's bacon. As the party could win seats in the more depressed areas almost without lifting a finger, the consequences of Labour's appalling internal mismanagement between 1980 and 1983 were minimised. As Peter Jenkins has pointed out, Labour contrived to win over 200 seats in 1983 when it had less than 28 per cent of the popular vote. In 1931, after a previous great split, it had won 31 per cent of the vote yet only fifty-two seats.[7] The impact of the inherent divisiveness of Thatcherite policies in the 1980s was maximised by electoral geography. By the end of the 1980s, it was difficult to argue against the proposition that a 'Disunited Kingdom' had emerged, with Labour championing a substantial minority of 'losers' and the Conservatives continuing to appeal to the vested interest of 'winners'.

It was not all one-way traffic. Although Thatcher won the Conservatives new working-class voters, her policies, populism and stridency alienated many in the professional and public sector-employed middle classes. For some, although hardly a significant proportion, the opposition was intellectual. They disapproved of what the leading Marxist academic Stuart Hall called Thatcher's 'authoritarian populism' and 'reactionary common sense'.[8] Thatcher could afford to treat left-wing intellectuals with contempt – and relished doing so. For far more, Thatcher's naked dislike of the public sector was the determining factor. It is likely, for example, that more teachers, health service workers and local government administrators in local government voted against the Conservatives in 1987 than ever before. Their salaries had been squeezed and their contributions to national life constantly belittled by a government that made no secret of its belief that national prosperity depended upon the vitality of the private, not the public, sector.

Only about 55 per cent of the middle classes supported the Conservatives in 1987, the lowest proportion since the end of the First World War. This did not threaten their electoral position. First, a fissure had opened up between the private and public-sector middle class. The former was growing in wealth and remained overwhelmingly Conservative. Second, the numbers of the middle classes were increasing every year and the Conservatives were quite happy to trade a slightly lower proportion of a much larger number – particularly as so many of the disenchanted middle classes voted for the Alliance rather than for what Thatcher called the 'real opposition', Labour. Fairness, of course, did not come into it. The Conservatives got a far larger proportion of the seats in the House of Commons than their share of the popular vote might suggest, and the Alliance far less. But so what? Life, as right-wing ideologues constantly preach, is not fair. Political parties, like individuals, make the most of what they have. In 1983 and 1987, the Conservatives made the political weather and could afford to be unconcerned about areas that seemed always to be shrouded in mist and drizzle.

SUPPLY-SIDE ECONOMICS

Thatcher used her political dominance to continue her crusade to transform Britain. In these years, she completed the rout of the trade union movement, reduced both the scope and the independence of local government (see Chapter 5) and subjected many of the professions to the alien rigours of the business ethic (see Chapter 6). Her economic policies, although subtly changed, continued to dance upon the grave of the Keynesian consensus. Hers remained a formidable agenda, driven on by a woman of ferocious energy who knew no life outside politics.

Economic policy was the key. Although the first Thatcher term of office had seen a substantial success, she regarded it as a period of frustration as well as change. She did not have the ministerial team she wanted and, even on the analysis of the true Thatcherite believers, the economic benefits of monetarism were frustratingly slow to appear. As one of Thatcher's most trusted academic advisers, the economist Professor Patrick Minford of Liverpool University, put it: 'In 1979–82 the fight against inflation dominated all else'.[9] As we have seen (Chapter 2), the rate of inflation almost halved during the course of 1982, so Thatcher could justifiably claim victory, at least in the short term. By January 1983, inflation stood at 5.4 per cent, the lowest level since 1970. Norman Tebbit gleefully predicted that Thatcher's government would be the 'first in over twenty years to achieve in office a lower average increase in prices than that of its predecessor'.[10] Inflation would not exceed 7 per cent again until after the 1987 election. The government, keen in this as in so many other matters during the 1980s to present statistics in the most advantageous light, constructed another index, which took the cost of mortgage interest repayments out of the equation. Not surprisingly (as Treasury civil servants had been asked to produce it for precisely this purpose), the alternative measure nearly always showed a lower rate of inflation during this period.

Critics, however, continued to point out that success in the attack on inflation had been partly accidental and in any event won at enormous economic, if not political, cost. Despite the ending of the recession in 1982, unemployment continued to rise. It reached a peak of 3.2 million in 1985, and the cost of unemployment benefit was one important reason why the overall tax burden on those in work continued to increase. Not surprisingly, unemployment statistics were massaged. The government made it less easy to qualify for unemployment benefit and then counted in the official figures only those 'unemployed and claiming benefit'. This reduced the political impact of the monthly figures. Between 1979 and 1996, Conservative governments adjusted the basis upon which unemployment was calculated no fewer than thirty-one times, almost invariably with the objective of reducing the raw figures. Nevertheless, the average unemployment rate in the United Kingdom, even according to deliberately doctored statistics, was 9.1 per cent in the years 1979–89, compared with 3.4 per cent in the period 1973–9 and 1.9 per cent during the largely boom period 1960–73.[11] In strictly economic terms, also, it cannot be claimed that the sharp reduction in inflation brought Britain any competitive edge. It was part of a worldwide trend in the early 1980s and, although the gap had narrowed, other nations within the European Economic Community could still boast both slightly lower inflation rates overall and stronger economies. In the early 1990s, Britain ranked only seventh in the list of the twelve European Union (EU) countries, measured in terms of their GNP.[12] Only Spain, Ireland, Portugal and Greece – all very late industrialising countries with substantial, inefficient agricultural sectors – ranked lower. Germany (even after absorbing the inefficient and underproductive East in 1990), France and the Benelux countries were much higher.

Most workers – and voters – however are unaware of comparative international statistics. They are much more concerned with material benefits, and the boom of the mid-1980s brought plenty of these. Real earnings in the 1980s grew by an average of 2.8 per cent. In the 1970s, only a 0.5 per cent increase had been achieved. Even during the latter stages of the post-war boom in the 1980s, real earnings had grown by only 2.1 per cent. As the boom of the 1980s was accompanied by easy credit, which fuelled massive increases in consumer expenditure, it is probable that living standards grew faster under Margaret Thatcher than under any previous Prime Minister. Certainly, what is now called a substantial 'feel-good factor' emerged, which Conservative politicians naturally exploited to the full in the run-up to the 1987 general election.

This factor was also successfully manipulated by Margaret Thatcher's most able Chancellor of the Exchequer, Nigel Lawson. Thatcher described him, with some justice, as 'imaginative, fearless and . . . eloquently persuasive' and quickly promoted him.[13] He first became Chancellor in October 1983 and held the post until a spectacular falling out with his boss over who was in control of economic policy exactly six years later (see Chapter 10). During most of this historically long period in office, Lawson played politics and economics more or less equally. He had made his name as the originator of the so-called medium-term financial strategy (see Chapter 2) and was expected, therefore, to pursue 'dry' policies such as keeping the money supply tight and reining in any tendency to excessive consumer expenditure, especially on imports. Instead, money targets drifted ever more into the background and had been almost forgotten by the time of the 1987 election. As he was one of the few ministers on the right of the party prepared to argue with Thatcher, he got his way more often than most. It later transpired that he was conducting some aspects of government economic policy without informing the Prime Minister. The 'Lawson boom' was crucial to the Conservatives' election success in 1987, although it stored up enormous problems thereafter when the bills had to be paid during the next economic recession at the end of the decade.

Thatcher and Lawson increasingly disagreed. However, the Prime Minister entirely approved of her Chancellor's policy on taxation, which continued to stress the virtues of low direct taxation as incentives to effort and entrepreneurial zeal. Lawson both reduced and rationalised the tax structure. The rationalisation was completed in March 1988 when Lawson announced an income tax structure comprising only two rates: the standard rate, at 25 per cent, and a uniform higher rate of 40 per cent. Tax cuts served their turn as propaganda in the 1987 election as they have in many others, enabling the Conservatives to present themselves as the party of low taxation. Lawson's rationalisation was also politically astute. As a low top rate affects a large number of only modestly wealthy people as well as the far smaller number of the genuinely rich, any proposal to tinker with the higher rate is open to the charge that it would penalise the middle classes as a whole.

The real irony is that the Tories did not succeed in cutting the overall tax burden. Taxation accounted for 38.5 per cent of GDP in 1979 and 40.75 per cent in 1990. The real increases were in indirect taxation, particularly VAT, and in compulsory National Insurance payments (which are additional direct taxes in all but name). Compulsory insurance payments, even more than VAT, are regressive: they take a much larger proportion out of the pay packets of the poor than those of the wealthy. The consequence of Thatcherite tax policies, as in much other aspects of economic management, was to increase inequality in British society. It is doubtful whether the least wealthy fifth of Britain's population – which of course included the large numbers of unemployed – shared in any in the benefits of the boom of the 1980s. The trend towards greater inequality between rich and poor, which had begun in 1977 under the Callaghan government, increased very substantially under Thatcher, whose policies were widely criticised as having created an 'underclass' not seen since Victorian times. To Thatcher's view of Victorian values, we shall return later (see Chapter 12).

The other major economic success that the government could claim concerned labour productivity. One of the most consistent reasons for Britain's long-term economic decline (which some economic historians argue went back to the last quarter of the nineteenth century) was that productivity per worker in Britain was much lower than in most other developed countries, although not the United States, which historically has a very large proportion of unskilled and recent migrant workers. Investors get weaker returns from the money that they put into low-productivity countries than they do from investment elsewhere. The

1980s saw a dramatic improvement in Britain's relative performance. Whereas in the 1970s Britain had a lower rate of productivity growth (0.6 per cent) than any of the seven largest industrialised economies – the so-called G7 group – during the 1980s the country had moved up to third place, behind only Japan and France. The rate of productivity itself had increased by approximately three times.

Critics of Thatcherite economic policy, however, put this apparently glittering success into wider perspective. Had so much of Britain's manufacturing industry (where low productivity was endemic) not been put to the sword during the recession of 1979–81, then the increase would have been more modest. The improvement depended upon massively increased investment in finance and other parts of the service sector; it served to confirm Britain's virtual disappearance as a leading manufacturing economy.

The numbers of workers in manufacturing industry had been falling since the mid-1960s. Between 1966 and Thatcher's coming to power in 1979, it declined by 15 per cent. The rate of decline, however, accelerated after 1979 and the numbers continued to fall during the economic boom of the mid-1980s. In the decade after 1979, 42 per cent more workers disappeared from manufacturing industry.[14] In 1979, manufacturing industry contributed 26 per cent to the GNP; by 1990, this had declined to 20 per cent.[15] Many new jobs were created to replace those lost in manufacturing during the recovery of the mid-1980s, of course. The overall labour force grew from 22.5 million to 26.9 million in the decade after 1979. However, these were disproportionately in those service industries, such as hotel work and tourism, in which low rates of pay, part-time working and limited job security all obtained. Highest rewards tended to be earned in the finance sector of the economy, where many of the decade's famous 'yuppies' (young upwardly mobile professionals) worked. Unsurprisingly, their years of easy wealth coincided with the zenith of Thatcherism.

As critics also pointed out, when the economy began to recover and consumers found more money in their pockets, their preference for imports remained voracious. Indeed, the miserable fate of so much of Britain's manufacturing sector during the first Thatcher government made it even more likely that consumers would look to Japan and, increasingly, elsewhere in the Pacific Rim for their motor cars and electrical goods. In consequence, balance of payments deficits continued to mount. In 1988, they reached the unprecedented level of almost £15 billion.[16]

Britain's emergence from recession in 1982 gave the government an opportunity to present election-orientated budgets. These gave far less prominence to monetarist criteria. They also provide further evidence that, whatever the public image, Margaret Thatcher was practical politician first and economic ideologue a long way second. She was, of course, well aware that her own long-term strategy of turning Britain around was not realisable from the Opposition benches. Thus, Geoffrey Howe's budget of spring 1982 was intended to give voters more spending money, mostly by increasing personal tax allowances and raising tax thresholds. The dose was repeated in 1983, three months before the election, when the mortgage tax relief limit was also increased (for the last time, as it turned out) to £30,000. Child benefit was also increased.[17] It is worth noting that revenues from North Sea oil, which were increasing substantially in the early 1980s, also enabled the government to offer inducements to voters. By the mid-1980s, indeed, Britain was an oil-rich nation and the government could use oil revenues to pay for the increased social security and unemployment benefits that the decline of the manufacturing base had necessitated.

Margaret Thatcher's determination to stick to a chosen course is one of the main characteristics that voters identify when (as they invariably do) they call her a strong leader. 'The lady's not for turning' became one of the favourite aphorisms put into her mouth by her speechwriters during the deepest days of the recession. She did not herself recognise the punning literary allusion to the play by the twentieth-century dramatist Christopher Fry. Yet, as we have seen, economic policy changed very significantly from 1982 to 1983 onwards. Although a 'medium-term financial strategy' still found a ritualistic place in budget speeches, fiscal targets were regularly loosened. Academic monetarists, angered by this, pressed in vain for policies to remove inflation from the economic equation altogether by maintaining the tightest of controls on the money supply. Having identified one major target – inflation – and having seen it decline to manageable, single-figure, proportions, however, Thatcher was much more interested in the political capital that would accrue from claiming success in this area than she was in pushing right-wing economic theory to its logical limits. Here again, she proved a populist politician of genius, not an ideologue.

PRIVATISATION

If control of inflation was the key economic objective during the Thatcher's first government, privatisation became the central goal during the second. Privatisation had three main aspects, all designed to reduce the influence of state regulation and control. There was straightforward denationalisation of publicly owned assets, subcontracting of government-financed goods and services, such as refuse collection and hospital meals provision, and reducing or removing state supervision or monopoly in areas such as transport regulation, telecommunications licences and the like.[18] As so often with Thatcherism, the assumed benefits of privatisation were at once economic, political and moral.

Compulsory sale of local authority houses to sitting tenants had increased the proportion of owner-occupied homes during the first Thatcher term. It had been an enormously popular policy. All Conservatives could support a strategy designed to strengthen the property-owning democracy. Council house sales undoubtedly created numerous Conservative voters among groups that had previously been solidly Labour; 55,000 public-sector houses had been sold in the first year of the Thatcher government, and this rose to a peak of 204,000 in 1982–3.[19] Owner-occupation increased from 55 per cent to 63 per cent in the decade after 1979. Opinion polls, meanwhile, also showed a strong preference for private, as opposed to nationalised, ownership of industry.[20]

Privatisation of companies promised even richer rewards. Taking major assets, some of which were loss-making anyway, out of public ownership would reduce government debt and raise revenue, which could be used for further politically popular cuts in the direct rate of income tax. The sums raised from privatisation were substantial. It has been estimated that it raised almost £19 billion in the years 1979–87.[21] Privatisation was also broadly popular across the Conservative Party, papering over those damaging splits between 'wets' and 'dries' which had surfaced so prominently during the first Thatcher government (see Chapter 4). It could also be presented to the electorate as a means of making money easily and with very little risk. The junior minister Richard Needham emphasised privatisation's populist appeal: 'The British have always been followers of horse-racing, who like to put a few shillings on a winner – privatisation was putting a few bob on a sure winner'.[22] It was a 'sure winner', of course, because the government could set the price of shares in recently nationalised industries and utilities now offered for private ownership and could, therefore, virtually guarantee profits for small investors.

Thatcher emphasised the moral dimension. Her political convictions told her that nationalisation was wrong. It burdened the state with ownership, which cost the taxpayer money. It was not the job of government to run businesses; businessmen were much better at that. Worst of all, collective ownership was the inevitable adjunct of socialism, and socialism represented a form of enslavement. In her memoirs, Thatcher considered the political, economic and moral dimensions of privatisation as all of a piece:

Privatisation, no less than the tax structure, was fundamental to improving Britain's economic performance. But for me it was also far more than that: it was one of the central means of reversing the corrosive and corrupting effects of socialism. Ownership by the state is just that – ownership by an impersonal legal entity: it amounts to control by politicians and civil servants . . . Through privatisation – particularly the kind of privatisation which leads to the widest possible share ownership by members of the public – the state's power is reduced and the power of the people enhanced . . . Privatisation is at the centre of any programme of reclaiming territory for freedom.[23]

Privatisation, of course, was under way before 1983. British Petroleum, British Aerospace and the British Sugar Corporation had all been taken into private hands by the end of 1981. Mercury had also been given a licence to compete with the state-owned monopoly British Telecom. Mobile telephone networks, still uncommon enough in the 1980s to be symbols of 'yuppie' lifestyle, had also been licensed. The Conservative election manifesto of 1983 made much of the movement towards greater freedom of competition. However, the pace of privatisation quickened rapidly after the election. The talisman of wider share ownership was the privatisation of British Telecom in 1984, on terms deliberately designed to benefit the small investor. Thatcher's dream was of genuine popular capitalism, and she looked forward in her Manichean way to the time when shareholders (good symbols of freedom) would exceed trade unionists (bad symbols of restrictive practice) in number. This was a far from unattainable objective as the government had no qualms about bribing the electorate to participate in share ownership by rigging the rules of share flotations. Initial purchase prices were invariably set artificially, and attractively, low, virtually guaranteeing quick profits for those small shareholders who chose to sell quickly. Meanwhile, restrictions on trade union activity (see below, pp. 38–40) made membership ever less eligible. The privatisation of British Gas in 1986, for example, was accompanied by an almost unbelievably crass advertising campaign based on the creation of 'Sid', the streetwise popular capitalist with simple lessons in share ownership for the general public. Crassness and successful advertising are, of course, close allies. The gas flotation was oversubscribed five times and fortunate beneficiaries rejoiced.

Thatcher's campaign for popular capitalism worked extremely well on one level. Shares in going concerns made available at artificially low prices were easy to sell. Important breaches had also been made in the argument that a civilised society should keep those utilities on which all depended in public hands. The very notion of public ownership became deeply unfashionable. The Earl of Stockton, who, as Harold Macmillan, had been one of the Tories' most successful Prime Ministers during the period of the Keynesian consensus, attacked privatisation as 'misguided'. He spoke to the Tory Reform Group in 1985 about the dangers of getting rid of the Georgian silver before moving on to the furniture and the Canaletto paintings. The press quickly rendered this as 'selling off the family silver'.[24] People appreciated Macmillan's wit, as they had been doing for thirty years. Few, however, really listened to the serious message behind the *bon mot*. Privatisation offered quick and easy rewards. Public ownership, in contrast, seemed outdated. Perhaps even the metaphor that Macmillan used struck the wrong note; it reminded people that these were the words of a titled gent, born alike to privilege and the exercise of easy power over others.

On another level, however, privatisation was less successful. The base of share ownership did broaden considerably. There were 3 million private shareholders when Thatcher came to office and almost 11 million when she left it.[25] However, the new shareholders were hardly the generation of risk-taking, wealth-enhancing popular capitalists of Thatcher's dreams: doughty class warriors imbued with a hatred of public ownership. Many small shareholders kept their stocks only long enough to realise quick profits and then sold them back again to the large institutions. The long-term financial beneficiaries of privatisation were the pension fund managers. The interest of most ordinary citizens in stocks and shares, if sustained at all, was at one remove – in long-term pension plans that would take twenty years or more to mature. Even among those converted to speculation in equities, the stock market crash of October 1987 (see Chapter 10) provided a harsh lesson in financial realities; more than a decade later, so did the devastating effects of the long-term stock market decline from 2001 on maturing endowment insurance policies and on pension funds, especially when the latter were related to very low-yielding annuities. Popular capitalism had a spectacular downside.

Public support for privatisation rapidly dwindled when it was realised that, all too often, its theoretical benefits were belied by dubious, if not downright squalid, practice. Publicly owned monopolies were replaced not by vigorous competition from which consumers benefited in the form of efficient production of high-quality goods at low prices but by privately owned monopolies, which, all too often, offered the consumer service no better than before. Chief executives of these monopolies or near-monopolies – nearly all proven Conservative supporters – paid themselves outrageously high salaries while also taking up share options and pension rights. At the same time, they increased the profit expectations of their shareholders (who, of course, included themselves) by slimming down their workforces and asserting that they had become 'leaner and fitter'. Worse, ministers who had prepared the ground for privatisation of particular companies found their way onto the boards of those companies as soon as they retired, which, in some cases, was very quickly after public ownership had been surrendered. Thus, Norman Tebbit, who helped privatise British Telecom, sat on its board after he retired from the House of Commons. One of the directors of National Freight was Sir Norman Fowler, who had been Transport Secretary at the time of its privatisation.[26] The reputation for 'sleaze' that hung unhelpfully around Conservative necks in the 1990s (see Chapter 11) came into sharper focus with the privatisations of the mid- and late 1980s. One did not need to be a socialist or indeed any kind of anti-Thatcherite to view such developments with distaste. Public support for privatisation flagged, and the policy, although certainly not abandoned (there were too many easy financial pickings ahead for that) was no longer marketed as a vote winner.

TRADE UNION POLICY AND THE MINERS' STRIKE

If privatisation amply sustained capitalism, and especially those capitalists who helped fund the Conservative Party, then Thatcher showed in these years that she had not forgotten her promise to do more about labour – and specifically the trade unions. Just as she had given ample proof of her belief that managers, at least private-sector managers, should be left to manage free from state interference, so she also demonstrated how effectively the state could intervene by legislation that deprived workers of rights which had rarely been challenged before the 1970s. Strong trade unions threatened the free play of market forces. The trade union legislation of the first Thatcher government (see Chapter 2) was thus eagerly built upon by the second and third. The Employment Act of 1982 restricted the definition of a lawful strike to one wholly or mainly between workers and their own employers. Strikes in sympathy with other workers became virtually illegal. The Act also contained clauses that made 'closed shops' of exclusively unionised labour more difficult to sustain. Individuals who were dismissed for not joining a union were entitled to high rates of compensation. The Trade Union Act of 1984 required postal ballots at least every five years for all union offices and provided subsidies for holding them. The Trade Union and Employment Acts of 1988 gave individuals greater powers vis-à-vis their unions. They could no longer be disciplined for working during an official strike.

Crucially, also, the unions' legal immunity from prosecution for damages sustained during strikes was available only if a secret ballot of its members had been held and had provided a majority for strike action.[27]

Although acutely resented by many, Thatcher's firm stand against the trade unions was generally popular. She succeeded in enacting trade union reform where previous governments had either tried and failed or had not been inclined to try. This had been true of previous Conservative, as well as Labour, governments. Harold Macmillan had asserted, not entirely jocularly, that, alongside the Catholic Church and the Brigade of Guards, the trade union movement was an institution that no Tory government should ever tangle with.[28]

Public support, although by no means uniform across the country, was an important element in Thatcher's important victory in the miners' strike of 1984–5. Coal miners were the traditional élite of the trade union movement, and their industrial muscle had become legendary. Thatcher, of course, had been a member of the Heath government, which had been brought down by a miners' strike ten years earlier. She would not repeat his mistake. Far from trying to avoid another strike, however, there is considerable evidence that she actively courted a showdown with the miners under their aggressive and charismatic, but vain and politically limited, President, Arthur Scargill. She appointed Ian MacGregor, a trenchant free-marketeer who had been a success at British Steel, as the new chairman of the National Coal Board in September 1983. Thatcher praised his 'courage' as well as his business sense.[29] The government also prepared carefully for the possibility of conflict, stockpiling coal and trying to ensure that supplies from abroad could be imported at need.

Scargill was quite right to assert what Conservative ministers throughout denied: that defeat would see the rapid closure of most of Britain's pits and the destruction of the miners' distinctive community and culture. However, he failed to hold a miners' ballot beyond calling the strike. This deprived miners of moral authority for their action, at least in the eyes of public opinion. It also gave the new Labour leader, Neil Kinnock, who was himself MP for a mining constituency and very close to miners' culture but aware of what a political disaster Scargill was, the excuse to distance himself from the miners' leader. This deprived the miners of wholehearted Labour Party support during their strike. These factors, together with the appearance of a much more conciliatory breakaway union representing the profitable East Midlands mining area and an unusually mild winter, led to the miners' eventual defeat in the spring of 1985. Miners and their families had shown enormous courage, resource and self-sacrifice in defence of their pits and their way of life, but they fatally misjudged the power that the state, under a determined Prime Minister, could wield. The bitter irony was not lost on trade unionists, who reflected that this same Prime Minister wished to roll back the powers of the state – in the interests of free market capitalism.

Defeat was to prove as costly for the miners as victory was sweet for Mrs Thatcher. She mused that the strike had 'established the truth that the British coal industry could not remain immune to the economic forces which applied elsewhere in both the public and the private sectors'. She conceded that the industry then proceeded to shrink 'far more than any of us thought it would at the time of the strike'.[30] As the reason for this was that the industry had 'proved unable to compete on world markets', however, she appeared to view this dismal outcome with equanimity. The trade union movement, beaten down alike by recession, legislation and industrial defeat, cowered. Another major strike in defence of the restrictive practices of print workers was defeated in 1986. The mine workers' union lost 72 per cent of its members in the years 1979–86. The number of trade unionists as a whole shrank from 13.5 million in 1979 to 10.5 million in 1986, and fell below 10 million by the time she left office in 1990.[31] Margaret Thatcher appeared to have slain another of her dragons.

4 Thatcherism and the Conservative Party

CHANGE AND THE CONSERVATIVE PARTY

It might be thought that the business of the Conservative Party is to conserve. One of the main criticisms of Margaret Thatcher has been that she broke with Conservative traditions by leading the party in dangerous new directions. One of Thatcher's monetarist gurus, Milton Friedman, asserted – more, it has to be admitted, on a knowledge of economic theory than of political history – that she is not a true Conservative at all, but a nineteenth-century Liberal.[1] Her misleading assertions about Victorian values (see Chapter 12) might seem to offer support for this interpretation. The Conservative Party, however, has not historically been a party of narrow reaction. It has usually been receptive to new ideas, whether generated from within or outside. Looked at from this perspective, Thatcher's period in office, however much it shook up the country, hardly represents a betrayal of Conservative values.

Far more often than 'conserving' for its own sake, the Conservative Party in both the nineteenth and the twentieth centuries has been a party of change. When it attempted to defend the old political system against modest proposals for parliamentary reform, in 1828–32, it suffered one of the two largest electoral defeats in its history. Sir Robert Peel nursed the party back to health during the 1830s by adopting 'necessary reforms' and supporting major changes to legislation on the poor and on prisons, local government reforms, factory and mines as he sought to make the Conservatives responsive to the new industrial age. He then broke it on an issue of reformist economic principle – free trade generally and the repeal of the Corn Laws in particular – in 1846. The Conservatives have avoided overt splits ever since. It was Disraeli's Tories in the late 1860s and 1870s, rather than Gladstone's Liberals, who placed the greater trust in working men by giving a majority of them the vote.[2]

In the twentieth century, after internal divisions over tariff reform had caused a catastrophic election defeat in 1906, the party recovered in the second decade of the twentieth century. During the interwar period, when it was in office almost continuously, the Conservatives played to what were its now 'traditional' strengths of patriotism and support for reformist policies which united the nation. Both Neville Chamberlain's enthusiastic development of National Insurance policies begun by Lloyd George and the Liberals before the First World War and Tory slum clearance and housing programmes fitted naturally into this pattern of considered, moderate reform. After the Second World War, as we have seen (Chapter 1), so far from the party attempting to dismantle Labour's welfare state, the Tories participated willingly in the 'Butskellite consensus'. Harold Macmillan, perhaps the outstanding example of a one-nation, reformist Conservative, greatly expanded the house-building programme as a distinctive Conservative contribution to post-war reconstruction.[3]

The Tory Party, therefore, is not averse to change – sometimes radical and dramatic. Nor has it ever denied the existence of internal policy disagreements. Like the Church of England, with which it was for so long associated, although emphatically not under Thatcher, the Conservative Party had always been a broad church and reasonably tolerant of dissenting views. Margaret Thatcher's prescription for change should therefore have occasioned no special alarm. When her first Queen's Speech was presented in 1979, the right-wing journal *The Economist* presented a composite, artificial 'Queen's Speech', drawn equally from this and from Heath's in 1970. The exercise convincingly demonstrated how little were the apparent policy disagreements between the two Prime Ministers who, by this time, were bitter personal enemies.[4] The journal might also have made reference to the distinctive contribution of Enoch Powell. Powell's importance has been obscured by the circumstances of his dismissal from Heath's Shadow Cabinet over a speech that was widely interpreted as racist. Powell was the first heavyweight politician to mount a coherent attack on the post-war consensus politics from the Conservative right. Many of his ideas anticipated those of Joseph and Thatcher. It is a considerable irony of twentieth-century politics that by the time that Thatcher became leader, Powell had left the Conservative Party altogether.[5]

ROUTING THE 'WETS'

Thatcher's period as leader witnessed sharper, and more bitter, disagreements within the party than at any time since Joseph Chamberlain's campaigns for tariff reform and imperial preference more than seventy years earlier. Why was this? Two main explanations may be offered. First, Thatcher's style was deliberately confrontational. She made no secret of the fact that she intended to blow apart misbegotten notions of consensus. This was very difficult to square with 'one-nation' ideas that most Tory MPs believed to be the essence of modern Conservatism and also the party's strongest card at general elections. One-nation Tories had until the mid-1970s controlled the crucial levers of power within the party, notably Conservative Central Office and the Conservative Research Department. Thatcher had developed or appropriated her own structures – the Centre for Policy Studies, the Institute of Economic Affairs and a posse of academic economists – to challenge those who believed, in the words of Andrew Gamble, that Conservatism 'meant governing a society rather than managing an economy'.[6] She made it clear that hers was a struggle for the soul of the party.

Second, Thatcher was both a political and a social outsider. There was nothing particularly unusual or threatening about this in itself. Historically, the Conservative Party has always been ready to accept, and promote, men of talent from outside the charmed circle of aristocrats, country squires and wealthy bankers. The fact that both Benjamin Disraeli, from a Jewish intellectual family, and Edward Heath, a clever grammar school boy of humble background, could rise to become Conservative Prime Ministers is sufficient demonstration of this. Thatcher's own lower-middle-class background was in some ways surprisingly similar to Heath's. The difference, however, was that Thatcher, having risen within the party hierarchy and enjoyed its patronage, up to and including a Cabinet post in the Heath government, aspired now not to be absorbed comfortably into that hierarchy but to dismantle it. This was not the Conservative way. Conservatives were expected to work with the grain. Traditional Conservatism was much more comfortable with compromise and consensus rather than with the conviction and its associated confrontation which Thatcher not so much represented as demanded.

Few in her Shadow Cabinet understood at the beginning of 1979 how far she was prepared to go to achieve her vision. Her plain, unsophisticated ways were ridiculed in private and she was also the target of that snobbish hauteur which is one of the least attractive features of aristocratic Conservatism. One, who subsequently became a Cabinet minister under Thatcher, revealed his true feelings about her to a journalist in 1978:

She is still basically a Finchley lady. Her view of the world is distressingly narrow. She regards the working class as idle, deceitful, inferior and bloody-minded. And she simply doesn't understand affairs of state. She doesn't have the breadth.[7]

In a similar vein, James Prior, her first Employment Secretary, re-called that 'In the early days of Margaret's Cabinet, Ministers often used to pass notes to one another during Cabinet . . . . There were those which were very private, which said: . . . "She's got it all wrong" '.[8] In the early 1980s, Francis Pym offered the revealingly dismissive view that the real problem for the Tories was that 'we've got a corporal at the top, not a cavalry officer'.[9]

Cabinet colleagues such as Pym and Prior initially assumed that the process of government would soon 'civilise' Thatcher and bring her to see the greater wisdom of doing things in traditional, consensual ways. Some believed her 'conviction' statements to be either mere blustering propaganda or the unsophisticated rantings of a talented woman who lacked the necessary gloss that a longer experience of life at the top would eventually provide. The fact that Thatcher's first government contained a significant number of well-bred, one-nation Tories in the most senior positions – including Viscount Carrington as Foreign Secretary, Willie Whitelaw at the Home Office and Francis Pym at Defence – seemed to confirm their beliefs. In the parliamentary party at large, the upper middle classes and landed 'knights of the shire' still held prominent positions.

As we have seen (Chapter 2), at no point in the government of 1979–83 did Thatcher's Cabinet have a majority for monetarism. She used a combination of skill and cunning to avoid presenting the centre-piece of her economic strategy before Cabinet for discussion of basic principle. An important element in that cunning was her calculated use of femininity with men. Most of the political colleagues she dealt with had come from single-sex, public school backgrounds, which equipped them poorly to deal on equal terms with a determined, professional woman. One of her most devoted admirers, the aristocratic junior minister Alan Clark, who confessed to finding her physically attractive, nevertheless resorted to stereotypical sexist rant when she successfully argued against one of his schemes:

As the Prime Minister developed her case she, as it were, auto-fed her own indignation. It was a prototypical example of an argument with a woman – no rational sequence, associative, lateral thinking, jumping the rails the whole time.[10]

One of her foreign policy advisers, the Hungarian emigré George

Urban, found her on first acquaintance 'much softer and more feminine' than her television image. He believes that her 'perplexing charm' enabled her to be 'getting away with' political ploys and stratagems which a man would not.[11]

Certainly, James Prior, who found it 'an enormous shock' that the Howe budget of 1979 was 'so extreme', grudgingly recognised the effectiveness of Thatcher's tactics against Cabinet opponents: 'I realised that Margaret, Geoffrey [Howe] and Keith [Joseph] really had got the bit between their teeth and were not going to pay attention to the rest of us at all if they could possibly help it'.[12] Francis Pym, then Leader of the House of Commons, thought the 1981 budget an 'awful' piece of work: 'rigidly deflationary and thus highly controversial at a time of deep recession, yet the strategy behind it was never discussed in Cabinet and was only revealed to the full Cabinet on budget day itself'.[13]

The battle within the Conservative Party in the early 1980s is usually described as between 'wets' and 'dries'. 'Wets' were one-nation Tories; 'dries' were loyal Thatcherites, most of them conviction monetarists. Inevitably, the distinction is too crude. Some 'wets', for example Prior, Walker and Gilmour, were particularly critical of what they considered unrealistic economic theory. Others, such as Heseltine, wanted to use the powers of the state to pursue a more effective industrial strategy. Others again, especially in 1980–1, urged abandonment of monetarist policies on more pragmatic grounds: they feared electoral catastrophe. The 'dries' all exhibited loyalty to, shading into reverence for, Thatcher as a leader, but they were divided also. Howe and Lawson, by different routes, became convinced monetarists; John Biffen, an old ally of Powell, grew increasingly sceptical as the 1980s progressed and was never particularly close to Thatcher personally. Other 'dries', further from the centre of power, were patriots who supported Thatcher because they believed she would revive national fortunes and not give in to foreigners. Overall, however, the conflict between 'wets' and 'dries' as a whole was what mattered because it was a struggle for the future of the party and had wider than merely ideological implications.

In 1977, the most articulate spokesman of the 'wets', the old Etonian Sir Ian Gilmour, stressed the need for Conservatives to make constructive use of the state:

> . . . if people are not to be seduced by other attractions, they must at least feel loyalty to the State. This loyalty will not be deep unless they gain from the State protection and other benefits . . . Economic liberalism because of its starkness and its failure to create a sense of community is likely to repel people.[14]

Thatcher never believed that it was any business of government to create 'a sense of community'. Rather, it should release the energies of individuals who, one way or another, were imprisoned by the state. Her vision of Conservatism could hardly have been more different from that of Gilmour.

Why did the 'dries' win, and with what consequences for Conservatism in the last years of the twentieth century? Perhaps the most important reason was that the wets' tradition of compassionate Conservatism appeared to have failed. They were seen to have been willing accomplices of Keynesian demand-management, which had weakened the pound, sent inflation soaring and seen responsibility for the government uneasily, and inappropriately, shared between the elected government and a powerful oligarchy of class-obsessed trade union bosses. As one non-Thatcherite Conservative unattributably reported: 'the right wing smelt blood and with Mrs Thatcher they got tacit support from No. 10. Time after time we were told "you've had twenty years in charge, now it's our turn"'.[15] The 'wets' were never satisfactorily able to combat the argument that a crisis in the nation's affairs had arrived, which demanded a radical new approach. Norman St John Stevas, who was to become Thatcher's first sacrificial wet Cabinet lamb at the monetarist feast of the 1980s, told a journalist: 'I don't know whether it [monetarism] will work or not. Why is there no critique of it? Because no one has any alternative. There is nothing else to try'.[16] Thus was 'Tina' delivered into the world; '*t*here *i*s *n*o *a*lternative' became an acronym that the monetarist right would appropriate for devastating propaganda effect in the first half of the 1980s.

Alternatives did, of course, exist, as they always will in politics. The 'wets' did not follow them through partly out of a sense of responsibility for past failures and partly out of that bred-in-the-bone loyalty that Conservatives have for the party leader except when they fear imminent electoral defeat, or in the aftermath of such a defeat. They could also see the devastating consequences of the bloodletting in the Labour Party and, perhaps too readily, fell back upon overt loyalty to the leader as a better option than fighting for what they believed in. Thatcher ruthlessly exploited what she considered their infirmity of purpose.

The decisive leadership of Thatcher also stood in marked contrast with the pusillanimity of the 'wets'. The anonymous Cabinet minister quoted above praised Thatcher's 'remarkable grasp on government – there was no faltering from day one'. As we have seen (Chapters 2 and 3), Thatcher most impressed friend and foe alike with her decisive handling of crises. Many, including all of the 'wets', were convinced that she was steering the ship directly towards the rocks of electoral disaster, but none denied that she was steering it with an unfaltering hand. When Thatcher and her financial advisers responded to the disasters of the slump of 1979–81 with yet more deflation, she left her party opponents with no response except impotent anguish. She believed that they spoke only for a narrow and unrepresentative élite, whereas she was of the firm belief that her constituency was the 'ordinary' England of her own background:

> Deep in their instincts people find what I am saying and doing right. And I know it is, because it is the way I was brought up . . . in a small town. We knew everyone, we knew what everyone thought. I sort of regard myself as a very normal, ordinary person, with all the right, instinctive antennae.[17]

Thatcher was sustained by this inner conviction and used it to extend the limits of Prime Ministerial power. Another important reason why Thatcher won her battle with the 'wets' was that she was much more ruthless in using the theoretical, but generally underused, powers of the first minister to control agendas and limit the discussion of controversial items to those known not to be 'obstructive'. Additionally, she used her press office – and particularly the rumbustious Sir Bernard Ingham – to leak information, with the intention of damaging ministers who were falling out of favour. A political press far more interested in personality clashes than in policy discussions could be relied upon to do the rest by talking down, or sometimes up, the prospects of ministers at the next Cabinet reshuffle. Overall, Thatcher exercised more power more directly than any previous peacetime British Prime Minister.[18]

And all the time, and with much greater confidence after the 1983 election victory, she was culling 'wets' from the Cabinet. By 1984, virtually all of the prominent 'wets' – St John Stevas, Gilmour, Prior and Pym – had been sacked. Of the old Heathite guard, only Whitelaw (never an 'ideas man' anyway and supremely loyal to any Conservative leader of any persuasion at any time), Walker ('wet' but wonderfully efficient and useful as a token gesture towards diversity of opinion) and Hailsham (who, in any case, as Lord Chancellor, was hardly party political) remained. Howe and Joseph stayed on as old believers of varying temperament and conviction but, increasingly, the most powerful positions were occupied by Thatcher's own creations, especially Lawson, Tebbit and Brittan. During her second term of office, Thatcher's position was usually unchallengeable. She had achieved a most enviable position. By 1985, she had more experience than almost all of her Cabinet colleagues. She owed no debts of loyalty to those of substantially different political views. She could present herself as a winner – of one war and two general elections – and could look forward to more buoyant economic conditions in which to fight and win another election.

She had two other immense advantages: grass-roots support and a parliamentary party closer than ever before to both her views and her social background. Grass-roots support manifested itself most openly at the annual party conference. Party conferences are ghastly affairs. Ostensibly an opportunity to debate, and even decide, policy, since the last quarter of the twentieth century they have become synthetic love-ins at which the party faithful can press the flesh of the great, if not always the good. Television cameras meanwhile obsequiously and redundantly record speeches more likely to have been written by a team of researchers than a senior politician, delivered from an autocue with special attention to the 'sound bites' that will be uncritically broadcast on the evening news. Cogent development of either policy or argument has become almost an anachronism. Conference managers also ensure that form triumphs over content as images of cosy unity are presented to the television audience, whatever the reality might be.[19]

Conferences are disproportionately attractive to party activists, and activists tend to be well to the right, or the left, of whichever party they support. Most Conservative Prime Ministers privately shared the public's view of party conferences. They loathed them. Margaret Thatcher was different. She saw them as an annual opportunity to renew the faith and to rebond with right-thinking folk. It has been correctly observed that Thatcher was 'the only Tory leader this century to endorse with gusto the prejudices of most conference representatives'.[20] In her own mind, no doubt, she also considered that they represented precisely the kind of public opinion with which the Tory grandees were out of touch.[21] They strengthened her resolve not to compromise or turn back. Her advisers carefully stage-managed party conferences throughout the 1980s to emphasise Thatcher's leadership qualities. The ecstatic and ever-longer standing ovations which her annual conference speeches received were given maximum publicity. Under Thatcher, the party conference became almost a populist rally. Debate was shunted off into fringe meetings, which usually attracted limited publicity. The embarrassment of many 'wets' at all this vulgar contrivance was as palpable as Thatcher's enjoyment of it. It was an important part of the Americanisation of politics that took place in the 1980s and which took the Conservative Party further away from its English, landed roots.

THE CHANGING COMPOSITION OF THE PARLIAMENTARY CONSERVATIVE PARTY

The composition of the parliamentary Conservative Party under Thatcher changed considerably. Larger numbers of MPs were elected who shared

Margaret Thatcher's view of the world. Until the late 1970s, about three-quarters of Tory MPs had been educated at public school. The most important change between the 1920s and 1970s was the declining representation of MPs from those schools with the highest social prestige – Eton, Harrow and Winchester.[22] Between 1974 and 1987, the number of Tory MPs educated at any public school declined to about two-thirds. At the same time, Oxbridge-educated Tory MPs declined from 56 per cent to 44 per cent of the total, whereas those educated at provincial universities doubled to 26 per cent. Even those who represented the ancient universities had previously been educated at grammar or direct-grant schools. Although overwhelmingly university educated, therefore, the Tory Party was becoming less 'posh'.

The professions and business between them continued to provide about four-fifths of Conservative MPs during the 1980s. However, members tended to come either from the humbler sections of the established professions – more ordinary solicitors, fewer high-flying barristers – or from the newer rather than the more established professions – many more accountants, fewer senior bankers. Teachers and lecturers have always provided a considerably smaller proportion of Conservative than of Labour MPs. Among the business interests, the change was even more dramatic. A larger proportion of the extensive ranks of Tory MPs sitting on the back, and increasingly on the government, benches were self-made businessmen. The motor trade and the housing market were particularly well represented. At the same time, and probably directly related to the ascendancy of Thatcherite Conservatism, the numbers of substantial landowners (which had been declining for a century) declined even more quickly. Many felt that the times were out of joint. The hard-edged, market-led competitive world of Thatcherism was marginalising the older traditions of politics as a form of gentlemanly service. Paternalism and deference had been replaced by winners and losers. As one observer put it, the Conservatives were no longer the party of the estates but of the estate agents. Julian Critchley, the Shrewsbury-educated MP for the army town of Aldershot, talked of a takeover by the *garagistes*.

Making every allowance for snobbish exaggeration, the Tory Party under Thatcher was changing more quickly than at any time in the twentieth century. Change in the social composition and political views of parliamentary candidates was mirrored by a decline in political activism at grass-roots level. Thatcherism alienated progressive, paternalist and 'one-nation' Conservatives alike; many of these had been traditionally dominant in rural English seats. Thatcher's attack on local government (see Chapter 5) also induced the perception that local politics now offered neither prestige nor such obvious political opportunity for parliamentary candidates. This contributed to a withering of some previously vigorous Tory tap-roots.[23]

The turnover of MPs, especially on the Conservative side, was also unprecedentedly rapid. Almost three-quarters of MPs returned to the 1987 parliament had first been elected in 1974 or later. This naturally increased Thatcher's authority within the parliamentary party. As fewer and fewer MPs had known any other leadership, she was seen as the ultimate source of power and patronage. Also, many of the newcomers had been selected by local Conservative associations with a pronounced pro-Thatcher bias. Especially after Thatcher had proved herself as an election winner, the right-wing tendencies inherent in many local constituency parties asserted themselves. In others, the alienation and demoralisation of the paternalists gave right-wingers an opportunity to take over. In consequence, fewer and fewer Tory candidates of the old, consensual, one-nation school were selected. This change was enthusiastically supported by Tory Central Office, which, by the mid-1980s, was also firmly under Thatcherite control. The trend towards the selection of right-wingers continued after Thatcher left office. One-half of the Conservative members elected in 1992 had been MPs for ten years or fewer; most were right-wingers. Right-wing Conservative candidates continued to be chosen for at least a decade after Thatcher left office, although in the very strong Labour years of 1997 and 2001 far fewer of them were actually elected.

Although many of the new Tory MPs were wealthy, few had inherited their wealth. The emphasis was firmly on self-made success. A new breed of Tories appeared, such as David Bevan, who had made a fortune as an estate agent and who served a Birmingham constituency from 1979 to electoral defeat in 1992, or Steven Norris, whose money had been made from car dealing and who was an effective Transport Minister until his retirement in 1997 to resume his business career and his local government interests. Party managers played up this development as a distinctively Thatcherite phenomenon that encouraged merit and individual effort. They conveniently forgot that Thatcher's own upwardly mobile career – impressive enough in the early stages from grammar school to Oxford and degrees in both law and chemistry – had been massively boosted by marrying a millionaire businessman. It is quite likely that the nation owes Margaret Thatcher's appearance as an MP in 1959 to the financial ballast and the influential business and political connections that Dennis Thatcher was able to provide.

The parliamentary party has also become more professional. About one-half of the increased number of Conservative MPs first elected in 1983 or 1987 had experience as local councillors. To them should be added the growing number who won seats after working in Westminster or in Conservative Central Office as party research assistants or advisers. In consequence, far more MPs now regard politics as a full-time, all-consuming interest. In this, of course, they follow Thatcher's example, although significant numbers have chosen to retire early from parliament in order to take up better-paid employment or resume lucrative careers previously held alongside service in local government.

The advantages of these very substantial changes have been much de-bated. The Tory Party might be thought to benefit from having so many more MPs from relatively humble, lower middle-class, backgrounds who have improved themselves by their own talents and business acumen. Some have a much sharper understanding of the competitive, Thatcherite business ethic than their upper middle-class predecessors, whose experience of wealth had been through gentlemanly capitalism, helped along by a privileged education, influential social contacts and inheritance. On the other hand, it is possible to argue that self-made 'winners' too readily assume that their route to success is open to all who work hard and discipline themselves. Faith in the beneficence of the free market often goes hand in hand with both intolerance and even incomprehension of the efforts and needs of those whom life has treated less kindly. It is, after all, of the essence of competition that it produces losers as well as winners. Even the Victorians, so beloved of Margaret Thatcher, knew perfectly well that lack of success is not always the result of individual failings. In losing its paternalistic ethic, Conservatism in the 1980s became sharper-edged, more strident and less sophisticated.

The Palace of Westminster has, arguably, become both a duller and a less effective place for the presence of so many ambitious full-time politicians. This development is not unique to the Conservative Party, of course, but both the disciplines of government and the substantially larger number of Tory than Opposition MPs ensured that the conse-quences first became pronounced on the Tory side. Now that relatively few MPs are content to remain back-benchers, too few are prepared to say what they really think for fear of having their cards marked as 'troublemakers' by the Whips. Also, the absence of what Denis Healey once memorably called 'hinterland' in so many MPs has contributed to a narrowing of vision and the inability to take a well-informed view on complex matters. As anyone who reads *Hansard* for both the 1880s and the 1980s can readily testify, the quality of parliamentary debate has slipped alarmingly. Quality newspapers now cover parliament far less extensively than they did, preferring the witty and sardonic comment of gifted parliamentary sketch-writers to the turgid expositions of earnest but frequently untalented speakers. Although some politicians accuse editors of deliberately censoring the wisdom of the nation's elected representatives, the decision owes more to valid editorial judgement that little wisdom – as opposed to repetitive incantations of the party line – is actually dispensed there.

It is, of course, easy to exaggerate the virtues of the House of Commons in the late nineteenth and early twentieth centuries. Parliament has always contained its quota of the ignorant, the dishonest, the venal and the sleazy. However, developments in the last quarter of the twentieth century have made the House of Commons a less diverse, less tolerant, less humane and less broadly informed legislature than any of its predecessors. It is not an accident that the changes described here were accompanied by opinion-poll evidence showing sharply declining respect for the honesty, competence and even the value of professional politicians.[24] It would be ludicrous to suggest that these changes can be exclusively ascribed to Margaret Thatcher's leadership. Longer-term social, economic and demographic forces were also at work. However, it was a key objective of Margaret Thatcher to create a party that was more opportunistic, less deferential and less beholden to an old guard of privileged grandees. In this she succeeded. The extent to which local party organisations followed her preferences and prejudices in the selection of candidates who became MPs in 1987 and 1992 probably surprised even her. Thatcher transformed the face of modern Conservatism while, in the short term at least, consolidating her party's hold on power. It was a substantial, if not necessarily a beneficial, achievement.

5 The attack on the government ethic

I was determined ... to begin work on long-term reform of government itself. If we were to channel more of the nation's talent into wealth-creating private business, this would inevitably mean reducing employment in the public sector. Since the early 1960s, the public sector had grown steadily, accounting for an increased proportion of the workforce ... about 30 per cent in 1979. Unlike the private sector, it actually tended to grow during recessions while maintaining its size during periods of economic growth. In short, it was shielded from the normal economic disciplines which affect the outside world.[1]

THE CIVIL SERVICE

Although Margaret Thatcher liked, respected and trusted individual civil servants, and was by all accounts a kindly and concerned employer, she hated the civil service. The above extract from her memoirs shows why. She considered public sector employment a necessary evil and was determined to reduce its burden on the state. Civil servants were specially targeted. On Thatcher's analysis, they did not create wealth but reduced it. They took far too long to make decisions, their training inclining them to weigh all evidence carefully. Senior civil servants were a powerful element of the establishment élite, against whom Thatcher was waging *jihad* anyway. They had jobs for life, dispensing lordly advice, from the economic consequences of which they were invariably shielded. So attractive and responsible was the life of a senior civil servant that a disproportionate number of the ablest university-trained minds opted to apply for entry to the service rather than take their chance in the rough and tumble of commerce and private industry.

Civil servants were also the permanent professionals. They had an impressive record of persuading ministers, who generally stayed in a particular office for only a couple of years or so, that specific government policies were ill-advised. All of their training disposed them against 'conviction politics' and in favour of smooth administration along broadly consensual lines. They took pride in being able, even-handedly, to serve both Labour and Conservative administrations. It was easy for someone of Thatcher's background to conclude that these superior, unelected beings needed bringing into the real world. It is not surprising that her favourite television programme in the early 1980s was *Yes, Minister*, a brilliantly witty situation comedy that turned on the relationship between a malleable, spineless minister and an effortlessly superior civil service mandarin. The title was itself an irony: the programme invariably ended with the civil servant apparently agreeing – 'Yes, Minister' – when he had in fact manipulated the minister into accepting the approved civil service view. In the normal course of events, Margaret Thatcher did not 'do' humour. In offering a genuine tribute to all-round usefulness of her deputy, William Whitelaw, she asserted: 'I think that everyone should have a Willie' – and had to have the unintended joke explained to her. But she understood the point of *Yes, Minister* and was determined to do something about it.

Attempts to change the ethic of the civil service were by no means new. Both Harold Wilson and Edward Heath in the 1960s and early 1970s had attempted to inject a more managerial tone. Heath, indeed, had produced a portentously phrased White Paper *The Reorganisation of Central Government,* created a Central Policy Review Staff and looked forward to reducing manpower in the civil service.[2] Heath, however, attempted to reform from the inside. He was rapidly ensnared, diverted by other priorities and was, in any case, Prime Minister for less than four years. The Wilson and Callaghan Labour governments conducted an extensive review of central administration, which resulted in the abolition of 35,000 administrative posts and savings of almost £140 million.

Characteristically, however, Thatcher was more tenacious in her pursuit of her objectives. She came to office having, apparently, given far less thought and preparation to the machinery of government than had Heath. However, unlike him, she instinctively preferred working with 'outsiders' from the business world rather than establishment insiders. Her long period of office gave her the time to overcome resistance to change and enabled her policies to take root.

As so often, Thatcher's policies depended more upon instinct than on mature consideration of the issues. As Peter Hennessy put it, 'In 1979 Mrs Thatcher had more a gut-feeling than a game-plan'.[3] She was sure that Britain was overburdened by excessive administration and red tape. Almost three-quarters of a million civil servants cost every individual £3 per week. The service needed the brisk discipline of the market to eliminate waste and to achieve stated objectives. A leaner and fitter civil service would also give the Conservative Party ample scope for election-winning tax cuts. Thatcher looked to outsiders from the world of business to effect the necessary changes. John Hoskyns, the head of Thatcher's Policy Unit from 1979 to 1982, had made a fortune in the computer business during the mid-1970s and distrusted civil servants and trade unionists equally. His influential policy document *Stepping Stones* (1977) had identified trade unions as the main obstacles to getting Britain moving again. Civil servants were too often pessimistic and cynical: distrustful of, and unsympathetic to, new ideas. He also considered it a bad sign that the civil service unions were doing their best to block change. When examining ways of improving Britain's trading performance in the mid-1980s, Hoskyns was not surprised to find that 'few, if any, civil servants believe that the country can be saved'.[4] Thatcher herself recalled her dismay at the defeatism of a senior civil servant in the 1970s who argued that the height of realistic British ambition should be the 'orderly management of decline'.

Derek Rayner was seconded part-time from Marks and Spencer to set up an efficiency unit. His task, in Thatcher's brisk words, was to eliminate 'the waste and ineffectiveness of government' and also to encourage civil servants to think more positively.[5] It was Rayner who introduced senior civil servants to the paraphernalia of efficiency audits and management targets. Both he and Thatcher fervently believed in transferring the business ethic into the heart of government administration. As Thatcher put it, 'We were both convinced of the need to bring some of the attitudes of business into government. We neither of us conceived just how difficult this would prove'.

Rayner's strategy was not, however, overtly confrontational. He had experience of the workings of Whitehall and had developed from this a subtler understanding than his political mistress of its strengths as well as its weaknesses. He identified civil servants amenable to the managerial culture and used them to work with, rather than against, the administrative grain. His unit reported that Whitehall could save as much as £70 million per year and operate with a much smaller permanent establishment. By 1983, the civil service had lost 100,000 jobs. By 1987, efficiency savings were calculated to have reached £1 billion.[6] During Thatcher's period as Prime Minister, the number of civil servants was reduced by 22.5 per cent (from 732,000 to 567,000).[7]

The first Thatcher administration also saw the abolition of the Civil Service Department (CSD), which had been established in 1968 to oversee management and conditions in the service. By 1981, it had 5,000 employees, although the Prime Minister was entirely unconvinced of its value. The fate of the CSD was sealed by a long-running labour dispute in the civil service and an embarrassing dinner at which heads of civil service departments only succeeded in convincing Thatcher that their main objectives were defensive and negative. Its abolition also made it easier for Thatcher to determine appointments to the most civil senior posts. The retirement of no fewer than eight heads of department during 1982 and 1983 ensured that their replacements would be, if not exactly conviction Thatcherites, at least believers in change in general and the managerial approach in particular.[8] From this period dates the increasingly frequent charge that she appointed those known to favour her political views. Opponents have argued that Thatcher's determination to 'get things done' and to make the civil service more accountable led her to compromise its long-established and jealously guarded political neutrality.

Ironically, in view of their later disagreements (see Chapter 10), Thatcher's closest ally in the managerial revolution at Whitehall was Michael Heseltine. He sponsored a new management information system for ministers in the Environment Department and followed this up with a financial management initiative. These changes saw the introduction of those defined objectives, close financial controls and 'cost centres', already familiar to private industry, while making it easier for ministers to impose their will on civil servants. Heseltine explained the rationale:

> A civil servant may tell you that he is responsible for the permissible levels of pollution in the waterways of Britain. That is a worthy activity, but it does not tell you much about what he is doing. I wanted to know what standards had been set; whether higher standards were to be brought in, and when; what this would cost and how the benefits were to be measured'.[9]

Heseltine was proud that the development of precise targets enabled both greater productivity and a reduction in manpower to be achieved. The Department of Environment's establishment was reduced by almost 30 per cent between 1979 and 1983. The number of civil servants attached to the Ministry of Defence, to which Heseltine moved in 1983, was reduced by 20,000 in the years up to his resignation in 1986.

How effective, and how extensive, the imposition of managerialism upon the civil service has been is a matter of considerable debate. It has been pointed out that Thatcher was concerned more with ensuring that she had congenial advisers in place than with abstract theories of administration. Likewise, some ex-civil servants have asserted that Thatcher did not defeat the civil service's legendary capacity to absorb change without fundamentally altering either direction or ethos.[10] Even the impact of rapidly declining numbers has been questioned, as most of the losses were either in the highest ranks or in the industrial civil service. The great majority of civil servants remained in secure, pensionable employment unexposed to the rigours of the market place.

Reliance upon the civil service for policy direction, however, certainly diminished during the 1980s. One important consequence of Thatcher's profound dislike of its administrative ethos was that she circumvented it whenever she could. The most obvious indication of this was the number of policy advisers she brought into government who had no previous connection with the civil service. Most, of course, were businessmen. Some, however, such as Terry Burns or Alan Walters, were right-wing academics, free-marketeers refreshingly free, to her mind, from that leftist collectivism and cynicism that Thatcher believed to be the malign legacy of academic élitism. These advisers usually had a much more direct impact on the formulation of policy than did senior civil servants, who were taught to know their subordinate place. Thatcher was less amenable than any earlier Prime Minister to practised civil service arguments about why new policies could not work.

Thatcher's third government, from 1987 to 1990, took the most radical decisions in respect of the civil service. Sir Robin Ibbs, yet another business magnate brought in by Thatcher to shake up the mandarins, took over from Derek Rayner. His report *The Next Steps* initiated a major policy shift. It recommended the preservation of only a small core civil service that would continue to run the government machinery. Most civil servants would transfer to new executive agencies charged to 'deliver' specific services. These agencies would not be attached to ministries. The services to be provided covered a wide spectrum from vehicle licensing to Her Majesty's Stationery Office – the government's publisher – and from tax collection to the management of highways. The common denominator was the provision of services under tight budgetary controls to precise 'targets' and objectives. Thatcher left office before this process accelerated, probably irreversibly. By 1992, no fewer than seventy-two agencies were in place, employing almost 300,000 civil servants, roughly one-half of the total.[11] John Major's much lampooned Citizen's Charter initiative of 1991 was a logical extension of the philosophy. Government agencies were required to publish targets and to report on how they measured up to them. Throughout, the accent was upon service and accountability to the public as consumers rather than upon smooth administration. *Next Steps*, and the changed civil service culture to which it gave rise, represented the most radical change in government employment patterns and priorities for almost a century and a half. Not since the Northcote–Trevelyan Report of 1853 presaged the introduction of competitive examinations, rather than patronage, as the means of entry to the civil service had such a shake-up been attempted.[12]

LOCAL GOVERNMENT

Margaret Thatcher's policies on local government probably represented her sharpest break with the ethos of traditional Conservatism. Historically, the Conservatives were the party of local interests and identities, particularly English ones; many of its nineteenth- and early twentieth-century MPs saw it as their highest ambition to represent the interests of their constituents. They were sceptical of the influence of central government, preferred to advocate local solutions to local problems and generally agreed with Benjamin Disraeli's dictum that 'Centralisation is the death-blow of public freedom'.[13] Peter Walker's extensive reorganisation of English local government, undertaken in 1972 under the Heath government, although politically unpopular, aimed at improving local representative systems, not at undermining them.

Thatcher was sceptical of central government if it meant high taxes and control by a self-perpetuating élite. As we have seen, she was very much a provincial outsider from a non-conformist background. Where she most violently disagreed with many old-style MPs, however, was in her attitude towards the integrity and purpose of local government. She did not believe in it as a separate or alternative focus for public politics and she abominated what she saw as its inefficient, wasteful and all too often wrong-headed ways. Collectively, the town halls and municipal ideas of Britain represented yet another dragon to be slain.

In the 1970s, the Heath government had considered drastic action in respect of the Greater London Council (GLC), while local government had also been of increasing concern to the outgoing Labour government. Labour had reduced the level of grant support to local authorities and introduced cash limits on local government spending. Nevertheless, by the time Thatcher took office, local government accounted for no less than 28.1 per cent of public expenditure and for 12.4 per cent of GNP.[14] About 60 per cent of its activities were funded by central government anyway, and the legitimacy of this was highly questionable. Roughly three-quarters of the electorate voted at general elections, whereas less than one-third bothered to turn out for local government elections. If, as frequently happened between general elections, local elections produced anti-government majorities in town halls up and down the land, why should their powers not be curbed by a demonstrably more 'democratic' body – parliament? Kenneth Baker, who was minister in charge of local government in 1984–5, explained Conservative policy succinctly, if controversially:

A new generation of hard-left activists replaced old-style Labour moderates and deliberately decided to use town halls as a weapon against the Conservative government. Local government was to become a 'state within a state', the vehicle for delivering Socialism locally in the face of electoral rejection nationally.[15]

Thatcher determined to strip local authorities of many of their powers and to abolish the most troublesome ones. After councils had been instructed by the 1980 Housing Act to sell houses to tenants of three years' standing who wished to buy, the first Thatcher government reduced the grant subsidy to local authorities in the hope that this would restrain their spending. During the years 1980–6, the value of the central subsidy was reduced from 60 per cent of total local authority income to 49 per cent. Local government capital expenditure was, indeed, reduced. In the decade 1977–87, it declined, as a proportion of GDP, from 2.6 per cent to 1.3 per cent, although it should be remembered that this was part of a much longer-term development. In 1967, capital expenditure had been 4.1 per cent of GDP.[16] Most authorities initially responded not by slashing expenditure but by increasing rates. These rose by 27 per cent in the year 1980–1 and were still rising substantially after the Conservatives won the 1983 general election. In 1978–9, local authorities raised £23.2 million from rates while receiving £44 million in central government grant. Five years later, the figures were £27 million and £39.2 million respectively.[17]

Thatcher used her second electoral mandate to reduce local authority powers more directly. The Scots, who were not prone to voting Conservative anyway and so could safely be experimented upon, had already been introduced to the concept of 'rate capping'.[18] Local authorities which overspent were subject to financial penalties imposed by central government. A prolonged battle over local autonomy ensued, which was not a simple matter of 'left' versus 'right'. The respected Birmingham back-bench Tory MP, Anthony Beaumont Dark, told *The Financial Times* in January 1984, for example:

If this [rate-capping] Bill is only to be used against a few admittedly zany authorities, then it is unnecessary. If it is to be used like a gun to demand in the end the unconditional surrender of local powers to central diktat then it is the most retrograde piece of legislation ever introduced by a Conservative government.[19]

In 1985–6, eighteen local authorities (all but two of them Labour controlled) were rate capped.[20] The government won this acrimonious conflict for three main reasons. First, alongside the now characteristic steely Thatcher resolve on strategy – local government bashing – went an equally characteristic, but far less publicised, willingness to bend on tactics. Thus, in February 1985, the government revised upwards the rate limits of six local authorities (including four particularly trouble-some London ones), thus giving their councillors less political leverage to move from opposition to sustained outright defiance. Second, the authorities themselves found it difficult to maintain a united front. Some 'old Labour' councils were alienated by socialists and left extremists in others, whose priorities seemed to be not with the mundane issue of local government finance but with the heady rhetoric of defiance, law-breaking and even revolution. The particular needs and priorities of local authorities also differed widely. Third, the left extremists gave the government an immensely valuable propaganda weapon. Liverpool City Council, for example, had fallen into the hands of Militant Tendency, a revolutionary socialist organisation. The provocative tactics employed in Liverpool alienated both the Labour Party and other local authorities much more than it annoyed Thatcher.[21] Public opinion, influenced by sensationalist exposure reporting in the press, veered increasingly to the side of the government rather than the local authorities. What Arthur Scargill had done for the trade union movement in 1984–5 (see Chapter 4), the equally vain and even more preposterous Derek Hatton did for local government autonomy. When Liverpool, along with Lambeth, be-came the last councils to agree to set a legal rate in July 1987, Margaret Thatcher could claim another impressive triumph against socialism.

During the second Thatcher government, another significant nettle was grasped. The Local Government Act of 1985 proposed to abolish the GLC and six other metropolitan authorities entirely and to devolve their responsibilities to thirty-two separate London boroughs and to metro-politan districts. This provoked a spirited and skilful response, especially from the leader of the GLC, the left-winger Ken Livingstone, who had taken over as leader soon after Labour had won London in the local elec-tions of 1981. His decision to reduce London transport fares by 25 per cent was popular in itself but also pointed up the kind of decisions that only an integrated London council could carry through. The effective-ness of the pro-GLC propaganda campaign delayed abolition for a year. However, neither it nor the metropolitan authorities could indefinitely frustrate the political decisions of a determined central government with a clear parliamentary majority.

The pro-local government campaigners highlighted an important constitutional issue. The absolute sovereignty of parliament had never in the twentieth century been so nakedly revealed during peacetime as during the debates over the abolition of the metropolitan authorities. The absence of a written constitution leaves subordinate authorities without any redress against a decision made in parliament. In theory, the monarch can veto parliamentary legislation, but this has not happened since 1708 and the power is effectively extinct. The federal constitutions of Germany, the United States and many other democratic states would have prevented the actions of the Conservative government in 1985–6. It was a Conservative politician, Lord Hailsham, who coined the term 'elective dictatorship' to describe what he considered the inappropriately extended powers of a Labour government in the 1970s. Yet the term is much more appropriately applied to the Thatcher government in its dealings with local authorities – a government, be it noted, which never gained more than 44 per cent support from the three-quarters or so of those eligible to vote in a general election. From the mid-1980s, local government was directed by central government; only rarely was it consulted, and then on issues that central government considered peripheral to its main strategy. Thatcher, who purported to dislike 'big government', had increased the power of central government more than any Prime Minister before her.

Local government, having been broken by the first and second Thatcher governments, was converted into a competitive 'service enabler' by the third. Drawing upon earlier experiences, notably the deregulation of public transport under the Transport Act (1985) and the activities of the Tory authority of Wandsworth between 1982 and 1987,[22] the Local Government Act of 1988 required local authorities to put most of its existing services out to competitive tender and ensured that only commercial criteria should determine which organisations provided services. Paul Beresford, leader of the Wandsworth Council that claimed to have saved £24 million by contracting out services, explained that his strategy was:

> . . . the efficient management of services: to cut waste; to ensure high quality and to test all Council Services, where possible, against the private sector and to contract out, where appropriate.[23]

The operation of a large number of basic services was transferred from local authority to private-sector hands. This policy unfolded under the direction of Nicholas Ridley, a staunch free-marketeer who had taken over as Secretary of State for the Environment in May 1986 and served there until July 1989. It had patchy success. In some places, most services were provided efficiently by the private sector, and more cheaply than before. In others, the cheapest private bid proved anything but the best for consumers, who were badly served by new providers who had clearly underestimated, or otherwise miscalculated, the task they were taking on. Overall, it seemed that compulsory competitive tendering had enabled local government to make savings as high as 20 per cent, although more than three-quarters of the new service contracts were won by a unit of local authority-employed staff.[24] Even initially sceptical Labour authorities could see the value of a switch that enabled them both to rethink their service priorities and to curb trade union restrictive practice.

The integrated package of services previously provided by local government was dismantled by a government utterly convinced that the free market approach and unbridled competition were the only ways forward. As intended, also, the new policy continued local government fragmentation and enhanced the culture of management rather than that of administration. Along with the granting of new powers to a series of outside agencies, such as the urban development corporations, inner city enterprises and the Manpower Services Commission, the Conservatives continued to marginalise local government. These new agencies, furthermore, provided additional opportunities for the deployment of government patronage. Most of their directors were figures well known to hold at least Conservative, if not always Thatcherite, views.

Much the most controversial policy in respect of local government was the introduction of the 'community charge'. Widely known as the poll tax, this was introduced to replace domestic rates. The 1987 Conservative election manifesto promised reformed finance for local government and, as with rate-capping, new policies were tried out in Scotland first. The burden of rates varied with the size of the property on which they were levied. The new charge for local service would be levied upon each adult. For Margaret Thatcher, the great advantage was 'accountability':

> Of the 35 million local electors in England, 17 million were not themselves liable for rates, and of the 18 million liable, 3 million paid less than the full rates and 3 million paid nothing at all . . . many people had no reason to be concerned about their council's overspending, because somebody else picked up all or most of the bill.[25]

The 'somebody else', of course, was that property-owning group at the heart of Thatcher's support; she empathised with it like no other group in British society. An important subset of property owners was small businessmen, from which group Thatcher had herself sprung. The prospect of a uniform business rate, rather than the hugely different burdens that small businesses bore depending upon where they were located, was another part of the package. Accountability was one issue, but the Prime Minister was anxious to spread the burden of local government more widely. In this policy, perhaps uniquely during her eleven years in power, her political instincts proved disastrously faulty. A poll tax could not be presented to the public as anything other than regressive. It bore more heavily on those with limited incomes and hardly at all (as a proportion of income at any rate) upon the wealthy.

From its inception, the poll tax encountered stiff resistance. Many back-bench Conservative MPs – especially those in marginal constituencies – opposed it, feeling it to be a certain vote loser. Some influential voices, not least that of Nigel Lawson, the Chancellor of the Exchequer, were raised against it in the Cabinet. Opinion poll evidence told a uniform story: the so-called 'community charge' was deeply unpopular. Early projections had suggested to Thatcher that the charge per head would be less than £200 – hefty enough, but supportable. By early 1990, she was receiving revised estimates that it would be about £350, implying a charge for a family with two children of 18 and 20 years of almost £1,500 per year. Meanwhile, opposition to the introduction of the charge was mounting, generating the potential for massive public disorder. Advisers also told Thatcher that many who either moved accommodation frequently or were of no fixed abode would not put themselves onto the voting register, so increasing the likelihood that they would stay beyond the reach of the tax. Such voluntary disenfranchisement was an obvious threat to the democratic process, although how heavily this point actually weighed with Thatcher was debatable, as few of these marginal folk were likely to be Conservative voters anyway.

The resolution of the poll tax fiasco lies beyond the scope of this book, as it took place after she left office. Its important contribution to her fall is considered elsewhere (see Chapter 10). The fact that she continued to press ahead with such a deeply unpopular policy is significant. It emphasises what a resolute fighter she was. She had fought off severe opposition before and always won. She also knew that many notional party allies would always run for cover at the first sign of danger, or else use that danger to plot against her. The poll tax may also indicate, however, her increasingly insecure grip on political reality in the late 1980s. She seemed to believe that, by appealing over the heads of the political establishment to 'her' people – the ordinary house-owners of rural and suburban England – she would always be vindicated. She was wrong. It is not without irony that Britain's most determined and most powerful Prime Minister since the Second World War should be brought down on a measure concerned with local government – an area on which she had tested constitutional proprieties to their limit and on which she felt that she could mobilise her populist appeal most effectively.

6   The attack on the professional ethic

'All professions are conspiracies against the laity', wrote George Bernard Shaw in *The Doctor's Dilemma* in 1911. Margaret Thatcher would have had very little in common with Shaw, the Irish playwright, lover of music (he was a distinguished, if idiosyncratic, music critic) and socialist moralist who died in 1950, the year Thatcher fought her first, unsuccessful general election as Conservative candidate for the hopeless constituency of Dartford. On this one point, however, conviction Conservative and garrulous socialist sage were at one. Thatcher, too, was suspicious of professionals. She was irritated by the easy, apparently effortless, expertise many possessed, and considered the higher professionals a pampered élite. Professionals regulated themselves. In doing so, she thought that they winked at sloppy practice and casual inefficiency. They were insufficiently self-critical. However finely honed their skills, and however much their expertise was valued, Thatcher felt that they were insufficiently responsive to market forces – and thus a collective impediment to the achievement of the kind of world she wished to bring about. Professionals were particularly prominent defenders of that welfare tradition, especially in health and education, which had been inherited from William Beveridge in the 1940s and which had become an increasingly heavy burden upon the taxpayer. Thatcher's radicalism encompassed a critical approach to welfare state. Welfarism, in her view, had spawned a dependency culture; it militated against innovation, risk and economic achievement It is hardly surprising, therefore, that the professional ethic should be prominently in her sights.

THE NATIONAL HEALTH SERVICE

The National Health Service (NHS) presented particular problems for an ideologically driven Prime Minister. On the one hand, the administrative structure of the NHS was widely acknowledged to be both inefficient and wasteful. Some parts of the country were much better served than others. Also, its costs were extremely high, not least because universal provision of high-quality service since the NHS came into being in 1948 had increased life expectancy. More than twice as many people in the United Kingdom (1.6 million) were over 80 years of age in 1981 than in 1951, and the number would increase to 2.2 million by the time Thatcher left office. In 1991, 16 per cent of the population was over the male pensionable age of sixty-five, compared with 11 per cent when the NHS was founded.[1] Inevitably, the very old make heavy demands on scarce resources. Economically, the NHS was the victim of its own success. The Prime Minister's think tanks devised numerous schemes for reducing costs and introducing more market mechanisms into the service. A Central Policy Review Staff ('Think Tank') paper in the early 1980s proposed a package of measures – including the promotion of private health insurance, charging for doctors' visits and increasing prescription charges – designed to save between 10 and 12 per cent of the NHS budget.[2]

On the other hand, every opinion poll confirmed the British public's attachment to the NHS. For some it represented almost the only beacon of international excellence amid long-term post-war decline. Any tinkering was bound to be politically unpopular, and the radical options presented by right-wing think tanks could be electorally disastrous. In a widely reported, and by her opponents much derided, statement to the party conference in 1982, Thatcher declared: 'The National Health Service is safe with us . . . the principle that adequate health care should be provided for all regardless of the ability to pay must be the function of any arrangements for financing the NHS. We stand by that'.[3]

Thatcher's policy for the NHS followed a familiar pattern. Always the acute populist, she refused to follow the logic of her right-wing advisers either as far, or as fast, as they wanted. Important changes to the service were undertaken, involving cost-cutting by reducing the length of most hospital stays and the encouragement of 'care in the community' – particularly when that care was provided by the private sector. Health authorities were encouraged to look for efficiency savings; general practitioners (GPs) were allocated cash limits, which more or less dictated that they prescribe the cheaper of alternative drugs. Some ancillary services were contracted out to the private sector. However, financial commitment to the NHS remained strong. Between 1980 and 1987, the cash made available to it increased by almost 60 per cent while the share of public expenditure directed towards the NHS continued to increase.[4] In statistical terms, the government could make a strong case for saying that it remained committed to the health service. Politically, there was every reason for caution. As Thatcher confided in her memoirs, 'The NHS was a huge organisation which inspired at least as much as it exasperated . . . and whose basic structure was felt by most people to be sound. Any reforms must not undermine public confidence'.[5]

Margaret Thatcher's right-wing instincts replaced her electoral caution only after the general election of 1987 when, with spiralling NHS costs threatening almost on their own to destroy the government's commitment to reduced public expenditure, a new review was begun. The health service had been under almost constant review by both Labour and Conservative governments, but Thatcher promised that this one would be different. It would inaugurate the most far-reaching review of the service in its forty-year history.[6] She was as good as her word. The NHS White Paper *Working for Patients* (1989) unveiled the principle of the 'internal market', which proposed to separate 'purchasers' from 'providers'. About 300 'hospital trusts' would run large hospitals, and health authorities would 'purchase' their services. Money would follow resources. GPs, the first port of call for most NHS users, were brought into the new market system by being given their own budgets. They would thus have choice in where they referred their patients for further treatment. Choice was the carrot, economy the stick:

> Giving GPs budgets of their own also promised to make it possible for the first time to put reasonable limits on their spending – provided we could find ways of having some limit to the number of GPs within the NHS and to how much they spent on drugs.[7]

Beneath the incentives lay a thinly veiled attack on the medical profession itself. Thatcherism had convicted it of inefficient administration and insufficient contact with her real world – that of business. Thatcher's view was simple: 'Dedicated its staff generally were; cost conscious they were not'.[8] The management of the new trusts was to be put in the hands of business, rather than medical, experts and the Conservative Party scoured the business and management world for sympathisers to launch the new system. A predictable, and bitter, battle between the professional and the business ethic ensued. The British Medical Association (BMA), which boasts the proud record of opposing every radical health reform of the twentieth century, including National Insurance in 1911 and the National Health Service itself in 1948, spent much more on this anti-government campaign than on any other. The Association met its match in the bluff brutalism of the new Health Secretary, Kenneth Clarke, an overweight cigar smoker who came to his task of government profession-basher with both experience and relish. He was a gift to BMA propagandists: 'Question: What do you call a man who ignores medical advice? Answer: Kenneth Clarke', ran the double-edged joke. But Clarke could take a joke as well as he could dish out punishment. He also knew that he was on to a winner. His department had been given a budget of 'incentives' designed to split the profession and ensure, amid much rancour, that the first, lavishly funded, trust hospitals would be established. The first business managers – alert to every cost-cutting opportunity short of their own grotesque salaries – were installed along with them.

Thatcher had left office by the time the NHS reforms were in place, but they bore the hallmark of both her preferences and her prejudices. It is, therefore, appropriate to attempt what we might properly call an 'audit' of their short-term effectiveness. Medical anger was slow to abate, although those GPs who serendipitously discovered a talent for that financial management which had been no part of their training could see profit, if not objective merit, in the changes. BMA leaders such as John Marks continued to believe the reforms 'damaging to patients'.[9] Medical practitioners felt that constant financial surveillance impaired their general efficiency by engendering stress. The Durham medical husband and wife team Brian and Margaret Docherty, for example, estimated in 1994 that '80 per cent of GPs are disenchanted with their jobs, feeling increasingly that the new fund-holding powers leave the government with central control, while wasting money on newly created tiers of administration and accounting'.[10]

The most damaging charges were two. First, NHS reforms switched admittedly growing funding away from patient care and towards self-important and overweening administration. Second, the large number of financially independent trusts – all of which needed to show a 'profit on trading' – contributed towards increasingly inequitable treatment opportunities for patients. Structurally, this was always likely since the culture of competition – in this case between health trusts – deliberately superseded that of service. The National Health Service was ceasing to be 'national'.

The growth in managerial costs was truly staggering. Early in 1995, the Department of Health released figures which showed that the total salary costs of managers in the NHS increased by 283.9 per cent (from £158.8 million to £609.6 million) in four years – between 1989–90 and 1993–4.[11] This extraordinary development offers further evidence in support of the general observation that – whatever the intention of their begetters – all revolutions beget bureaucracy much more certainly than they beget improvement. In Thatcher's case, the 'culture of audit and financial accountability' assumed a pre-eminence greater even than a Prime Minister pledged to 'change everything' bargained for.[12]

Inequality between patients also seems to have increased since Thatcher's NHS reforms were put into operation. Some trusts flourished; others came near to bankruptcy – kept afloat more by political than by financial considerations. By the autumn of 1996, the BMA was reporting that the treatment of non-emergency patients was now more likely to depend upon whether fund-holding GPs or health authorities had any money left at the end of their financial year than upon how ill, or in how much pain, those patients were. Yet the paradox is that Conservative governments have continued to fund the health service more generously than any other element in the public sector. In real terms, funding on the NHS increased by 74 per cent between 1979 and 1995. One has to ask, however, whether misconceived ideology has seen too much of this money spent on the wrong things. It is difficult to dissent from the judgement of John Gray, who concluded that Thatcherite policies:

> . . . created a bureaucratic apparatus of internal markets that is both costly and inefficient, diverts scarce resources from patient care and threatens the autonomy of the medical professions. On any reasonable measure this experiment in imposing market forces on the NHS through the agency of a managerial revolution from above has been a ruinous failure.[13]

By the autumn of 1996, no fewer than thirty-four NHS trusts, statutorily required to break even, were in deficit and the Department of Health was anticipating that the health service as a whole would be £118 million in deficit. Successful trusts were dealing with more patients than they had budgeted for, so even these were falling foul of unrealistic financial constraints. Meanwhile, between 1990 and 1994 the number of available beds in NHS hospitals had fallen by an average of 2 per cent, this inevitably masking much larger falls in some areas. Barking in east London, for example, had 11 per cent fewer beds available over this period.[14]

EDUCATION

Thatcherite *dirigisme* was not likely to leave the education professionals in peace. Thatcher believed that too much money was being spent to achieve too little: 'increases in public spending had not by and large led to higher standards'. The Inner London Education Authority was singled out for special blame: it 'spent more per pupil than any other education authority and achieved some of the worst examination results'.[15] As with the NHS, Thatcher's criticisms went beyond mere prejudice. If, like Thatcher, you believed in the importance of both competition and examination success, then you would readily agree that these attributes were given relatively low priority in many comprehensive schools of the 1980s. If, like Thatcher, you believed that the education profession had not adumbrated a clear set of priorities, if you thought that civil servants in the Department of Education were in cahoots with teacher-trainers to frustrate ministers' policies, if you realised that too many of Her Majesty's education inspectors had been 'successful' teachers in schools whose values you deprecated, if you believed that the education establishment was a secret garden of cosy consensuality that valued 'personal development' above measurable attainment, then you would want to dismantle the entire culture. You would also expect fewer heavyweight battles. Parents were, on the whole, less protective of their children's schools than patients were of their doctors' surgeries, and the National Union of Teachers carried considerably less clout than the BMA.

As in other areas, notably economic policy (see Chapter 2), it is important to see Thatcher as an accelerator of change rather than as an initiator of it. As in other areas too, notably health, the most radical changes are 'end-loaded' to the last two or three years of her prime ministership. Debate had raged for at least a century about the alleged inadequacies of the British educational system, widely considered insufficiently 'practical' and catering adequately for only a privileged minority of pupils.[16] The comprehensive experiment of the 1960s rapidly proved as controversial as the '11+' selection examination, introduced under the 1944 Butler Education Act, had been. It was the Labour Prime Minister James Callaghan who, in a famous speech at Ruskin College in Oxford in 1976, called for a Great Debate on the subject. He asked fundamental questions: Why were so many pupils leaving school with inadequate levels of literacy and numeracy? Did the secondary curriculum meet the needs of most pupils? Were public examinations fit for purpose?

Callaghan, therefore, wanted to go back to basics, although he was anxious to stress the importance of carrying the teaching professionals with him. Interestingly, Keith Joseph, who served as Education Secretary until Kenneth Baker took over in 1986, regretted that he had not followed this advice: 'Don't make the same mistake as I did of attacking the teachers'.[17] Thatcher, as ever, had no compunction about smiting opponents hip and thigh, and the educational establishment was certainly considered to be an important part of 'the opposition'. Education was, of course, the only departmental ministry of which she had Cabinet experience and, on the strength of it, she roundly informed Joseph that he had 'an awful department'.

As ever, Thatcher brought passion and conviction to a debate not of her instigation. Her preferred solutions encompassed the usual incompatible objectives of greater central controls on distrusted professionals, increased financial accountability, wider 'consumer' choice in a quasi-free educational market and elements of privatisation. Education Acts in 1980 and 1986 extended parental choice of school and gave school governors wider powers, which, as it turned out, few of them properly understood or actually wanted to discharge. The government intended school governors to reflect local community interests, and encouraged business interests to get more involved. It also wished boards of governors to institute more rigorous checks on complacent or incompetent teachers. Few had any such intention. Many 'governed' consensually and at a distance, if at all, while head teachers 'managed' governors' meetings and hoped to operate much as before. Indeed, it became as difficult to find willing and competent governors for some schools as it had been to find interested or competent overseers in the years before Poor Law reform in 1834.

The Prime Minister was, however, able to round up her usual, and usually unloved, suspects in local government. Throughout the 1980s, both powers and funding were systematically withdrawn from local education authorities (LEAs). LEAs were asked to jump through ever more administrative hoops on a lower budget and with reduced income. Between 1979 and 1986, public spending on schools was reduced by about 10 per cent in real terms.[18] During the period 1984–7, the government fought, and largely won, a number of pay battles with the teacher unions. Education funding was finally increased, by about 4 per cent, in the last years of the Thatcher administration, largely in order to fund the implementation of new departures enshrined in the Education Act of 1988.

This important Act offered the by now characteristically inconsistent Thatcherite mixture of free market ideology and tighter state control. The management of state schools became concentrated in the hands of head teachers and governors as local education authority involvement rapidly waned. Schools were given financial inducements to opt out of LEA control altogether. In most authorities, the professional teacher advisory service was either pared down or withdrawn. Parental choice was to be paramount; it became theoretically easier to choose schools outside an individual's local authority.

Kenneth Baker believed that a large number of comprehensive schools were failing children and believed that comparisons of educational attainment with other industrial nations were becoming increasingly unfavourable. What nine out of ten German sixteen-year-olds achieved, for example, seemed to be within the compass of only four out of ten English pupils at the same age. For him, 'the key to raising education standards across the country was a national curriculum'.[19] He was not surprised to learn that what he called 'the education establishment in university departments of education' were deeply suspicious, although the inspectorate was considerably less hostile.

Baker decided that only central direction would do. He believed that far too many schools lacked firm direction, 'adrift in a sea of fashionable opinions about what children should not, rather than should, be taught'. Thus, a National Curriculum with compulsory subjects and defined content was imposed on all state schools. The confusingly named 'public schools', which operate in the private sector and to which almost all Cabinet members sent their own children, could adopt the new curriculum, in whole, in part or not at all as their governors determined. Thatcher wanted from the National Curriculum a simple, compulsory structure that would provide reliable evidence about school and pupil performance and measurements that could inform parents' choice of schools. The education professionals proved surprisingly resilient in their ability to respond by producing a curriculum neither simple nor easily assessable.

Its design was fatally flawed. No National Curriculum, as such, was ever designed. Instead, work on the ten 'core' and 'foundation' subjects that were supposed to take up 80 per cent of curriculum time was delegated to separate small groups of subject and professional experts. Faced with what they clearly saw as a wonderful, and wonderfully unexpected, opportunity to define their subject, they produced intricate and complex structures which – had they ever been implemented – would have taken up about 150 per cent of curriculum time, utterly bemusing most non-specialists in the process. Margaret Thatcher, who kept closely abreast of developments in the secret educational garden, needed her famous ability to survive on four hours' sleep a night as she ploughed through the voluminous complexities which the subject experts devised. History, which she simply considered to be 'an account of what happened in the past' (whose account one wonders?) based upon 'knowing dates', drew her particular anger:

> In July 1989 the History Working Group produced its interim report. I was appalled. It put the emphasis on interpretation and enquiry as against content and knowledge. There was insufficient weight given to British history. There was not enough emphasis on history as chronological study.[20]

Kenneth Baker, a history graduate himself, later commented upon his old boss's simplified views. Thatcher 'saw history as a pageant of glorious events and significant developments, with our small country having given the world parliamentary democracy, an independent judiciary and a tradition of incorrupt administration'.[21] Baker saw the irony in all of this; Thatcher certainly did not. She had the history curriculum extensively revised, and somewhat simplified, by a National Curriculum Council 'Task Group'. Again, however, the professionals refused to concede lists of dates and the memorising of factual knowledge at the expense of historical understanding or ritual obeisance before what one then junior civil servant impishly described as 'heroic icons'. Similarly, the mathematics working party was not to be deflected from its preference for the understanding of concepts over mental arithmetic and the rote learning of formulae and multiplication tables. In English, battles royal raged over the primacy of literary canon of great works and, in particular, how much Shakespeare it was advisable for fourteen-year-olds to study.

The National Curriculum Assessment Structure, based on complicated attainment targets and a ten-level scale, found little favour with the Prime Minister. She noted acidly that her Education Secretary had 'warmly welcomed' the report that recommended this structure, whereas she (most unusually!) admitted that she had 'no opportunity' to study it 'having simply been presented with this weighty jargon-filled document in my overnight box with a deadline for publication the following day'. It survived beyond Thatcher's term of office, although her instincts about it proved correct. It had to be considerably simplified once the experts tried actually to *use* it to assess real children.

The National Curriculum, then, lumbered bureaucratically into the 1990s and Thatcher was forced to concede defeat on important matters of detail to the experts. She won, however, on her essentials: a centralised structure of agreed learning and the means – however crude and flawed – for quantifying school performance. The new General Certificate of Secondary Education, which replaced the old, divided GCE ordinary level (O level) and Certificate of Secondary Education in 1988, gave even higher-profile measurements of pupil and school attainment. Results showed steady improvement, suggesting that a much larger proportion of sixteen-year-olds were capable of gaining the equivalent of five passes at the old 'O' level under the new system than the old. Professionals seemed to be doing their job. Inevitably, however, critics – mostly from the Tory right – complained about declining academic standards and argued that results had been inflated by excessive reliance upon insufficiently policed coursework. GCE advanced level (A level), disliked by most education professionals as too narrow, survived as the 'gold standard' of educational attainment. The same critics complained that it had become debased by the examination boards that allowed the pass and high-grade rates to rise for fifteen consecutive years. 'Better teaching', said the professionals; 'easier exams', riposted the critics. As the examination boards destroy almost all old examination scripts, the issue could not be resolved either way even after a long and frustrating survey undertaken in 1995–6 by the Schools Curriculum and Assessment Authority.

GCSE and A-level results became the crucial variables in new, published school league tables.[22] These the educational professionals criticised as inadequate because they contained no means of assessing either the quality of the intake or the amount of value a school had 'added' to an individual pupil's attainment. Thus, a school in a working-class catchment area with few educational traditions might be helping pupils towards high achievement although it would rank lower (and seem 'worse') than one that selected a large number of very bright pupils for admission and did less with them. League tables, however, could be readily understood by most of those who bothered to read them. The scrutineers' priorities were at least as much social as educational. Many wished to ensure that neither James nor Jocasta went to a 'working-class' school anyway. House prices within the catchment area of 'good schools' increased more rapidly than did those outside them, a trend which accelerated at the turn of the century. The National Curriculum did nothing to halt the pronounced trend towards the residential zoning of comprehensive schools and de facto selection by area. Parental choice, a central plank of Thatcherite education policy, is of very limited value when many of those which the league tables suggest are the 'best' schools are hugely oversubscribed.

CRIME

Crime and criminal policy had surprisingly limited impact on political debate until the 1960s. Since 1945, criminologists, Home Office officials and politicians had maintained a broad 'Butskellite' consensus on the best means to control crime and to maintain public order. The number of notifiable offences in England and Wales increased steadily but did not exceed 1 million per year until the mid-1960s. The increase of 111 per cent over that decade, however, saw it emerge prominently in the then Conservative Opposition's election manifesto in 1970.[23] Thereafter, crime remained a significant electoral issue. The Conservative Party appropriated crime as 'its' issue, calling for increased expenditure on police and longer sentences for wrongdoers. Home Secretaries promising tougher action against criminals were guaranteed rapturous receptions at party conference. The disorder associated with strikes and extremist political parties during the 1970s kept the issue in the forefront of debate. Thatcher took it over gladly, knowing crime to be a matter of growing concern among 'her' people, particularly the lower middle classes. During the 1979 general election campaign, she asserted that 'the demand in the country will be for two things: less tax and more law and order'.[24]

Almost the first action of the Thatcher government in May 1979 was to announce that recommendations for police and army pay rises, due to have been implemented by the outgoing administration only in November, were to be met in full, backdated to 1 April and paid immediately. It was a symbolic announcement of the government's law and order and defence priorities. In contrast with the severe squeeze on public funding elsewhere, expenditure on the criminal justice system increased from £2 billion in 1979–80 to £3.9 billion in 1984–5.[25] In the first three years of the Thatcher government, almost 10,000 additional police were recruited, bringing the complement to about 120,000. 'Short sharp shock' treatment for young offenders in detention centres was introduced and a major prison-building programme was put in train.[26]

Thatcher's attack on the professionals was much more oblique in the area of criminal policy than it was in the health service or education, but her targets rapidly became clear enough. The Thatcher years were notable for a shift in emphasis towards 'community-based' approaches to crime and crime prevention. The Home Office pioneered a 'situational crime prevention' strategy. This relied on making it harder for criminals to attack prime 'targets' and thus reduce the potential for that opportunistic criminal activity that contributed so heavily to recorded crime statistics and which was so common among teenage and young adult working-class males, statistically the most criminally inclined social group. The widely publicised policy had some marked success, notably in the proliferation of Neighbourhood Watch schemes and the development of ever more sophisticated security devices. Not surprisingly, Situational Crime Prevention worked best in prosperous areas. Here owner–occupiers could afford to invest substantial sums in anti-theft devices. Many were also amenable to homilies such as those offered by the Home Office minister John Patten in 1988: 'Individual responsibility for one's own property and responsibility towards the wider community are both important in reducing the opportunities for crime'.[27]

Neither tough Tory stances on crime nor 'community action' or substantially increased expenditure on law and order had much impression on the crime figures; rather the reverse. The number of recorded crimes rose by between 5 per cent and 7 per cent per year during Thatcher's period in government, the number of notifiable offences in Britain increasing from about 2.5 million per year to about 4.5 million. Motor vehicle theft, vandalism and burglary increased particularly rapidly during the 1980s.[28] As R. Evans says, 'The enormous costs and limited effectiveness of the criminal justice system became a grievous concern for a Conservative government intent on reducing taxation and promoting policies which deliver "value for money" and "cost-effectiveness" '. Professional criminologists were not slow to offer their explanations for the huge increase in recorded crime during the Thatcher decade. The overwhelming majority of the profession related crime to deteriorating social conditions. Criminologists offered substantial evidence in support of the positive correlation, especially between urban deprivation and decay, youth unemployment and levels of recorded crime.

Thatcher was entirely unpersuaded by such professional opinion. Of course, she did not trust what was a notoriously left-leaning professional group anyway. More important, she remained convinced that crime was a moral, not a social, issue. Echoing the views of so many party activists, she blamed the decline of authority 'of all kinds – in the home, the school, the churches and the state'. In the wake of the 1981 riots (see Chapter 2), the media came in for their share of blame too: 'the impression [was] given by television that . . . rioters could enjoy a fiesta of crime, looting and rioting in the guise of social protest'.[29] Her views depressed the professionals. Attempts to put them into practice failed miserably, yet there is no evidence that they did her anything but electoral good. Despite all empirical evidence that Thatcher's policies failed to work, crime remained a 'Tory' issue throughout the Thatcher years. One criminologist summed up the frustrations and bemusement of an entire profession:

> . . . the Conservative party retains its supremacy as the party of 'law and order'. It has managed to persuade a large section of the electorate that the rising tide of crime is not to be explained by the widened divide between rich and poor, the undermining of public goods and services, the emasculation of local government, and the lauding of competitive individualism to the detriment of collective responsibility. Rather crime is to be ascribed to evil individuals . . . generally young persons, subject to insufficient control by parents who have a duty to police their behaviour.[30]

What is the balance sheet from Thatcher's attack on the professional ethic? Two contradictory conclusions suggest themselves. First, she succeeded in pushing through almost all of her main objectives. In doing so, and again as intended, she shook the professionals up, causing fundamental reappraisals of objectives and values. Most of her changes, furthermore, stuck into the 1990s. The culture of performance indicators and league table measurements remained a rampantly besmirching aspect of life under New Labour after 1997. Given the virulent opposition that Thatcher's innovations encountered at the time, their durability represents a substantial achievement. Left to the professionals, few, if any, of the key changes discussed in this chapter would have come about. As with so much of her legacy, flawed and controversial although it has been, few spoke in the 1990s of dismantling it. She reshaped the agenda. Second, however, she seems to have overlooked the crucial point that the service sector of an economy is necessarily labour intensive. The morale of its labour force is, in consequence, crucial. Most of the changes alienated most of the professionals they affected. For those called upon to 'deliver' the new services, the regular consequences were longer working hours and higher stress levels. Even the language has changed. NHS trust managers now routinely 'deliver' health care while teachers 'deliver' academic or vocational courses – much as milkmen used to deliver milk. The language of the market place has seeped insidiously, and malignantly, into professional parlance.

Achievement has been less impressive than the scale of innovation. New approaches failed to reduce levels of crime in the Thatcher years. The NHS was fundamentally remodelled along business lines, although neither to its benefit nor to the liking of its users – or 'clients' as they were sometimes called. Surprisingly perhaps, the educational establishment won more battles than the medical establishment, although on matters of detail, not broad policy. Schools, encouraged to operate as small businesses, began to advertise their wares in glossy and expensive brochures, which, for some, take budget precedence over textbooks. Successful teachers have been encouraged, even required, to enrol on finance and business administration courses. Promotion tends to mean more time selling services or managing budgets and much less teaching children. Schools increasingly compete with one another over 'intake'. The status of ordinary school teachers, like the real value of their salaries, has declined. As in the health service, early retirement packages have been eagerly sought while a sense of being undervalued has become pervasive. If the professions were tamed by Thatcherism, then this was at substantial cost in both human and economic terms and to little discernible benefit.

7   Thatcher abroad I

Europe

PERCEPTIONS AND CONTEXT

Thatcher's lack of knowledge about the intricacies of foreign affairs was a major reason why many senior Conservatives underestimated her in the early years of her leadership. Although she travelled abroad regularly while leader of the Opposition, her background, education and earlier political experience had given her none of that breadth of vision that her Conservative predecessors enjoyed. As Education Secretary in the Heath government, she acquired no experience in foreign affairs. She was not a linguist and tended to be suspicious of foreigners, first because, for a front-ranking politician, she did not know many of them and, second, because she usually could not speak their language. Her simple patriotism was nourished much more in the East Midlands and the Home Counties than through those broader imperial contacts that were part of the family connections of all her predecessors, except Edward Heath. At the beginning of her premiership, she was, in fact, a little Englander.

What was Britain's position in world affairs when Thatcher became Prime Minister? It is tempting to characterise it in terms of rampant decline. Britain had, after all, given up almost all of its early twentieth-century empire, that largest agglomeration of territories upon which 'the sun never set' and which had been the source of such patriotic pride. The 'retreat from Empire' was, in fact, a more protracted affair than is often realised, although ceding independence to what had once been the 'black empire' took place largely over a twenty-year period from the late 1940s to the late 1960s. The process of adjustment was, therefore, an abrupt one, the more so since Britain had been laggard in moves towards creating closer ties with Europe. When Britain was invited in 1955 to participate in negotiations that would lead in 1957 to the establishment of a 'Common Market' of six leading western European powers, including France and Germany, it held aloof. The Chancellor of the Exchequer,

R.A. Butler, argued that Britain should remain involved in free trade initiatives only. Proposals for 'the creation of a common organisation for the peaceful development of atomic energy and the establishment of a common market in Europe, seemed likely to involve duplication with other arrangements or were fraught with special difficulties'.[1] Culturally and emotionally, closer links with the Empire still seemed for many a more eligible alternative than closer relations with Europe.

Perceptions changed as imperial possessions dwindled and the EEC established itself as formidable organisation with great potential for future development. As early as 1961, under Macmillan, Britain made efforts to join an organisation of which it could have been a leading – if not the dominant – partner four or five years earlier. However, both his application and that of Harold Wilson in 1967 fell foul of a veto by the French President, Charles de Gaulle, who feared that British entry would massively, and dangerously, increase US influence in Europe. De Gaulle's fears were not irrational. As Winston Churchill had noted in 1948, Britain's overseas interests could be represented as three interlinked circles – the British Empire and Commonwealth, the wider English-speaking world and what he called a 'United Europe', in reality anti-communist western Europe, which was being supported economically and militarily by US aid.[2] At least until the 1960s, it would have been a small minority of British people who considered the European 'circle' as important as the other two. Nevertheless, the decline of Empire, and some sharp lessons from the United States (not least over its lack of support for the Anglo-French invasion of Suez in 1956) that the so-called 'special relationship' with Britain should no longer be considered an equal one, promoted a deal of querulous introspection.

It was, of course, during Edward Heath's government that Britain signed the Treaty of Accession to the Common Market in January 1972, becoming a full member of the European Economic Community on 1 January 1973. Although she had no direct involvement in the negotiations, Thatcher was a member of the Conservative government that took Britain into Europe.

As Thatcher's relationship with Europe was so fraught for much of the 1980s, it is worth remembering that Edward Heath – temperamentally much more European inclined than she – nevertheless had his battles with his new partners. He was unable to do anything to unstitch a narrowly protective, uncompetitive Common Agricultural Policy, designed to benefit French peasant farmers more than anyone else. Well aware of what a divisive issue Europe was for both major political parties, he pursued economic objectives – not least in the field of regional development – much more than he did common social or technological ones. This was likely to backfire, first because the spectacular growth of European markets was slowing in the wake of the oil crises of the early 1970s and, second, because the government's evident lack of wholehearted enthusiasm for European developments rankled with many continental politicians, some of whom reflected that British behaviour was retro-spectively validating de Gaulle's decision to block British entry. Well before Margaret Thatcher's handbag began swirling around the council chambers of Europe, Britain was established as an 'awkward customer' or '*non-communitaire*'. Thatcher did not create scepticism about the value of closer links with European partners, but she was to exploit it to devastating and damaging effect.

THE EUROPEAN LEARNING CURVE

It is significant that Thatcher wanted to learn about 'abroad' for herself and from her own perspective. She was noticeably cool about Foreign Office briefings and she did not always trust her Foreign Secretaries to advance British interests. Her first Shadow Foreign Secretary was Reginald Maudling, who soon complained of being ignored:

> The problem was that contact between us was very little. I asked to go with her on her various visits overseas but I was courteously refused . . . What was more difficult still was her method of pro-ducing speeches on foreign affairs. I was not consulted in advance about whether she should make a speech on foreign policy at any given time.[3]

Thatcher took the first opportunity to sack Maudling, whose lan-guid, superior indolence she found as insufferable as his left-centre Conservative views. But even with advisers and ministers in whom she reposed greater confidence, she was always likely to announce, or change, policy without consultation. In foreign affairs, much more than in economic policy, she was prone to shoot from the hip.

She also made no secret of the fact that she had little time for the élite corps of the Foreign Office. She believed that the Foreign Office too frequently acted as if it were separate from, indeed superior to, other branches of government. Successive Foreign Secretaries, in her view, had been wrapped by their civil servants in a silken bureaucracy. In her view, while they were taught the intricacies and mystiques of diplomacy, they were too inclined to sell Britain short. Foreign Office orthodoxy was culturally inclined to prevarication and to consensus. She thus looked for every opportunity to clip Foreign Office wings. In terms of broad

strategy, she was her own Foreign Secretary. Over Anglo-American relations, over the Falklands War (see Chapter 8) and over negotiation with
the EEC, she invariably took the lead. During complex negotiations with
the EEC in 1980 over a financial rebate, for example, she packed her
Foreign Secretary off to Brussels: 'Peter Carrington, having received his
mandate from me', was how she later described the incident in a typical
passage from her memoirs. Geoffrey Howe, her Foreign Secretary for
six years, from 1983 to 1989, both a less confident and, in diplomatic
terms, an infinitely less experienced figure than Carrington, also played
second fiddle, although it has been suggested that Thatcher lost faith in
him because he had become 'a Foreign Office man'.[4]

Thatcher was also averse to working from Foreign Office briefs. One
of the most significant foreign policy statements of the Thatcher years
– her Bruges speech of September 1988 (see below) – was drafted by
her private secretary, Charles Powell, and not by the Foreign Office.
The silken skills of Powell were an extraordinarily useful complement
to Thatcher's more abrasive style – not least because, whatever he may
have thought privately, Powell proved an entirely loyal articulator of her
prejudices.[5] The observation that, in foreign affairs at least, he operated
more as Deputy Prime Minister than as private secretary had more than
a grain of truth.

Margaret Thatcher's objectives and methods in foreign affairs were
characteristically straightforward: she put Britain's interests, as she
interpreted them, first, and her ways could be jarringly direct. She noted
almost triumphally, concerning one of many fraught negotiations with
Common Market partners: 'I know nothing about diplomacy, but I just
know and believe that I want certain things for Britain'.[6] The 'certain
things' she wanted above all were three: increased respect for Britain as
a leading power in possession of both nuclear weapons and a permanent
(if anachronistic) seat on the Security Council of the United Nations; a
close alliance with the United States; and pretensions to closer European
unity put firmly in their place.

The key to understanding Thatcher's foreign policy is that she was
prone to regard Americans as honorary Englishmen (*sic*) and Europeans
as real foreigners. Her early visits to the United States in 1975 and
1977 had gone down well with hosts who shared her unrestrained free
market ideas. It was characteristic that she immediately broke with the
diplomatic convention that leaders of opposition parties do not openly
criticise the government when on foreign soil. Thatcher was no diplomat
and, when challenged, robustly retorted to the then Prime Minister,
James Callaghan that 'It's not part of my job to be a propagandist for a
socialist society'.[7] She formed an instant rapport with Henry Kissinger

in 1975 and asserted, perhaps prematurely, that 'I feel that I have been accepted as a leader in the international sphere'.

'MY MONEY'

Thatcher had none of Edward Heath's sympathy with the European ideal. Nor did she share his view that Britain's future lay in ever closer contacts with the EEC. She was suspicious of the EEC's tendency to that bureaucratic grandiosity which she knew in her bones was inimical to 'freedom'. This was the central theme of her speeches during the campaign for the first direct elections to the European parliament:

> We believe in a free Europe, not a standardised Europe . . . We insist that the institutions of the European Community are managed so that they increase the liberty of the individual throughout the continent. These institutions must not be permitted to dwindle into bureaucracy. Whenever they fail to enlarge freedom the institutions should be criticised and the balance restored.[8]

This distinctive critique was something with which her European partners would become all too familiar.

In the first year of government, however, her main priority was not bureaucratic but financial. Ever since joining the EEC in 1973, British contributions to the Community budget had considerably exceeded its receipts, and Thatcher was determined to get a large rebate. She set her eyes on an immediate transfer of £1,000 million to the UK Exchequer, although how this figure was arrived at – beyond the desire to wave very large round figures in pounds sterling in front of Germans and Frenchmen – was never clear. Her negotiating strategy was alien to the culture of the Community. She set out her stall and defended it, inflexibly and repetitively. She told her European partners in Strasbourg in June 1979 that she could not 'play Sister Bountiful to the Community while my own electorate are being asked to forgo improvements in the fields of health, education, welfare and the rest'.[9] A summit at Dublin in November almost broke up in disorder when Thatcher adamantly refused to dance to the weary Community quadrille of coded language and bluff, followed by graceful, mutually anticipated, concession at the fifty-ninth minute of the eleventh hour. When she said she wanted 'my money' back, she meant it and refused to back down. The German Chancellor, Helmut Schmidt, feigned asleep as she ranted on. The French President, Valéry Giscard d'Estaing, was openly contemptuous, describing Thatcher as *la fille d'epicier* – the grocer's daughter.

Neither man realised that such insults, both implicit and explicit, were grist to the Thatcher mill. She genuinely *did* believe that national interests came before Community ones. She *did* feel a genuine sense of injustice. Most important of all, she knew that her stand – dismissed throughout Europe as coarse, vulgar and unintelligent – was mightily popular among 'her' people in Britain, the only constituency in which she was truly interested. Aided by the predominantly right-wing tabloid press, she turned European contempt into domestic popularity by employing a calculated measure of xenophobia. It was an excellent example of Thatcherite populism in action.

Less populist, but at the core of growing Conservative discomfiture over Europe both in the Thatcher period and beyond, was the issue of sovereignty. Soon after Thatcher left office, the prominent Tory intellectual and MP David Willets asserted that 'political sovereignty means more to us than to many continental countries; it is more closely linked to our sense of nationhood'.[10] For Thatcher, what she called 'British democracy, parliamentary sovereignty, the common law, our traditional sense of fairness' were all threatened by developments in Europe.[11] In reality, what Europe threatened was not so much British nationhood as Thatcher's world economic view, based on free markets, low taxation and very limited state intervention. Key elements of the European ideal incorporated trade protection (the Common Agricultural Policy was an excellent example), closer cooperation within a geographically defined Community and collectivist social policies, paid for, if necessary, by higher taxes. Furthermore, for many Europeans there remained the ultimate objective of a federal European state. Although she was too shrewd ever to be forced to make the choice, Thatcher was at root more of an international free-marketeer and a supporter of global capitalism than she was an English nationalist. Her growing hatred of the European Community (EC) owed even more to its collectivist aspects and its commitment to 'improving' social policies than it did to its challenge to British sovereignty. Playing the patriotic card, however, won greater political dividends.

Thatcher could claim reasonable success when, in 1980, she won about two-thirds of 'her' money back after the EEC conceded a three-year deal of rebates totalling £1,570 million. Thatcher – wanting the lot – accepted the deal reluctantly and only after considerable persuasion by Viscount Carrington. Her aristocratic and experienced Foreign Secretary was, in fact, privately as aghast at Thatcher's negotiating tactics as were Giscard and Schmidt. However, he entrusted to his memoirs only that diplomatic language which came so naturally when he spoke of her 'firmness and intransigence' as the 'key factors in getting us a proper settlement'. He sardonically noted: 'I cannot pretend that the resultant atmosphere made all our foreign relations easier to conduct'.[12] His mistress did not give a hoot.

THE COMMON AGRICULTURAL POLICY

Budget grumbles over funding continued until the Fontainebleau summit in 1984, when agreement was reached to reduce the British budgetary contribution to a level broadly related to the country's GNP and not, as before, considerably in excess of that. The most contentious EC issue during the middle years of Thatcher's period in office – and directly related to budgetary rows – was the Common Agricultural Policy (CAP). She called the policy at various times 'wasteful','extravagant' and 'Mad Hatter economics'; it took up almost 70 per cent of the entire EEC budget when she came to power.[13] By the mid-1980s, CAP subsidies totalled $22 billion per year.[14] Her criticisms had point. The CAP had been a foundation stone of the original Common Market, and its main purpose was protectionist. The system of guaranteed prices for farmers was designed to ensure continuity of production and stability in food markets. As there was no prospect of mass starvation in one of the world's richest areas, the CAP defaulted to uncovenanted benefit to often very inefficient small producers. Farmers as a whole were subsidised to produce, and produced, far more than the Community needed. 'Butter mountains' and 'wine lakes' resulted, and surpluses were 'dumped' at rock-bottom prices, often in communist Eastern Europe. The effect on a vigorous capitalist free-marketeer like Margaret Thatcher of a protectionist system that gave communists subsidised food can readily be imagined. A further illogicality of the system was that CAP subsidies tended to benefit inefficient more than efficient farmers, and British farmers were relatively efficient.

Thatcher wanted to be rid of the CAP, bag and baggage. The policy would never have been put in place had Britain – an industrial nation with a relatively small agricultural sector – been a founder member of the Community. As it was not, and as farmers were an immensely influential interest group in both France and Germany, there was no prospect of abolition, as Thatcher recognised. One of her main strengths as a conviction politician was the recognition that conviction and practical politics frequently point in opposite directions. When they did, and despite the steely public image, she was a firm believer in Voltaire's dictum: '*Le mieux est l'ennemi du bien*' [The best is the enemy of the good]. She had gained rare approval in Europe in 1986 for signing Britain up to the Single European Act, which would provide a free internal market, involving unrestricted movement of goods, labour and capital by 1992.[15] She wanted to exploit the opportunity to gain further concessions, rather than waste it by tilting at an unchallengeable Community icon. The result was an agreement at Brussels in February 1988 on a package of measures – including automatic price cuts beyond certain production levels – which reduced agricultural surpluses and confirmed substantial rebates to Britain.

The paradox of Thatcher's decision over the Single European Act should not go unremarked. The most stridently anti-European of British post-war Prime Ministers acquiesced in European legislation which, by qualified majority voting, would over-ride the preferences and policies of democratically elected national governments. As one commentator has observed:

> ... the Single European Act accelerated the process towards wider European integration, ultimately leading to the Maastricht Treaty in 1991 and the establishment of a single European currency in 1999, two issues which did so much to create the divisive faction-alism within the Tory Party.[16]

The Act was no dead letter. Numerous European 'directives' followed on a range of economic and social issues, including health, safety, holiday entitlement and the maximum length of the working week. For right-wing 'Euro-sceptics' in the Conservative Party of the mid-1990s, this degree of intervention represented a fatal compromise with the principle of national sovereignty. It is hardly surprising that they were too embarrassed to place the blame for this 'treason' where it properly lay – with Margaret Thatcher.

The last two years of Thatcher's prime ministership were all downhill, in European as in other ways (see Chapter 10). The enormities of the CAP had spurred a right-wing group of about seventy Conservative MPs to form a 'European Reform Group'. The title was misleading. The group really wanted to wreck rather than reform. Its profoundly anti-Europeanism reopened deep wounds within the party. Temperamentally, Thatcher was as anti-European as most. Politically, she knew that she needed to maintain a party balance, although this was becoming increasingly difficult. Furthermore, during her years in power she had forged useful links within Europe, notably with the Gaullist Prime Minister Jacques Chirac. Personal contact eventually smoothed out some of the rougher edges of her anti-Europeanism.

BRUGES AND BEYOND: HOLDING BACK A FEDERAL EUROPE

Many in Europe wanted to use the Single Market as a bridgehead to both closer economic cooperation and the creation of Europe as a fully federal state. Thatcher was extremely sceptical of the former and implacably hostile towards the latter. It did not help that one of the main supporters of such moves was the President of the EC Commission, Jacques Delors, who held the position from 1985 to 1995, and who was a cultivated Frenchman, an intellectual and a socialist. In 1988, he chaired a committee that drew up the strategy for European economic and monetary union, immediately dubbed the 'Delors plan'. The strategy had three 'phases': first, movement towards common membership of a European Monetary System (EMS); second, a central bank with control over the monetary policy of member states; and, third, the use of a single currency throughout the Community. Delors showed himself an interventionist in other ways too. He had no inhibitions about involving himself in the internal politics of member states, visiting the British Trades Union Congress in 1988 and – to great acclaim – regaling its delegates with his vision of a federal, socialist Europe.

Thatcher, who recognised Delors' abilities, hated his politics. What Delors welcomed as federalism, Thatcher interpreted as 'the erosion of democracy by centralisation and bureaucracy'.[17] She was particularly concerned that Commission advice and directives increasingly asserted EC powers to 'interfere' in the affairs of member states on issues as divergent as social security and subsidies for the arts. She believed, against the general view of her European colleagues, that Delors was abusing his powers by issuing directives that lacked the unanimous support of EC member states.

Her response was the Bruges speech of 20 September 1988. It was born of deep frustration that, despite her best efforts, Europe was moving in the wrong direction. In it, she declared that nations had, and must retain, distinctive identities. Britain would play no part in fostering 'some sort of identikit European personality'. She resisted any idea of a 'European super-state exercising a new dominance from Brussels' and called instead for 'willing and active co-operation between independent sovereign states' as 'the best way to build a successful European community'. She was careful also to include references to Europe outside the EC. To the frustration of Foreign Office officials, who had wanted a speech that would mend fences and emphasise the government's commitment to the EC as an institution, she gleefully stated: 'We shall always look on Warsaw, Prague and Budapest as great European cities'. One of her key objectives, as she later put it, was a 'wider, looser Europe'.[18]

The Bruges speech has widely been considered 'Gaullist' as it advocated strong government following clearly defined national priorities. There is, indeed, much of the Gaullist heritage in Thatcherism, not least in its invocation of pride and the importance of patriotic resurgence. De Gaulle, however, had the very considerable advantage of being able in the early 1960s to shape early development of the EEC. Much of the EEC was French, as it were, by design. Thatcher, by contrast, was in the late 1980s still the abrasive European outsider, and she was unlikely to increase British influence by mere assertion, however eloquently phrased. As always, however, she kept at least one eye on the British electorate. She could also engineer a warm reception for her message in the British press. Especially from 1982 onwards, British newspapers were predominantly Thatcherite on most foreign policy questions, and especially so when she was banging the patriotic British drum. The speech did not, however, prevent substantial Conservative losses in the European parliamentary elections a few months later. Thatcher blamed damaging, and politically significant, divisions within the party over Europe and not the Bruges speech.

Bruges aimed at putting a break on any headlong rush towards Euro-federalism. Monetary union nevertheless proceeded apace. Support grew for an 'Exchange Rate Mechanism' (ERM), a device whereby interest rates would be allowed to fluctuate only within defined bands. The overall objective was currency stabilisation as the basis for more secure investment. ERM was almost universally supported within the Community. Both the Chancellor of the Exchequer, Nigel Lawson, and the Foreign Secretary, Geoffrey Howe, wanted Britain to join the ERM. Thatcher, worried as ever about national sovereignty implications, was hostile. But, by the end of the 1980s, she was both isolated within the Community and increasingly beleaguered within her own party.

After much havering, she eventually consented to Britain's joining the ERM in October 1990, only six weeks before she lost office. Her memoirs make it clear that she agreed under duress and against her own better judgement: 'I had too few allies to continue to resist and win the day'.[19] In retrospect, it is clear that Britain went in at far too high an exchange rate, and probably also at the wrong time. Entry to the ERM ensured that the European issue would continue to fester within the party. The country was in any case forced out again less than two years later by a sterling crisis (see Chapter 11). The big political and economic battles on currency union remained to be fought. Thatcher had certainly not resolved the internal contradictions of Conservatism over Europe.

THE EUROPEAN RECKONING

Overall assessment of the success of Thatcher's European policy depends upon one's view of the EC, or European Union (EU) as it prematurely and pretentiously called itself from 1994, as a whole. Opponents of closer European unity argue that most of Thatcher's policies were successful. She used her formidable mastery over detail, her cool head for figures and her ability to concentrate for long periods on the most apparently trivial issues to negotiate substantially reduced budgetary contributions for Britain. She firmly rebuffed moves towards greater unity and peeled away some of the woollier idealism of '*l'esprit communitaire*'. One favourable critic called her early achievement 'remarkable' – imposing on the European community 'a Thatcherite interpretation . . . of economic policy [while] manipulating and dominating the community issues'.[20]

In all this, she also rang resonant chords with 'her' people at home. She believed that most of the French and German ministers with, or against, whom she worked had agendas just as narrowly nationalist as her own. Only their longer membership of the Community, which had enabled them to incorporate their countries' own priorities into its structure during the 1950s and 1960s, made them seem more pro-European. Blatant rudeness and disdain for the conventions of diplomacy she excused as bringing welcome directness and honesty to the negotiating table. A senior French diplomat dismissed Thatcher thus:

> That woman is an old-fashioned nationalist with no feeling for the European ideal. She reckons merely in terms of accountancy, not the broader political vision that is needed . . . Seen from Paris, the British government appears to express little belief in the need to develop the Community's institutions.[21]

Thatcher saw what the diplomat clearly intended to be a stinging rebuke in quite different terms. The 'European ideal' she regarded as humbug; 'accountancy' is crucial to good management, in the nation-state just as naturally as in the home; too many of the 'Community's institutions' – not least the appalling CAP – needed deracination rather than 'development'. As for 'political vision', Thatcher thought one person's vision to be another's impractical idealism. She presented herself as realist, albeit one with firm convictions. Her Bruges speech (see above) offered an alternative, and more practical, vision of European development:

> Let Europe be a family of nations, understanding each other better,

appreciating each other more, doing more together, but relishing our national identity . . . Let us have a Europe which plays its full part in the wider world, which looks outward not inward, and which preserves the Atlantic Community – that Europe on both sides of the Atlantic – which is our noblest inheritance and our greatest strength.[22]

The speech demonstrates that this most 'practical' of Prime Ministers could waffle with the best of them, but the specific message indicates how much she differed from the pro-Europeans. Insidious reference to Europeans 'on both sides of the Atlantic' reminded critics where her true loyalties lay.

The main criticisms of Thatcher's European policy are two. First, she failed to realise what she was signing Britain up to in the Single European Act. Her natural sympathisers had greatest reason to rue this spectacular piece of political naiveté. Second, she frequently wasted important opportunities by aggressive posturing. Such posturing was – more often than she allowed – followed by a standard 'Euro-fudge' anyway. Britain, largely because of the dominant perception in the 1950s that both its Empire and its US alliance were more important, had been a late entrant to the EEC. When it joined, in 1973, the British economy was far weaker vis-à-vis the major nations of the Community than it would have been in 1957. Britain did, however, have both a longer-established political democracy and at least as substantial a tradition of worldwide influence. These assets could have been used to build up a position of political equality, if not leadership, especially since the North-Sea oil-boosted British economy recovered quickly in the early 1980s, giving the country more opportunity to pull its weight cooperatively within Europe. In short, Britain had much that the Community needed. Thatcher withheld them in a sustained orgy of spleen, scepticism and penny-pinching precision. Any vision she had was all too clearly non-European. The close relationship she built with President Reagan suggested that Thatcherite Britain remained both strategically and emotionally much more attached to an Atlantic than to a European axis.

The long-term danger remained that the United States, by the early 1990s the world's only superpower, and one which was becoming less 'European' not only in temper but in ethnic composition with every passing year, had less interest in Britain than Britain had in the United States. A grossly unequal, if not sentimental, American alliance, anachronistically buffed as a 'special relationship' seemed a perverse preference over growing influence in a self-confident and economically advanced European power bloc. The assertion that close links with the United

States were not incompatible with constructive membership of the EC cut little ice.

The EC in the 1980s too often saw a once powerful, but now substantially diminished and geographically pretty remote, state on the north-west fringes of Europe trying to relive past glories under a formidable, but formidably wrong-headed, leader who refused to accept that medium-sized European nation-states could make effective and constructive contributions only through close collaboration with each other. Critics of Thatcher's EC policy bemoaned a decade of fractious wasted opportunity. In the late 1980s and early 1990s, Britain hedged, remained 'difficult' and negotiated opt-outs from measures designed to improve intra-Community trade, banking and social conditions. All too often, the constituency being addressed was not the Community but a disunited parliamentary Conservative Party. As Glynn and Booth have put it, Britain 'faced the prospect of continued relative decline on the fringes of a European community moving towards ever closer integration'.[23]

8 Thatcher abroad II

Defence and the Americas

ANGLO-AMERICAN CONTEXT

The Americas were crucial to Margaret Thatcher during the 1980s. She looked most naturally for support and friendship to Ronald Reagan, US President from 1981 to 1989, a like-minded right-winger, although the mind at his disposal was a good deal less powerful than hers. Her political fortunes were rescued from what seemed terminal decline in early 1982 by a brief and successful war with Argentina over sovereignty in the Falkland Islands. She is both temperamentally and materially drawn to the United States, as her phenomenally lucrative and empathetic lecture tours there during the 1990s demonstrated. 'Atlanticism' was a key element in British foreign policy during the 1980s.

Thatcher acknowledged its importance in a typically grandiose assessment made soon after she left office: 'The United States and Britain have together been the greatest alliance in the defence of liberty and justice that the world has ever known'.[1] Ignoring the fact that alliances are almost invariably made for far more pragmatic reasons than these, it is easy to see why the two countries had developed a long-term understanding. Most of the United States's early leaders were of British origin and, once the new state's independence was conceded by Britain in 1783, there was far more to bring them together than keep them apart; ethnicity, mutually beneficial trading relations and separate non-competing spheres of territorial influence were three which held good for most of the nineteenth century.

In the twentieth century, the United States fought two wars alongside Britain, although in both cases only eventually. In the Second World War, the US contribution was decisive when Britain, alone of Hitler's European opponents, survived to carry on the fight after 1940. Britain entered the Second World War as one of the leading imperial powers; the United States ended it as one of two antagonistic 'superpowers'. Its determination to build up western Europe as a geopolitical counterpart to the evil Soviet empire brought the United States more decisively into European affairs than ever before. Britain was seen as the mainstay of that European policy. Winston Churchill, whose own mother had been American, deliberately delivered his famous 1946 'Iron Curtain' lecture in a US institution with an apposite name – Westminster College, Fulton, Missouri.

The two nations have been sufficiently close allies since 1945 to warrant the frequently used description 'special relationship'. However, it was not an alliance without strain. Quite apart from specific, short-term disagreements, most notably Eisenhower's feeling that he had been maliciously misled by Eden over Britain's aggressive intentions at Suez in 1956, longer-term tensions were never far from the surface. The United States wanted Britain to take the lead in a strong western European phalanx against the USSR. At least until the late 1950s, Britain continued to see itself as a nation if not as powerful as the two superpowers then clearly more powerful than the rest. Its worldwide interests were, therefore, too important to risk dilution by membership of the Common Market. The United States (albeit usually privately) considered this self-perception unrealistic. Britain's relative economic decline became ever more apparent. Its worldwide role was also enormously diminished as it quit most of its old imperial possessions between the late 1940s and the early 1960s. Dean Acheson's observation in 1962 that 'Great Britain has lost an Empire and has not yet found a role' was more than a neat aphorism. It conveyed in code widespread US frustration with its ally's pretensions. Britain's independent nuclear status was both a costly piece of self-advertisement for a declining power and a further source of US annoyance. Britain could exert massive influence in an important, but precisely defined, sphere – Europe – but chose instead to posture as a great power to embarrassingly limited effect. US frustration was only increased by the fact that de Gaulle vetoed British membership of the EEC in the early 1960s on the grounds that Britain was too 'American' and insufficiently 'European'.

The 'special relationship' in the years before Thatcher, therefore, was often a matter more of style than of substance. It benefited both sides to assert its indissoluble existence and, indeed, genuinely warm relationships developed between national leaders; Kennedy and Macmillan in the early 1960s and Carter and Callaghan in the later 1970s stand out. Beneath the surface, however, relationships were not as 'special' as they seemed and were becoming less close. For example, Heath's Europeanism saw him support the EC over the United States during the trade protection squabbles of the early 1970s. The reality was that

Britain wanted a relationship more 'specially' than the United States. Yet Britain had less to offer to the United States than many of its political leaders thought. By the 1970s, the United States was not so dominated politically or culturally by Anglo-Saxons as it had been. A multicultural nation with growing Pacific interests in respect of both trade and defence gave the United States ever more powerful reasons to look at least as much west as east.

AMERICAN LOVE AFFAIR

What the United States had for Margaret Thatcher was both impeccable free trade credentials and a down-to-earth 'can do' mentality. Culturally, she was always much closer to the United States than to western Europe. The United States contained, so she believed, far more people with a practical business approach and far fewer intellectuals, theorists and ironists who presumed to tell her – in elegant, superior tones and at great length – what was not possible. Her love affair with the country was reciprocated, with characteristically American interest. Each of her many visits was accompanied by fawning attention, not least from the White House, and by a series of soft-centred, high-profile television interviews designed to show Thatcher as the quintessence of strong leadership, although always loyally pro-American.

It seemed that Britain had finally delivered to the United States the true successor to Winston Churchill. Thatcher, the consummate politician, never lost an opportunity to quote from the 'Winston' she hardly knew – except in his stroke-diminished dotage. Indeed, in 1983 she was in the United States to receive the 'Winston Churchill Foundation Award'. The citation read 'Like Churchill, she is known for her courage, conviction, determination and willpower. Like Churchill she thrives on adversity'.[2] It was a good job that no one told the awarders that much of Churchill's 'adversity' derived from political failure and from his frequently appalling relations with the Conservative Party, from which he was semi-detached for most of the 1930s. It is not clear either whether Thatcher knew that, during his period as a successful Liberal minister in an Asquith government which massively increased income taxes on the wealthy, Churchill enthusiastically increased the power of the state over people's lives. By the 1980s, however, these historical inconveniences could be swept under welcoming red carpets. The fact that Thatcher was a woman provided that essential 'human interest angle' without which the domestic US market could not be captured. Margaret Thatcher, no less than Grace Kelly or Katharine Hepburn, was a star – and she loved it.

Not surprisingly, Thatcher considered Ronald Reagan her kind of ally. She enthused:

> He was a buoyant, self-confident, good-natured American who had risen from poverty to the White House – the American dream in action – and who was not shy about using American power or exercising American leadership in the Atlantic alliance. In addition to inspiring the American people, he went on later to inspire the people behind the Iron Curtain by speaking honest words about the evil empire that oppressed them.[3]

Reagan's reciprocal admiration was fulsome. He felt that she showed 'the true grit of a true Brit'. She had energised British business which 'woken from the long sleep of socialism, are our feisty competitors in world markets'. Thatcher 'brought about a resurgence of those things Great Britain has always stood for'. He recognised that, despite occasional disagreements, she remained 'a friend of the American people . . . who shared the same basic outlook'.[4]

Many of Thatcher's speeches to US audiences were suffused with Cold War rhetoric. Her speech on receiving the Winston Churchill Foundation award was typical:

> The Soviet leaders . . . do not share our aspirations: they are not constrained by our ethics, they have always considered themselves exempt from the rules that bind other states. They claim to speak in the name of humanity, but they oppress the individual. They pose as the champion of free nations, but in their own empire they practise total control. They invoke the word democracy, but they practise single-party rule by a self-appointed oligarchy. They pretend to support the freedom of the ballot-box, but they are protected by a system of one man, one vote – and one candidate.[5]

Thatcher saw close Anglo-American relations as the key to safeguarding the interests of the free world against increasing challenges. The 'evil empire' had confirmed its true nature when it invaded Afghanistan in 1979. The outbreak of war between Iran and Iraq in 1980 indicated how Islamic fundamentalism could further destabilise the Middle East, since 1945 already a notoriously volatile area. Israel's invasion of Lebanon in 1982 only confirmed the pattern. Thatcher also believed that the maintenance of Britain's independent nuclear deterrent was the most effective contribution that Britain could make to the 'special relationship'. She authorised replacement of the now ageing Polaris submarine with first

Trident I and, in 1982, the updated and more expensive Trident II, pur-
chased from the US government. Although Trident II was acquired on
particularly generous terms – a consequence, it was said, of Thatcher's
ability to charm Reagan – it still cost £9 billion.[6,7] Meanwhile, the ar-
maments industry in both countries anticipated substantial profits from
subcontracts.

The closeness and interdependence of US and British defence policy
was emphasised by the stationing of US Cruise missiles in British bases
from 1983 to 1988. In April 1986, Thatcher permitted the United States
to launch bombing attacks against Libya from bases in Britain. No other
EC leader allowed the United States similar licence. Throughout the
1980s, European statesmen criticised the British government for taking
an insufficiently critical or independent stance in its relationship with
the United States. It was a major cause of tension with EC partners
(see Chapter 7). Thatcher had a ready response, which reflected her
anti-European prejudices as clearly as it was designed to strengthen
US resolve in Europe. In a speech to the US Congress in 1985, which
dealt with the western alliances' response to the Soviet empire as well
as international terrorism, she left her audience in no doubt that Europe
should continue to acknowledge its debt to US assistance both during
the Second World War and during the post-war period of reconstruction:
'The debt the free peoples of Europe owe to this nation, generous with
its bounty, willing to share its strength, seeking to protect the weak, is
incalculable. We thank and salute you.'[8]
She did not miss the opportunity to embarrass European allies by stressing her awareness that many in the United States considered Europeans
ungrateful for their generation of largesse. She intended that she should
be exonerated from any such charge:

> From these shores, it may seem to some of you by comparison with
> the risk and sacrifice which America has borne through four dec-
> ades and the courage with which you have shouldered unwanted
> burdens, Europe has not fully matched your expectations.[9]

The creation of a new Europe 'of many different histories and many
different nations' she envisaged as a development that would enable that
Europe 'to share the load alongside you'. Most of her fellow Europeans
saw the new Europe developing rather as an effective counterweight to
the growing power of the United States.

Defence policy was a priority for Thatcher, and arms dealers enjoyed
a bonanza during the 1980s. The Prime Minister's son, Mark, was one
of many to benefit. As so often, politics and populism went hand in

hand. Defence was usually a 'Conservative' issue, but it had a much higher political profile during the 1980s for two reasons. The first was 'the Falklands factor' (see below) and the second was the collective lunacy that afflicted the Labour Party for much of the decade. Michael Foot fought the 1983 election on a self-indulgent parade of socialist conscience; nuclear disarmament was a key feature. Neil Kinnock's usually deft footwork deserted him on defence during the 1987 campaign. Thatcher, never one to miss an easy target, savaged Labour's defence policies on both occasions. At the last Tory conference before the 1987 election, she told adoring delegates that 'A Labour Britain would be a neutralist Britain. It would be the greatest gain for the Soviet Union in forty years. And they would have got it without firing a shot'.[10] Both opinion polls and post-election analyses confirmed that the public shared Thatcher's view that it had been 'the balance of nuclear forces which had preserved peace for forty years'. Defence was a major vote-winner for the Tories in the 1980s. Opponents could debate both the validity and the morality of the *policies*, but the *politics* she got incontestably right.

TENSIONS IN THE 'SPECIAL RELATIONSHIP'

Although Reagan's presidency inaugurated a period of close, even suffocating, personal warmth between the two national leaders, the United States never remotely regarded Britain as an equal partner in the alliance. Important defence and foreign policy changes took place without consultation. In 1983, for example, Reagan announced a radical new Strategic Defence Initiative (SDI). As this depended on the use of complex antiballistic missile systems, the new policy was rapidly christened 'Star Wars', following the title of the immensely successful science fiction film released six years earlier. SDI was a source of particular worry for Europe. If its use (as the boffins claimed) could render the United States impregnable to any nuclear attack, why should the United States continue to spend huge amounts of money via the North Atlantic Treaty Organisation (NATO) in defence of western Europe?

On this point, at least, Thatcher shared European concerns. She used her influence with Reagan to ensure that what was clearly one of his major enthusiasms was placed in a broader context. This objective, it has to be said, was shared by some of Reagan's own advisers, who were well used to blunting what they saw as impractical initiatives from the Pentagon. At a meeting in Camp David just before Christmas in 1984, Thatcher stressed that Britain had no desire to stifle research into Star Wars but insisted that the new strategy be seen alongside, and not as a replacement for, nuclear deterrence. This accommodation survived to the end of Thatcher's prime ministership, by which time the imminent collapse of the 'evil empire' was changing all defence perspectives anyway. Thatcher's business antennae were alive to the commercial benefits of SDI. In 1985, she ensured that British firms were the first in NATO to participate with the Americans in research and development contracts associated with the project.[11]

The US invasion of the Caribbean island of Grenada in October 1983 was another important initiative taken without consulting Britain. The United States moved in response to requests from other Caribbean islands fearful that events in Grenada, where a Marxist regime had been toppled and replaced by another extreme leftist group, would destabilise the whole region. Two crucial points arise. Grenada was a member of the Commonwealth. Irrespective of any special relationship, therefore, Britain could reasonably expect to have been consulted. Certainly, the Queen, who was Grenada's head of state, thought so. She was 'reported to be furious – as much with Mrs Thatcher as with . . . the Americans about being deliberately or carelessly ignored'.[12] Second, as Britain had intervened to such effect over the Falklands, why was it so supine over Grenada eighteen months later?

Thatcher publicly concentrated on the consultation element. She did, after all, have access to the President unequalled by any other world leader at the time. He had written to her two days before the invasion informing her that he was giving the idea 'serious consideration' and saying that he would welcome her own thoughts.[13] Privately, he had no intention of changing his mind. Privately too, as her memoirs later revealed, Thatcher was vexed. She was, she said, 'strongly against intervention' in Grenada and sent a message to Reagan advising against an act that would be interpreted as 'intervention by a Western country in the internal affairs of a small independent nation'. She told him that she was 'deeply disturbed' by his action. She was, however, unable to change US policy.[14]

Without intending it, Reagan's action humiliated the British government. Only the day before the invasion, the Foreign Secretary, Geoffrey Howe, had told parliament that he knew of no American invasion plans. Thatcher noted that 'I felt dismayed and let down by what had happened. At best the British government had been made to look impotent; at worst we looked deceitful'.[15] It was clear to most observers that the Grenada intervention demonstrated that the United States was as likely to intervene in an area of the world in which it considered its interests directly challenged as was the USSR. The parallels with Afghanistan in 1979 were much closer than either Thatcher or Reagan were prepared to admit. The Grenada invasion was naked power politics; the diplomatic niceties of consultation did not come into it – British Commonwealth or no British Commonwealth.

It was a Conservative journal, *The Spectator*, which pointed out the weakness of Thatcher's position on Grenada:

> During the Falklands War, Mrs Thatcher very unwisely chose to generalise her justification for recapturing the islands as a vindication of the principle that aggression should not pay, whereas the sensible argument was simply that Britain would not allow British land and people to be taken over by a foreign power. Now the United States has been thoroughly aggressive and of course there is nothing that Mrs Thatcher can do and very little that she can say about it. It serves her right for always being high-falutin about the cause of liberty, instead of practical about the defence of Britain.[16]

THE FALKLANDS

For many, the reconquest of the Falkland Islands in May 1982 represents the high-water mark of Thatcherism. In early April 1982, Argentina, which had long claimed sovereignty over the British Falkland Islands in the remote South Atlantic (and had in 'the Malvinas' its own name for them), mounted a successful invasion, deporting the British governor to Uruguay. The decision was taken by a military leader, Leopoldo Galtieri, who come to power in a coup only a few months earlier. Thatcher, embarrassed by an invasion she clearly believed could have been prevented by better Foreign Office intelligence, was determined to recover the islands as swiftly as possible. Within days, an emergency session of parliament voted to dispatch a task force on a mission of reconquest. The leader of the Opposition, Michael Foot, gave notably warm support. He argued that Britain had 'a moral duty, a political duty and every other sort of duty' to recover the islands.[17]

The military expedition roused fierce passions, but success was swift and, as these things go, relatively painless. About 250 British and almost 1,000 Argentinian troops lost their lives in a conflict that lasted only three weeks and which demonstrated both the skill and efficiency of the British military and naval machine – at any rate against a demonstrably weaker opponent. The logistical problems encountered in waging a war 8,000 miles distant were also triumphantly overcome.

Thatcher won high praise in the country for steering a straight, no-nonsense course against a clear aggressor who had invaded British territory. The British victory raised the nation's prestige internationally and enhanced the national sense of self-worth. For some romantics, it was long-delayed retribution by the British for the fiasco of Suez. Its political benefits for Thatcher were immense and she capitalised on them to brilliant effect. Her populist genius was seen at its height during her speeches in the immediate afterglow of victory:

> We have ceased to be a nation in retreat. We have instead a newfound confidence – born in the economic battles at home and tested and found true 8,000 miles away . . . .We rejoice that Britain has rekindled that spirit which has fired her for generations past and which today has begun to burn as brightly as before. Britain found herself in the South Atlantic and will not look back from the victory she has won. When we started out there were the waverers and the faint-hearts, the people who thought we could no longer do the great things we once did, those who believed our decline was irreversible, that we could never again be what we were, that Britain was no longer the nation that had built an empire and ruled a quarter of the world. Well they were wrong.[18]

'Winston' could hardly have done better; indeed, he did not. He lost the election of 1945, whereas the 'Falklands factor' was the single most important factor in the large Conservative election victory of 1983 (see Chapter 3). The Falklands War was overwhelmingly popular in Britain, as a genuinely national struggle with the lives of British troops at stake. Public opinion polls suggested an 80 per cent approval rating of the British response to send a task force to reconquer the islands. The Tory Cabinet minister James Prior found 'incredible support for Margaret in the pubs' of his constituency, Lowestoft.[19] Of the political parties, only Plaid Cymru (the Welsh Nationalists) opposed going to war, probably because of the long-established Welsh contingent in the Argentinian region of Patagonia. Labour MPs quickly expressed their support. The few open doubters, mostly from professional and intellectual backgrounds, were quickly made to feel the strength of popular support, especially in the working men's clubs.

The press, as so often with Thatcher, was mostly on the loyal side of triumphalist. The *Sun* consolidated its already substantial hold on the popular market by conducting a war campaign of unprecedentedly crass and distasteful xenophobia. The *Daily Mail* and *Daily Express* offered less strident, but equally unswerving, support. Most of the quality newspapers argued that 'freedom was indivisible' and that unprovoked aggression compelled a military response. *The Financial Times*, invoking cost–benefit analysis, was more sceptical. Outright opposition came, as expected, from the left-centre quality newspapers, the *Guardian* and the *Observer*. Thatcher probably calculated that their small-circulation, hand-wringing, opposition was an advantage. Almost none of 'her' people read them anyway. Those who did were disproportionately well informed and articulate but, politically, of no account. Their opposition showed that the British press was free to say what it liked; Britain was, after all, going to war to preserve freedom.

The overwhelming victory justified what was actually a considerable gamble. Few other leaders would have taken it. Having taken it, furthermore, she was determined to see things through to their conclusion and to ensure that both she and the British people as a whole took pride in a remarkable achievement. She recalled the reaction of the Soviet military: 'years later I was told by a Russian general that the Soviets had been firmly convinced that we would not fight for the Falklands, and that if we did fight we would lose. We proved them wrong on both counts and they never forgot the fact'.[20]

After the heady rhetoric, and after noting both a huge military triumph and a brilliantly orchestrated propaganda coup, it is worth recalling at this distance of time what Britain was fighting *about*. The Falklands were a remote group of islands in the far South Atlantic, of no strategic significance, and on which lived 1,800 mostly British subjects. The islands had been acquired by Britain in 1833 in somewhat dubious circumstances and Argentina had long laid claim to them. Most in the Foreign Office recognised that the Falklands were an anachronistic imperial burden. Frequent attempts were made to broker a peaceful resolution of the disputed claims. These had continued throughout the years 1979–82.

It is hardly surprising, therefore, that others – far less hostile to Thatcher than Soviet generals – should have wondered whether Britain had taken leave of its senses in the spring of 1982. Ronald Reagan supported his ally in a statement that Argentina was clearly the aggressor and that the United States would supply such war materials as Britain might request. Behind the scenes, however, there was bemusement. The US Secretary of State, Alexander Haig, for example, reported the reaction in the State Department:

> In the early hours of the crisis, most of the staff shared the amusement of the press and public over what was perceived as a Gilbert and Sullivan battle over a sheep pasture between a choleric John Bull and a comic dictator in gaudy uniform.[21]

The Europeans were no more flattering. The French and German governments gave guarded support but could not understand why Britain was committing itself to the huge expenditure of a war – and the indefinite expense of maintaining thereafter a deterrent presence almost within shouting distance of the South Pole – in such circumstances. The French newspaper *Le Monde* was ruder, likening Thatcher's adventure to the famous French satire *Clochmerle*, in which local dignitaries lose all their dignity over something entirely trivial – the siting of a public lavatory.

Rational and longer-term calculations might be made by those not directly involved. Thatcher had to take immediate decisions and sell them to a British audience. She took the former courageously and did the latter brilliantly, emphasising the moral dimension. British military intervention was right: not to intervene would be cowardly; Britons never would be slaves. The islanders themselves were British subjects and had unequivocally expressed their support for any action which led to British troops recovering their territory. Thatcher cut through awkward questions about whether the conflict could have been honourably prevented. She ignored the clear evidence of inadequate policy-making on the Falklands in the years before 1982. In her view, she was faced with a crisis and dealt with it by invoking British patriotism. She knew in her bones that she was right, but she was equally aware of the immense political value of success. She understood that intangibles such as 'freedom' and 'patriotism' are more politically charged than desiccated calculations of strategy. In the Falklands War, her leadership gave the British people a success that most of them rejoiced at, while raising the country's stock internationally.

The Argentinian occupation provoked the resignation of the Foreign Secretary. Lord Carrington denied that he misread the signals about an imminent invasion but decided to go anyway, as the ranking minister. He had, as he put it:

> . . . a sympathetic understanding that the whole of the country felt angry and humiliated . . . . Inhabitants of a British colony – men and women of British blood – had been taken over against their will. Diplomacy had failed to avert this. Military reinforcement had not been tried. Deterrence had been exposed as a bluff.[22]

Carrington's was one of the last examples of unprovoked ministerial resignation on grounds of principle when the minister concerned had no immediate responsibility for proven incompetence and wrongdoing.

Many aspects of the Falklands War remain controversial. Pertinent questions were raised to which ministers never satisfactorily replied: did the government exhaust all diplomatic avenues before ordering the task force into action? Was it motivated by the desire to teach a demonstrably weaker regime a sharp lesson? Was the Prime Minister motivated more by the lure of glory than the need to save lives? The playwright and diarist Alan Bennett dwelled sardonically upon this last aspect when he read in June 1982 that the Argentinians had capitulated: 'A ceasefire with 250 of our forces dead, one for every twenty civilians in the Falklands Islands – the price, Madam says, of freedom.'[23]

It will not possible to provide authoritative answers until all the official documents are released, which will not be until 2012 at the earliest. Meanwhile, however, controversy over the Argentine cruiser the *Belgrano* must suffice to suggest that the Falklands affair is not a simple matter of truth, justified retribution and a staunch demonstration of the superiority of the British way. Michael Heseltine, who became Defence Secretary in January 1983, it is now clear, colluded with officials in his ministry to conceal the truth about the circumstances in which the *Belgrano* was sunk on 2 May, when still a considerable distance away from the Falklands, with the loss of more than 300 lives.

A civil servant in the Ministry of Defence, Clive Ponting, was prosecuted under the Official Secrets Act for leaking accurate, but classified, information to the Labour MP, Tam Dalyell. Ponting revealed that the 'official' version of the reasons for sinking the *Belgrano* was, quite simply, untrue. The decision to sink the cruiser had not been taken, as both Prime Minister and Defence Secretary John Nott had continuously asserted, by a British submarine captain in the South Atlantic who feared that the cruiser represented an immediate and direct threat to the British task force. At the time it was sunk, the *Belgrano* was not even sailing towards the task force. The decision was taken by a War Cabinet, which knew a great deal more about location and context than it admitted at the time. It is not irrelevant to remark that the decision to sink the *Belgrano* was taken during a period of furious diplomatic endeavour led by Peru, which had produced a peace plan with good prospects of averting a war altogether. Controversy will continue to rage on whether Thatcher, having made her moral stand and sure of the support of majority British opinion, was implacably opposed to any course of action except a just war.

Heseltine pressed vigorously, but unavailingly, for Ponting's conviction. Ponting did not deny what he had done, but claimed in court the higher duty to reveal the truth, rather than conceal it to preserve the embarrassing fact that the public had been consistently and intentionally lied to not only during the war (which might have been excusable) but for as long after it as ministers could get away with. Despite the strongest possible hint from the judge in his summing-up that the evidence against Ponting justified a conviction, twelve arbitrarily selected members of the public ignored his advice.

Ponting's acquittal did Thatcher no political damage. Detailed raking over the embers of what the overwhelming majority of the British public wanted to consider an unalloyed triumph was of interest only to political opponents, pedants and those intellectuals whose faint-hearted equivocations she so despised. Her memoirs on the subject are characteristic. She vaporised about the 'large amount of dangerous and misleading nonsense [which] circulated both at the time and long afterwards about why we sank the *Belgrano*'. She asserted that the government was responding to a 'clear military threat' and that the decision to sink was accordingly military, not political. This may well be true; we still await the full evidence. However, it is significant that she made no reference to the elaborate government cover-up of 1982–4 and did not reflect on how that cover-up might impugn the image she so skilfully cultivated for honesty and plain speaking. The name of Clive Ponting makes no appearance in Thatcher's full and scholarly index.[24] Heseltine, whose bluff had been called and whose behaviour had been far less honourable than Carrington's, apparently never considered resignation over the Falklands himself.[25]

9   Thatcher abroad III

The bringer of freedom? Principle, pragmatism and the limits of power

'Dealing with Margaret Thatcher was like taking alternate hot and cold baths'.[1] Helmut Kohl's assessment gives some idea of the personal impact Thatcher had on other world leaders. She could be personally charming and she grew to enjoy international diplomacy as she gained in experience, but she was never a comfortable colleague. In European diplomacy, her substantial specific achievements were of limited general importance because it was clear to fellow leaders that both her priorities and her sympathies lay elsewhere. Being alternately wheedling and strident, therefore, was of little use. International leaders dislike being lectured or harangued and Thatcher's diplomatic style incorporated too much of both.

Appearances, however, can be deceptive. Thatcher was a more cautious, and certainly more temporising, world leader than the strident image implies. She also developed a perceptive understanding of what was achievable. When she came to power, she wanted a resolution of the long-running dispute over the independence of Southern Rhodesia, which, since 1965, had been governed by white colonials led by Ian Smith in what the Foreign Office prissily told the BBC to refer to as 'the illegal Smith regime'. Among the nationalist leaders queuing to take over when negotiations brought 'majority rule', Thatcher much favoured Abel Muzorewa, a moderate black bishop she trusted, over Robert Mugabe, a black Marxist she did not. Additionally, Muzorewa had been the only senior black politician to stand in an election arranged by the Smith government in April 1979. Mugabe, who had been leading a civil war against Smith, had boycotted the elections.

Lord Carrington was able to persuade Thatcher that endorsing Muzorewa would be interpreted internationally as 'a device to perpetuate the white man's rule behind an amenable and unrepresentative black front'.[2] Thatcher, recognising that 'unpleasant realities had to be faced', opted for all-party talks to be held in London. From these, a peaceful transition to majority rule ensued and it was Mugabe who became the independent Zimbabwe's democratically elected leader. Rather against the steely image, the Prime Minister understood the need for compromise on what was widely considered a sensitive human rights issue. She informed the House of Commons in March 1980 that the government would accept the result of what she called 'free and fair elections'.[3] Mugabe was invited to undertake an official visit to the United Kingdom in 1982, when Thatcher congratulated Zimbabwe on effecting 'reconstruction and rehabilitation . . . at remarkable speed' and looked forward to increasing British investment in the newly independent country. Mugabe was personally congratulated for his tireless efforts 'to consolidate the independence of his country and improve the quality of life of his people'.[4] Offering these tributes to an ideologically offensive and, as things turned out, increasingly idiosyncratic and profligate ruler evidently came within the parameters of 'unpleasant realities'.

Unlike the Queen, Thatcher was never a great admirer of the Commonwealth, not really seeing what such a polyglot organisation was *for*. She also felt that it contained too many uncouth leaders and too many uncongenial and ideologically unsound regimes. Nevertheless, she understood that settling the Rhodesia issue would smooth Commonwealth relations at the beginning of her term of office. It would also win international approval. Her summary was characteristically crisp and simple. It also demonstrates why the raging internal struggle between practical politician and ideologue was usually won by the former:

> It was sad that Rhodesia/Zimbabwe finished up with a Marxist government in a continent where there were too many Marxists maladministering their countries' resources. But political and military realities were all too evidently on the side of the guerilla leaders.[5]

Pragmatism tempered principle in other high-profile foreign policy issues too. As we have seen, she was determined to stand up to Argentina over the Falklands (see Chapter 8) in 1982, and her determination was reinforced by the knowledge that she had the support of the United States. She was, however, in no position to stand up to China in 1984 – a far more powerful and even nastier regime – over the handing back of Hong Kong. Thatcher had gone to Peking in the autumn of 1982 hoping to do a deal on the basis of which Britain would concede sovereignty to China in 1997, according to the terms of the ancient Treaty of Nanking, signed in 1842. In return, she hoped that the Chinese would permit indefinite continuance of British administration in of one of the liveliest and most profitable money markets in the Far East. The Chinese, who did not recognise the validity of the treaty anyway, saw no reason to concede so much.

The final agreement that Hong Kong should become Chinese in 1997 was signed in December 1984. Thatcher's speech on the occasion acknowledged that the negotiations had been difficult but asserted that both sides had been able to 'draw on a shared fund of goodwill' in order to reach a resolution that provided 'the assurances for the future which Hong Kong needs in order to continue to play its unique role in the world as a financial and trading centre'.[6] She asserted that the agreement 'fully meets the political requirements of Britain and China, as well as the interests of the Hong Kong people'. This was a roseate assessment. True, the agreement recognised that different economic systems might coexist in a single state. 'One country, two systems', the Chinese called it. In reality, however, the Chinese had entered no binding commitments to preserve capitalism in Hong Kong; Thatcher could offer no guarantees to its citizens that their economy, still less democracy, would survive. She acknowledged that the deal, although eventually reached with sufficient overt expressions of Anglo-Chinese goodwill to send the Hong Kong stock exchange soaring, made only the best of a bad job. Crudely, she had caved in to what she called 'an intransigent and overwhelmingly superior power'.[7] Those Hong Kong citizens fearful of living under Chinese rule and anxious to move to Britain did not fare well. In 1989, the government refused to grant citizenship to 3 million Hong Kong residents who held British passports, although a Nationality Act passed the following year did permit up to 50,000 middle-class professionals and entrepreneurs from Hong Kong to take citizenship and move to Britain.

By 1987, Alan Clark, the romantic imperialist and indiscreet junior minister at the Department of Trade and Industry, was remarking that British influence in Hong Kong was already severely reduced: 'One more piece of wealth and real estate that has been allowed just to run through our fingers'.[8] The crackdown on dissidents in China after June 1989 confirmed Thatcher's own fears and emphasised the fragility of the assurances made only five years earlier. Thereafter, however, things quietened down. Having made their anti-democratic political point, the Chinese authorities were content to continue their own slow process of trade liberalisation and modernisation, using the eventual acquisition of Hong Kong as an effective staging post. The territory passed peacefully into Chinese control in July 1997.

Thatcher had few successes with the communists of the Far East. Her influence, however, became substantially greater in communist Eastern Europe. Here she showed both prescience and prejudice. She did not foresee the imminent collapse of her 'evil empire'; indeed, as she later admitted, she substantially miscalculated both its speed and its implications. In June 1990, for example, on a visit to the Ukraine, she looked forward to that state's continued contribution to the development of the Soviet Union and asserted that London and Kiev would never exchange ambassadors.[9] Nevertheless, she assessed the internal contradictions of communism before the disintegration of the Soviet Union in 1991 much more shrewdly than did most of her contemporaries. The conviction politician in her also reinforced her perception: something as unnatural and inhumane as communism *could not* survive indefinitely.

From the mid-1980s, she made a point of visiting eastern Europe as often as she could. When relations with the Soviet Union were frosty in 1984, she made a well-publicised visit to Hungary, which had made a number of small-scale, market-led reforms. She was gratified at the warmth of the reception she received during a walkabout in a Budapest street market. She attributed this to her 'reputation as a strong anti-communist political leader'. Her visit also confirmed her view that there were no communist people, only communist regimes. The people in them 'retained a thirst for liberty'.[10] She visited Poland in November 1988, where she spoke freely with the Solidarity leaders and visited the Gdansk shipyard that had seen the rebirth of the Polish liberation movement in 1980 and whose workers now cheered her to the echo. She also spoke plainly to the Communist Party leader General Jaruzelski about the need for change. Once more, she noted the essentially non-communist 'spirit' of an enslaved people, yearning for freedom. Once again, she offered them hope. Once more, she found what she was programmed to find: socialism 'doing its usual work of impoverishment and demoralization'.[11] In September 1990, only two months before her fall, she revisited Hungary and also Czechoslovakia, both of which had by then cast off the Soviet yoke and were 'coming to grips with the communist legacy of economic failure, pollution and despondency'.

Thatcher visited the East in part because she enjoyed preaching the superior virtues of capitalism and being received by ordinary people either as a liberator and sage. In a kindly, if patronising, way she lectured the Hungarians on her second visit. She particularly welcomed the recent election of what she called a 'really genuine centre-right government' and suggested that economic growth would be faster in their country than elsewhere in the East because Hungary had begun its own privatization policy. She continued: '. . . perhaps we can help because we have been through the experience of privatising many big companies and nationalised industries in Britain'.[12] The previous day she had been in Prague, where she addressed the Czech Federal Assembly, lecturing them on the superior virtues of 'a free Parliament and the rule of law' which, she asserted, 'We in Britain have had the good fortune to enjoy ... for some eight hundred years'. She hoped that her visit would 'encourage our businessmen to come here and invest' but most of all she looked forward to the reshaping of Europe:

> What gives us the greatest pleasure ... is to see Czechoslovakia, and indeed Poland and Hungary, return once more to their rightful place in Europe ... We never accepted during the Cold War years that Eastern Europe should be permanently outcast ... Now that the Cold War is dead, and the barriers down, we must not lose time. The momentum which brought your freedom must now be harnessed to the task of reuniting Europe.[13]

Thatcher enjoyed being feted as the high priestess of political and economic freedom. She was, however, playing European politics as well. She knew as well as anyone that Britain's failure to join the European Common Market in 1957 had marginalised the country as a European power. During the 1980s (see Chapter 7), she had fought both French and Germans tooth and nail over a number of key economic and political issues. The collapse of the eastern bloc represented a fresh opportunity to recast Europe and reduce long-established Franco-German domination of the EEC. Thus, as the Soviet Union lurched towards collapse, Thatcher's became more concerned to ensure that the result was not mere fragmentation. Her vision encompassed a pan-European economic union – a kind of super-Zollverein. Her position on closer political ties was unequivocal. 'I do not believe in a federal Europe and I think to ever compare it with the United States of America is absolutely ridiculous'.[14] She believed that the more states across Europe cooperated within her 'reunited Europe', the less likely was the outcome of a 'European superstate' which blurred national identities and imposed 'alien' regulations. It was, in fact, the perfect riposte to the pretensions of Jacques Delors (see Chapter 7).

She was particularly wary of Germany. During the major defence review of 1981, an exercise designed to cut costs and whose structure was in the event distorted by the consequences of the Falklands War (see Chapter 8), the size of the British army on the Rhine hardly changed. British army and air force personnel totalled about 65,000 in the late 1980s. Thatcher's abiding suspicion of Germany was one reason why the British defence budget in the second half of the 1980s was comparatively large: 5.5 per cent of GNP compared with only 3.8 per cent for Britain's European allies in NATO.[15] NATO was for Thatcher the central defensive bulwark against Soviet imperialism. As she told a press conference after a NATO summit in 1988: 'I am a passionate believer in NATO, in its solidarity as a defender of freedom'. It was still, in her belief, being threatened by the Soviet Union whose 'central objective is to separate western Europe from the United States'. Thus, she continued, well knowing how much her words would grate with other EU leaders who wanted to develop a more distance relationship: 'Our first priority must be to preserve the organic link between Europe and the United States'.[16]

It has been suggested by one of her erstwhile foreign policy advisers that an important element in Thatcher's foreign policy thinking was pure anti-German prejudice:

> She didn't hide her cordial dislike of all things German (forgetting, it seemed, the Teutonic descent of the English nation, of the English language and of the Royal Family) aggravated by her distaste for the personality of Helmut Kohl . . . The contrast between herself as a visionary stateswoman with a world-view and Kohl the wurst-eating, corpulent, plodding Teuton, has a long history in MT's imagination.[17]

She seemed to share the unreasoned views of many British people of her generation that Germany, which had during the twentieth century been the cause of two world wars, could never be trusted. She is said to have confided to one of her foreign policy advisers in 1989, as the Berlin Wall collapsed and as Helmut Kohl placed the reunification of communist east with capitalist West Germany at the centre of his policy:

> You know, there are things that people of your generation and mine ought never to forget. We've been through the war and we know perfectly well what the Germans are like and what dictators can do and how national character basically doesn't change.

In like vein, she remarked to the German Ambassador at a dinner to mark forty years of Anglo-German alliance, of all occasions, that 'You need another forty years before we can forget what you have done'.[18]

She refused to accept the overwhelming view of both the other EC members and the Americans that West Germany had been a model liberal democracy since 1945 and that the much larger and richer West could safely be trusted to absorb East Germany into an effective and representative regime, which would add to the stability of Europe rather than detract from it. Not surprisingly, this was also the view of the Foreign Office. As we have seen (Chapter 7), Thatcher's initial, and visceral, position on the Foreign Office was that whatever they advised was likely to be wrong.

Confirmation of what might be termed Thatcher's 'Germano-scepticism' comes from her own memoirs.

> I do believe in national character, which is moulded by a range of complex factors: the fact that national caricatures are often absurd and inaccurate does not detract from that. Since the unification of Germany under Bismarck . . . Germany has veered unpredictably between aggression and self-doubt . . . The true origin of German *angst* is the agony of self-knowledge . . . a reunited Germany is simply too big and too powerful to be just another player within Europe. Moreover, Germany has always looked east as well as west, although it is economic expansion rather than territorial aggression which is the modern manifestation of this tendency. Germany is thus by its very nature a destabilising rather than a stabilising force in Europe.[19]

Her campaign to delay, if not halt, German reunification, however, had little chance of success; indeed, it was probably counterproductive. In the late 1980s, the Russians were too preoccupied with their own internal crises to pay heed to Thatcher's warnings. Within the EC, Thatcher's unique diplomatic style (Chapter 7) militated against the formation of an anti-German alliance. President Mitterand of France, whom Thatcher distrusted as an urbane, but slippery, socialist, was hardly likely to be deflected by any intervention of hers from the Franco-German axis that had provided the motive force of Europeanism for much of the decade. If Helmut Kohl wanted a united German state, then Francois Mitterand would not stand in his way. To the frustration of diplomats and the Foreign Office, therefore, Thatcher's stance only increased British isolation in Europe.

Visits to eastern Europe, however, continued to sustain both her self-regard and her sense of mission. She developed a useful personal relationship with Mikhail Gorbachev, Soviet leader from 1985 to 1991. She met him first just before he became leader, and famously declared in a television interview with the BBC journalist John Cole that 'We can do business together . . . we believe in cooperating on trade matters, on cultural matters, on quite a lot of contacts between politicians from the two sides of the divide.'[20] She found him, as indeed he was, a far more flexible and intellectually stimulating figure than the frozen Marxist stereotype. She deliberately chose a visit to the Soviet Union in the spring of 1987 as a launching pad for her successful re-election campaign. She used her good relations with Gorbachev to demonstrate to the British public that she was a key player on the world stage, able to move easily between the superpowers. Pompously, however, she slapped down a British reporter who asked about the significance of her visit for the domestic political scene: 'I am on a historic mission representing my country'.[21] Again she rejoiced at the 'rapturous' reception she received both in Moscow and in Tbilisi (Georgia). An interview on television also reinforced the image of a strong, but compassionate, leader who had come to the heart of the evil empire to speak directly to its good, but downtrodden, people and offer them hope. She later stated that she could sense 'the ground shifting underneath the Communist system . . . The West's system of liberty which Ronald Reagan and I personified in the eastern bloc . . . was increasingly in the ascendant'.[22]

By the end of her period in office, she was seeing Gorbachev, wrongly as it turned out, as the man to who would effect the transition of the Soviet Union into a free market supporting liberal democracy. She told an interviewer in February 1990 that Gorbachev would 'win through' because he was 'pursuing policies which will bring the Soviet Union a prosperity and an importance far greater than they have ever had before'.[23]

It would be easy to dismiss Margaret Thatcher's frequent eastern forays as pandering to little more than the lady's self-regard and love of flattery. That there was an element of both is beyond dispute, as anyone reading the unintentionally revealing sections of her memoirs will immediately see. However, Thatcher genuinely *was* influential in the East. The image of the 'Iron Lady', which a Soviet newspaper had helpfully conjured for her as far back as 1976 and which she sedulously cultivated thereafter, was extremely useful. For many struggling against communism, Thatcher was an inspiring figure. She had won a war; she was not afraid of speaking her mind; she had been more forthright than any western leader in voicing hatred of an evil empire that oppressed them. Is it any wonder that Thatcherism won so many converts there? Even in the West, her political leadership could be inspirational, as was instanced in Spain by the election in March 1996 of a Thatcherite free-marketeer, José Maria Aznar, who became the first right-wing leader of that country since the long rule of Generalissimo Franco. To most EU diplomats, however, Thatcher seemed capable only of boring on about British interests, narrowly, and perhaps wrong-headedly, conceived. In the East, her reception was quite different. Thatcherism championed the values of the free market. Thatcherism supported national self-determination. Thatcherism inspired visions of the triumph of liberty over the darkness of socialism. Thus what at home brought high unemployment, rising inequality and the excesses of vulgar capitalism, meant something altogether more benign in the tottering and ramshackle eastern bloc of the 1980s.

Thatcher's prescriptions were eagerly absorbed as the necessary medicine to destroy the dark contagion of Bolshevik tyranny. Thatcher herself might posture almost as a new Alexander II, not Tsar- but capitalist-liberator. Only cynical Western eyes, and perhaps not many of them in 1990, could predict that these newly independent eastern states would lurch from one extremism to another. The reckoning came only after she had left office, when it became all too clear that Thatcherism was hardly better at generating instant prosperity – except for the privileged and sharp-shouldered few. Only time could teach the follies of excessive reliance upon entirely unregulated markets. Only experience could demonstrate how seamless was the transition from party apparatchik to capitalist spiv. Disillusion did set in, of course, as is indicated by the remarkable successes of communist candidates in free elections held in eastern Europe during the 1990s.[24] As we have seen, even a mature political democracy adapts only with difficulty to the kind of shock which Thatcherism administers to the body politic. Its impact on states with little or no such tradition is much more intoxicating and the full effects cannot yet be assessed. That Thatcherism had a huge impact, however, is undeniable. Thatcher herself raised Britain's profile and status in the world. Even outside the Soviet Empire, Thatcherism became widely valued as a valid set of precepts to halt the long and sterile march of state authority and influence. For a time, at least, it seemed to have the measure of those malign internal contradictions of Keynesian demand management: an ever-growing state, printing money and rising inflation. Thatcherism may have beguiled more than it benefited, but it certainly changed things.

10 The fall

During her long prime ministership, Margaret Thatcher's political demise was frequently prophesied and, by her many critics, eagerly awaited. It was widely felt that she could not survive the desperate economic depression of 1980–1, for which her government's economic management was directly responsible. Many in her own party hoped that she would not. Her recovery after the Falklands campaign and her substantial election victory in 1983 silenced Tory doubters for a while. However, it is reasonable to date the background to her eventual fall not to 1990 but to 1986, the year of the Westland affair and the consequential resignation of Michael Heseltine.

Westland was, in one sense, a political storm in a teacup. The financial difficulties of an ailing west of England helicopter company would not normally be the stuff of Cabinet crisis. However, they were portents of something much bigger. Westland gave an early indication of the deep divisions within the Conservative Party over Europe and it was not coincidental that it would eventually be the challenge to her leadership of strongly pro-European Michael Heseltine which brought the Prime Minister down. Westland is also a useful place to begin because it was the first occasion on which she seems to have thought herself vulnerable to a party coup against her. She later confided in her memoirs that, at the height of the crisis, 'I was considering my own position', knowing perfectly well that 'there were those in my own Party and Government who would like to take the opportunity of getting rid of me'.[1]

Heseltine, as Defence Secretary, wanted to bale the Westland Company out, using funds provided by a European consortium. Leon Brittan, the Industry Minister, backed by No. 10, favoured a rescue bid from the US company Sikorski. The disagreement assumed critical proportions for two reasons. First, Heseltine was becoming increasingly alienated both by Thatcher's authoritarian style of government and by her evident preference for US links over European ones. Second, what might – and should – have remained a battle within the Cabinet became a public scandal because of leaked confidential material clearly aimed at discrediting Heseltine. Although a specific leak was traced to Brittan's department, there had clearly been collusion with No. 10, possibly orchestrated by Thatcher herself. Brittan was forced out of office. Thatcher's own position might have become parlous had a forensic parliamentary debater like the young Robin Cook been in charge of the Labour assault rather than Neil Kinnock, all passion but no precision when presented with the rare opportunity of a Prime Minister lacking confidence and actually prepared to admit mistakes.[2]

Westland raised important doubts about the Thatcher government's style and policy. It also left Heseltine, much the most ambitious rival to the Prime Minister, out of office and with time to plan future strategy from the back-benches. The large election victory of 1987 removed any immediate threat to Thatcher's position and made her less cautious (see above, Chapter 5). Beneath the surface, however, it soon became clear that all was not well. Thatcher's government style seemed to become even more personal and less accountable. Ministers complained privately that she trusted unelected advisers more than she did them; she also set up ad hoc groupings of personal advisers on important policy matters, rather than have them discussed at Cabinet in their formative stages. Generally, she honoured the conventions of Cabinet government more in the breach than in the observance. This had been the cause of Heseltine's departure.

The contrast between the first and second halves of her prime ministership is striking. In the earlier phase, she was generally able to choose when to remove ministers she did not trust. By the mid-1980s, she appeared to have fashioned a Cabinet with as many sympathetic and well-disposed ministers as it is feasible to secure in that diverse coalition of interests that every major political party must comprise. In the last three years of her prime ministership, however, she lost ministers to resignation at times which were often highly embarrassing.

The resignation of Norman Tebbit immediately after the 1987 election set a doleful pattern. There were strong compassionate reasons for his departure. His wife had been crippled by an IRA bomb during the Tory Party conference of 1984, and Tebbit wanted to devote more time to her care. Thatcher preferred to believe – at least for public consumption in her memoirs – that this was Tebbit's sole reason for going: 'his reasons were as personal as they were admirable. I did bitterly resent his decision. I had too few like-minded supporters in the Government, and of these none had Norman's strength and acumen'.[3] The truth was not so simple. Behind the scenes, the 1987 election campaign had been a divisive one for the Tories. Tebbit, as Party Chairman, bringing Thatcher news about how her personality grated with the public, found himself the archetypal messenger being blamed for the message. In a characteristic gambit, the Prime Minister took her own initiative, employing a different advertising agency, which, not surprisingly, presented less personally wounding findings.[4] This was one incident among several as a previously close relationship became decidedly frosty. Tebbit went in 1987, at least in part because he felt his authority being undermined. His shrewdness, intelligence and plain, thuggish ability to intimidate were much missed by Thatcher.

Allegations of excessive power from No. 10 were also the key reason for the yet more damaging departure of the Chancellor of the Exchequer, Nigel Lawson, in October 1989. He and Thatcher fundamentally disagreed about entry to the EMS and about the exchange rate policy to be followed before entry. Considerable evidence also exists to suggest that the Prime Minister resented Lawson's increasing tendency to push his independent opinions while on overseas trips. Lawson was much the most economically literate of Thatcher's Chancellors, a forceful personality and well able to punch his then considerable weight.[5] When Thatcher made it clear that she favoured the advice being given to her by her economic adviser, Alan Walters, to that of her own Chancellor, Lawson responded that either Walters went or he did. In the event, both departed. Substantial damage was done by this very public evidence of disaffection. Thatcher could hardly afford to lose someone of Lawson's quality while complex financial negotiations over Europe were in train (see Chapter 7). The already prevalent reputation was strengthened of a Prime Minister who traded on the strength of conviction leadership yet who could not tolerate equally strong opinions in others.

Downing Street influence was not restricted to the Prime Minister. Ministers either temporarily or permanently out of favour tended to be 'talked down' in unattributable briefings held by Sir Bernard Ingham, Thatcher's Chief Press Secretary throughout her premiership. Ingham, a Yorkshireman of Labour origins, with a temperament which veered uncertainly between the bluff and the brutal and a highly developed sense of his own importance, delighted in passing political black-spots onto lobby journalists, knowing that they would be written up eagerly for the next day's quality papers. Thatcher, who called him 'the greatest' of her supports, probably never understood how much resentment the Ingham press machine caused.[6] In her last years of office, this almost certainly worked against her, as it gave Conservative politicians of much greater significance than Ingham a lingering sense of resentment. When it comes to their own careers, politicians, like most people, have long memories.

Ingham also contributed to Thatcher's lack of sensitivity about her true political position by the late 1980s. Unlike most politicians of the modern era, she was relatively uninterested in what the press said about her. Her job, as she saw it, was to lead; the press's was to comment on her leadership. Responding to hostile press criticism – and there was no shortage of it – was a sign of weak leadership. Ingham's role was to produce a digest of the day's key press coverage, which Thatcher could absorb almost at a glance. The problem, however, was that Ingham had frequently 'planted' stories – usually favourable to the government – which duly appeared in Thatcher-supporting newspapers such as the *Sun* or *The Times*. Ingham had himself therefore been at least partially responsible for the cast of press coverage on which Thatcher relied. It is reasonable to assume that, until it was too late, she learned little about the negative stories which might have provided a truer picture of her weakening support within the party. Inured to success (often against the odds and in the face of massive unpopularity) over a decade, she was now unprepared for failure.

Six weeks after the Lawson resignation, Thatcher faced her first leadership challenge, from an obscure left-wing, pro-European Tory backbencher, Sir Anthony Meyer. She and her entourage mismanaged this. As Charles Powell later admitted, Thatcher and her entourage greatly underestimated the importance of a challenge from someone he loftily dismissed as 'this insignificant man'.[7] Thatcher's easy victory was not the point. The *contest* was the point. It gave sixty Tory MPs the opportunity of a secret ballot to demonstrate that the Prime Minister did not have their confidence. In a party whose two rationales might be said to be loyalty to the leader and election victory, this was deeply significant. Thatcher had won the Conservatives three successive elections, given them a lease on power for a generation, and yet a back-bencher of whom almost no one outside Westminster had heard could demonstrate her vulnerability. In any case, her real opponent was not Sir Anthony Meyer but Michael Heseltine. Over the next twelve months, while all Westminster insiders realised that the next year would see another, and much more threatening, challenge, Heseltine fixed on a mendacious mantra, which he solemnly intoned to enquiring political journalists. He 'could foresee no circumstances' in which he would oppose Thatcher in a leadership contest. No one, least of all Thatcher, believed him. Heseltine, she knew, had many faults: lack of a sense of political opportunity was not one of them.

During the leadership crisis of November 1990, Thatcher was evidently as bemused as she was resentful about the 'disloyalty' which she believed destroyed her. As a Prime Minister of eleven years' standing, she felt that she should have been able to draw on a much greater fund of loyalty, especially from ministers, most of whom owed their careers to her preferment. Now, one by one, in a lachrymose parade to her private room in the House of Commons, they told her she must go. Although her fall was the result of a complex interaction of factors, she should certainly have been asking sharper questions of Sir Bernard Ingham as to its cause. Too few ministers in November 1990 felt that they could rely enough on her loyalty to them in the long term for them to pledge it to her in the short. They had observed how many of their predecessors had been treated. They also noticed how important leaks from those close to the Prime Minister had been in stimulating adverse press comment about their chances of survival at the next reshuffle.

The actual contest of November 1990 was precipitated by two factors. The first stemmed from several causes and was ultimately the more important. A large number of Tories felt that the next election was unwinnable under Thatcher's continued leadership. The year of 1990 was a very difficult year for them. Partly because of Lawson's earlier policies to prepare Britain for ERM membership, interest rates had soared to 15 per cent, making the homeowners' mortgages ruinously expensive while the value of their houses was also tumbling. Inflation – the key evil of Keynesianism in Thatcher's eyes – had recently risen above 10 per cent again. Whatever its economic merits – and few were prepared to back it even on these grounds – the poll tax (see Chapter 5) was proving a public relations disaster. At the end of March, a demonstration against it in London's Trafalgar Square degenerated into rioting and 400 policemen were injured. Thatcher, preferring as ever to recall the horrors of public disorder rather than the depth of feeling to which it had given rise, stated simply: 'I was appalled at such wickedness'.[8]

Two more of Thatcher's long-serving ministers, the shrewd Norman Fowler and Peter Walker, that long-preserved yet entirely symbolic proof of the Prime Minister's tolerance to wets, chose to resign early in 1990. A third, the clever but unguarded Etonian right-winger Nicholas Ridley, was forced out for telling a journalist – actually Nigel Lawson's son – even more prejudiced things about Germany than Thatcher privately believed: 'I'm not against giving up sovereignty in principle, but not to this lot [meaning a German-led federalist European community]. You might just as well give it to Adolf Hitler, frankly'.[9]

The Cabinet seemed to be falling apart. Those few experienced ministers who were left openly, and embarrassingly, squabbled on another key European issue – the EMS. Opinion poll findings were dismal, confirming that 1989 losses in the European elections were no flash in the pan. The newspapers talked up the prospects of a Labour victory, perhaps soon. Back-benchers need the electorate to sustain their pension contributions and their often profitable links to private industry at least every five years. Many, not all in marginal constituencies, were decidedly jumpy by the summer of 1990. By early November, one of the most besotted of all Thatcherite loyalists, Alan Clark, was recording in his diary: 'The papers are all very bad. Tory party falling apart, the death blow, that kind of thing. Something in it, I fear, unless we can get a grip on events.'[10]

The second precipitating factor in Thatcher's departure was the resignation of Sir Geoffrey Howe on 1 November 1990, or more accurately the resignation speech which he made in the Commons twelve days later. Howe was by a considerable stretch the most senior minister in the government after Thatcher. He alone had a record of continuous Cabinet service under her since 1979 and he had held the two most senior offices of state below the premiership – Chancellor of the Exchequer and Foreign Secretary – for four years and six years respectively. He was not, however, a high-profile minister. People tended to remember not him, but what was said about him – most notably Denis Healey's wounding jibe that being attacked in parliament by Sir Geoffrey was like being savaged by a dead sheep. Howe had, however, left his best for last and was determined to prove that the old bruiser's famous put-down was somewhat less than the whole truth.

He was no longer Foreign Secretary, having been removed from that office much against his will in July 1989 for excessive Europeanism and possibly also for excessive deference to the hated Foreign Office official line. He had insisted on the honorary title of Deputy Prime Minister but took little comfort from it; his star was clearly on the wane. Thatcher's ever more strident anti-Europeanism chafed with him throughout 1990 but he was goaded to resignation by some spectacular words on the subject in answer to a question from the Leader of the Opposition. He believed that Thatcher's stance on Europe was diminishing the nation's influence where it mattered.

His resignation speech was as action packed as anything in his political life. It contained a cogent recantation of monetarist policy, which he himself had implemented as Chancellor a decade earlier, and the accusation that Thatcher's dithering about entering the European monetary system had caused the recent damaging increase in inflation. He also included a withering denunciation of the Prime Minister's 'nightmare image' of a EC stalked by malevolent anti-democrats who wanted to destroy national sovereignty. He had already said enough to earn a place in the pantheon of twentieth-century parliamentary political speeches. But he had not quite done. His final sentence was dynamite: 'The time has come for others to consider their own response to the tragic conflict of loyalties with which I have myself wrestled for perhaps too long.'[11]

Michael Heseltine had been presented, gift-wrapped, with just the opportunity he said he could not foresee, but for which the last four years of his life had been a preparation. The very next day he announced that he would be a candidate for the leadership of the Conservative Party.

Only during the last ten days of an eleven and a half year premiership did both luck and political judgement desert Margaret Thatcher at the same time. She did most things wrong from the day she knew she must fight another leadership battle until she emerged, tear-stained, from the steps of No. 10 Downing Street to return her seals of office to the Queen. And yet she so nearly won. She chose the wrong team and was rewarded with an appallingly mismanaged campaign, which ended up underestimating Heseltine's support by about seventy votes.

She also decided to be prime ministerial and represent her country at a European Security and Co-operation Summit in Paris rather than bargain or wheedle for Tory backbench votes in London. This was, in its way, fitting. Europe had brought her low and it was appropriate that her prime ministership should in effect end there with the news, telephoned through to the British Embassy in Paris on 20 November, that she had failed, by four votes, to obtain the required majority over Heseltine to be declared winner on the first ballot. In total, 178 Conservative MPs had failed to back her, and most insiders calculated that existing support would haemorrhage away in any second ballot. And yet she initially opted to fight on, barging a surprised BBC reporter out of the way to seize a microphone within minutes of hearing the result and announce that she intended to contest the now necessary second leadership ballot. It looked rude and it sounded impetuous. The real calculations were being made that Tuesday evening not by her (she was fulfilling a diplomatic engagement at the opera) but by her ministers in London. Only their procession to her Commons office more than twenty-four hours later finally persuaded her to release her grip.

Nigel Lawson, no longer in government but still very close to many Cabinet colleagues, knew why ministers deserted her:

> . . . there were many, particularly among her ministerial colleagues, who had allowed their loyalty to get the better of their judgment in the first ballot but would not have done so in the second. Those reasons boiled down to one: the conviction that Margaret had become an electoral liability, and that the Conservative Party could win the coming general election only under a new leader.[12]

The resignation announced, she produced a feistily demob-happy performance in the House of Commons, in which she lambasted the Labour Party as of old for its temporising nature and for betraying the British people.[13] This may have induced a retrospective sense of guilt in some Tory deserters. At all events, enough rallied around Thatcher's own chosen successor, John Major, to ensure that he comfortably defeated Heseltine in the second ballot from which she was now an enforced absentee. Because a third candidate, the Foreign Secretary Douglas Hurd, had also entered the contest, Major polled fewer votes in winning the leadership than Thatcher had done in – effectively – losing it. This reflection did not ease her often graceless retreat to the fringes of political life. Her memoirs make clear her sense of betrayal. She gives a blow-by-blow account of the interviews which took place with almost all of them in the Prime Minister's room in the House of Commons on the evening of 21 November and concluded:

> I was sick at heart. I could have resisted the opposition of opponents and potential rivals and even respected them for it; but what grieved me was the desertion of those I had always considered friends and allies and the weasel words whereby they had transmuted their betrayal into frank advice and concern for my fate.[14]

No matter; she was gone. The next day, the *Guardian*, never a friend to Thatcher, published a one-word reader's letter which recalled, with savage irony, the lady's response to success in the Falklands almost a decade earlier. The letter read: 'Rejoice!'.

THE MYTH OF MARTYRDOM

The manner of Thatcher's departure, and her own evident bitterness about it, had an enormous impact on the politics of the 1990s, which is considered in more detail in Chapter 11. It is as well to deal here with a myth entitled 'the martyrdom of the blessed Margaret'. The tone, for those who believe it, is well set by one of the great toadies of British politics. Woodrow Wyatt was a Labour MP for more than twenty years before professing his admiration for Thatcher's politics in the 1970s, leaving the party and writing increasingly sycophantic pro-Thatcher newspaper pieces. He was rewarded with a life peerage in 1988. Part of his journal entry for 22 November 1990 reads thus:

> The fateful day. Twenty-seven years ago John Kennedy, President of the United States, was assassinated. She was assassinated this

day ... That fearful crew, the Tory party, had let her down. She
was reported as saying her Cabinet hadn't got any balls yesterday
and she was quite right ... We [he and other members of his Club]
all agreed that it had been a most shameful episode in Tory Party
history ... How I wish Margaret had consulted me about her campaign managers and the style of her campaign earlier and properly
... My brave darling, my heart bled for her.[15]

The surprising thing about this self-indulgent and lachrymose guff from
a grown man of great experience and some sophistication is not its appearance but, purple passages aside, the typicality of response. Most of
those who remained Thatcher supporters – a sadly diminished band in
the upper echelons of the party by 1990, it must be admitted – did indeed
believe that she had been betrayed.

Bernard Ingham was as loyal to the Thatcher myth in the 1990s as
he had been to his political mistress herself during her years in power.
He pointed out to anyone who would listen that Thatcher was had been
stabbed in the back by her own ministers. These were the very people
from whom she had a right to expect greatest loyalty, because – in
almost every case by 1990 – she had promoted them and nurtured their
careers. His observations were characteristically bluff: Had Thatcher lost
a general election? No; she had proved one of the Conservatives' most
spectacular winners three times in succession. Had Thatcher lost the
confidence of parliament? No; the parliamentary majority of 101 that she
had won in 1987 had barely been diminished since then and she could
easily win any vote of no confidence. Had she lost the leadership election she was in the process of fighting? Emphatically not; she had been
within four votes of knocking Heseltine out in the first ballot. Was she
less popular with the Conservative Party in the country? The evidence
of the annual party conferences continued to show that Thatcher was
lauded only this side idolatry. So, the only explanation was 'betrayal'.[16]
'St Margaret' was a martyr to treachery from those who thought only of
their own ambitions and not either of their party or their country.

Thatcher herself was not to be outdone. Her memoirs left no reader
in doubt of what she thought of government ministers who 'had decided
to dispense with my services', although she had headed governments
which – as she modestly put it – 'had pioneered the new wave of economic freedom that was transforming countries from eastern Europe to
Australasia ... restored Britain's reputation as a force to be reckoned
with in the world' and achieved 'our historic victory in the Cold War'.[17]

Thatcher's fall was, in truth, a far less unusual, still less shocking,
occurrence than these passages of purple prose imply. There is no

convincing zealots, of course, but the reality of Thatcher's fall is both more prosaic and more typical than the Wyatts and the Inghams suggest. The twentieth-century Tory Party was both more loyal to successful leaders and more ruthless in dispatching wounded ones than are other parties. Virtually all Labour leaders, although they usually had to fight tooth and nail to preserve party unity, have gone at times of their own choosing. Conservative leaders have been pushed with surprising frequency. Arthur Balfour, despite winning back substantial support in the elections of 1910 after the Liberal landslide of 1906 was in effect forced to resign in his political prime in 1911 when the Conservatives lost their battle with Asquith and Lloyd George over the powers of the House of Lords. A parliamentary rebellion in a Conservative-dominated House of Commons sent Neville Chamberlain on his way in 1940. Although Anthony Eden formally resigned on grounds of ill-health in 1957, he was not at death's door and would have found it very difficult to hang on after the disasters of Suez. His successor, Harold Macmillan, was also under enormous pressure when a conveniently troublesome (though not, as it turned out, cancerous) prostate gave him an excuse to resign six years later. He too faced a leadership challenge he would have found it difficult to resist with back-benchers fearful that their party stood no chance in the forthcoming election against the modernising Labour leader Harold Wilson. Macmillan's successor, Lord Home, was given his marching orders months after he turned a likely Conservative rout in 1963 into the narrowest of defeats at Labour's hands one year later. And Thatcher herself knew all about the political demise of Edward Heath early in 1975 (see Chapter 1).

The plain truth is that Conservative leaders are punished both for losing general elections and for looking likely to do so. Labour, which was until 1997 was much more used to electoral failure, has traditionally been much more indulgent of it. In the Thatcher case, Nigel Lawson's unsentimental assessment was spot on. Her own fall was as efficiently dispatched as had become normal. Politics is a rough, unforgiving trade and the Conservatives play it more ruthlessly than their opponents. Thatcher died by its rules although, as we shall see, she did not intend to go quietly.

11 The legacy I

Politics – Thatcherism after Thatcher

SHOUTING FROM THE WINGS

Enough time has passed since 'the fall' to make at least a preliminary evaluation of the impact of Margaret Thatcher. Two things can be said with certainty. First, even after the sharpest-edged memories of a famously divisive decade in British life have faded, Thatcher remains as controversial as she ever was. No one can seriously dispute that she mattered – more so than any other twentieth-century politician with the exception of Winston Churchill and, perhaps, Lloyd George. She was one of the very biggest players on the political stage. Second, she cast a long shadow over the actors who followed her. The second half of chapter will investigate whether Tony Blair in particular, and New Labour in general, follow more a Thatcherite legacy than an old Labour one.

It is a commonplace of political reputations that they nosedive in the years immediately after leaving office. It might almost be said that the greater the impact, the bigger the negative correction. In the early 1990s, there were signs that this might be happening with Thatcher. In the short term, John Major proved a great relief, if only because he was *not* Thatcher. Many commentators considered that his emollient, consensual style was precisely what the nation needed after more than decade being dragged along Margaret Thatcher's political assault course. Thatcher took no prisoners; Major, or so it seemed during a sure-footed period leading up to his election victory in 1992, saw no need for a prison.

Sensing a changing mood, one of the nation's most distinguished commentators tried in 1991 to cut Thatcher's political reputation down to size:

> Large claims were made for Mrs Margaret Thatcher as a great Prime Minister: but they are melting before our eyes like the snows of spring. My prediction is that history will judge her as

just above average, below C.R. Attlee and H.H. Asquith, who has better claims than she to being a great peacetime Prime Minister, but above Harold Macmillan and Harold Wilson.[1]

Now history plays a long game and its muse is famously capricious with reputations, but, from the perspective of the early twenty-first century, Alan Watkins's grandiloquent evaluation looks simply silly. Little of broad political significance that happened in the 1990s can be explained without acknowledging the longer-term influence of Thatcher.

It is difficult to imagine her successor John Major dissenting from this judgement. For him, the first eighteen months, when he thought he had exorcised the Thatcherite spectre, were much the best. In 1991, his government announced the abolition of the hated poll tax and its replacement, from 1993, by a council tax which took account of the value of property in its assessments. 1991 also witnessed the brief, successful Gulf War against Iraq as a subordinate allied partner with the United States. Success in what was widely interpreted as a just war against Saddam Hussein further sweetened the public mood. Lowered inflation and bank rates provided further reasons for Conservative optimism. Consumer price rises declined from 9.5 per cent in the last year of the Thatcher administration to 3.7 per cent in 1991–2.[2] The next general election, which most Tories had considered unwinnable under Thatcher, came in the untroubled spring of 1992 and proved an unexpected triumph for Major. His apparently open and emollient personality contrasted sharply with Thatcher's. This advantage was effectively exploited by Conservative election managers and particularly by the Party's shrewd chairman, Chris Patten. Major could take personal satisfaction from the fact that more people (14.1 million) voted for his Conservative government in 1992 than had done so for Thatcher in any of her three election victories.[3] Indeed, no party leader has ever won a larger number of votes than Major achieved in that election.

The electorate may have heaved a collective sign of relief in April 1992 that they no longer had Thatcher around to polarise opinion. As the most authoritative study of the election suggested, '1992 must be seen more as a vote to give John Major his chance than as an endorsement of Mrs Thatcher's record'.[4] Many doubtless expected that, the election over and a personable new Prime Minister able to celebrate his own – rather than an inherited – parliamentary majority, Thatcher would vanish into the political mists. Some hope. After 1992, his government was dogged by Thatcher at almost every turn.

The last century and a half has witnessed two decades during which important aspects of political life seemed to be dictated either from the real or the political grave. If the 1860s were for Queen Victoria a decade of self-indulgent, duty-shirking mourning for her prematurely deceased Prince Albert, then the 1990s were for 'Queen' Margaret a decade of fulminating, self-absorbed rage and repinement at what she saw as a treacherous dethronement and its malign effects. She had supported John Major as her successor partly because of his charm but mostly because she believed him both more malleable and more naturally 'Thatcherite' than any plausible alternative. If she could not remain as leader, then she at least looked forward to acting as 'a very good back-seat driver'.[5]

She soon had cause to believe that she needed not just to offer a few suggestions about clutch control but to wrench the steering wheel from its new owner and turn the entire vehicle around. Major was a sore disappointment to Thatcher on two levels. First, she considered him a poor leader who failed to deal decisively, as she had always done, with political crises and who also cut a poor figure on the world stage. Second, she thought that he failed to follow her example – and especially so over Europe.

In two areas – taxation policy and privatisation – Major appeared loyal enough to the legacy. He kept rates of direct taxation low, at 25 per cent for the standard rate and 40 per cent for the higher, although taxes as a whole were raised in the 1993 budget. Privatisation continued. In particular, Major embarked on one specially high-profile initiative – the disastrous break-up of British Rail in 1995. The main objective was to swell depleted Treasury coffers with quick injections of sell-off cash, although Major also held some half-baked notion that different companies, decked out in attractive new liveries – recalling a non-existent golden age in the 1920s – would provide a more efficient service under competitive conditions. As much of British Rail's track ended up being operated by only one privatised passenger company, it was difficult to see how customers were expected to benefit from a competitive environment. They were, however, irked and confused by a multiplicity of offers and catchpenny deals which in practice restricted choice over when, and where, to travel.

At any event, privatisation engendered in Railtrack perhaps the most spectacularly mismanaged and inept company in twentieth-century business history, run as it was by people who knew little or nothing about railways and who pensioned off most of those who did – the skilled engineers – to save costs and increase dividends for shareholders. The political fall-out was substantial. Major was accused of creating a 'poll tax on wheels'. It was widely believed that even Margaret Thatcher, sceptical of the value of public transport and the high-priestess of privatisation (see Chapter 3), knew that rail privatisation was a non-starter.

Overall, Major was no keeper of the Thatcherite flame. Public expenditure, expressed as a percentage of GDP, edged inexorably upwards – from 39 per cent in the last year of the Thatcher government to 44 per cent in 1997.[6] Rates of growth in GDP and, especially, consumer expenditure, were lower in the 1990s than in the 1980s, allowing Thatcher's supporters to claim that weaker political leadership led to diminished economic rewards.[7]

On no subject after she left office did Thatcher swing her famous handbag to such telling effect as on Europe. She included some wounding comments in the second volume of her memoirs, in which she accused Major of conniving in the destruction of British sovereignty.

> I knew that John Major was likely to seek some kind of compromise with the majority heads of government who wanted political and economic union . . . I could well understand that after the bitter arguments over Europe which preceded my resignation he would want to bind up the wounds in the Party. But I was not prepared for the speed with which the position I had adopted would be entirely reversed.[8]

The forced withdrawal of the government from the ERM in October 1992 provided an appropriate backdrop. Thatcher could remind her followers that she had been a reluctant entrant to ERM (see Chapter 7), having been persuaded against her better judgement by her Cabinet colleagues – led by Major. Quitting the ERM turned out to have considerable economic benefits but it was a political disaster, not least because neither the Prime Minister nor his Chancellor, Norman Lamont, gave the impression that they were in control of events. As the Home Secretary, Kenneth Clarke, sourly noted, 'this is the first time I've been in a government which hasn't got an economic policy'.[9]

In 1992–3, Thatcher opposed ratification of the Maastricht Treaty, which, among other things, promised to increase the size of the EC and which looked forward to the framing of a common EU defence policy. Major argued to parliament that the Maastricht changes were relatively trivial and that British diplomacy had secured a number of crucial 'get-out' clauses to frustrate any dangerous moves towards federalism and common sovereignty. Thatcher, knowing how much store her old enemy and arch-federalist Jacques Delors (see above Chapter 7) placed on Maastricht, and fearing the combined power of France and Germany to swing the EU behind their own interpretations, was having nothing of it.[10] She helped to foment a parliamentary rebellion against Maastricht. As Major ruefully noted in his memoirs: 'By the early autumn of 1993 she was telling friends that she hoped for a leadership contest a year before the next general election, and for Michael Portillo to win it'.[11]

Thatcher used her immense residual influence in the party, and in particular in the constituencies, to undermine Major. He aggrievedly noted in his memoirs that he had not expected her 'to flout traditional party discipline in a way so damaging to the government'.[12] This was to forget that Thatcher was no traditional Conservative. Unlike the great majority of her predecessors, and very much against the grain of party tradition, she despised loyalty in what she saw as a losing cause as much as she hated compromise. By contrast, Major always preferred consensus and good personal relations to the driven certainties and ferocious arguments on which Thatcher thrived. Undeniably, he would have found it easier to stamp his authority on a poisonously divided and leaky Cabinet had not those whom Major privately dubbed 'the bastards' known that their preferences and prejudices were those of Thatcher and of the right-wing Thatcherite back-benchers who had come into parliament at the Tory electoral triumphs of 1983 and 1987.

She eventually got her way over the leadership contest. In a desperate attempt to restore some authority over what were now openly warring factions in the Conservative Party, Major resigned its leadership in 1995 and sought a fresh mandate through election from the parliamentary party. This he received, because those Cabinet colleagues who might have defeated him, particularly Michael Heseltine and Michael Portillo, refused to stand in a first ballot – although both doubtless hoped that (like Thatcher in 1990) Major would fail to get enough votes in that ballot against his only opponent, John Redwood, to confirm that he had authority over the party. In the event, with Redwood a risibly less effective candidate than Heseltine had been five years earlier, Major received forty more votes than Thatcher had done, even although the parliamentary party was some forty smaller in 1995 than in 1990. He immediately claimed decisive victory, although his memoirs told a different story. He revealed there that the votes he received were only three more than the minimum he had calculated he needed to stay in office.[13]

This success availed him little. Fresh European rows broke out, it seemed, almost weekly. These were extravagantly written up in the broadsheet newspapers. John Major later recalled that his government was 'mortally wounded over Europe, our blood was in the water'.[14] Meanwhile public interest, driven by a prurient populist press, turned its attention to 'sleaze'. This took several forms. Sexual scandals took pride of place, especially for the Sunday newspapers, and the libidinous antics of leading Conservatives such as David Mellor, Tim Yeo and Stephen Norris were paraded before a slavering public. Major himself must have been living on tenterhooks, aware that an earlier affair with Edwina Currie – a pushy self-publicist whose own brief ministerial career as Tory health minister had come to grief under Thatcher in 1988 after a politically unwise declaration that most of Britain's eggs were infected with the *Salmonella* bacterium – could be revealed at any time.

Recurrent sexual scandals were a severe embarrassment for a Prime Minister who had urged his ministers that the government should 'get back to basics' in terms of the values that he believed ordinary people understood. Revelations of shady financial deals and personal impropriety, however, were probably more damaging. Both a Cabinet minister, Jonathan Aitken, and a Party Vice-Chairman, Jeffrey Archer, were jailed for perjury arising from scandals revealed during the Major years. Tim Smith and Neil Hamilton were also forced to resign from minor government posts, amid maximum damaging publicity, for accepting money from the businessman and owner of Harrods, Mohammed Al Fayed.

If Thatcher made little comment about sleaze, and in any case played a less prominent role in public life as the 1997 election approached, her overall influence on the Major government was decidedly unhelpful. Major did not lose the general election of 1997 purely because of Thatcher's influence. The impression his own indecisive leadership gave of a rudderless, as well as a feuding, party would probably have led to defeat anyway. However, 1997 was a Conservative disaster. It represented the biggest defeat the party had suffered since the election of 1832, immediately after the passage of the First Reform Act. The 336 Conservative MPs returned in 1992 dwindled to only 165, against 419 supporting the incoming Labour government. Of that paltry number, none was elected from either Scotland or Wales. It had been widely noted that Thatcher's economic policies did devastating damage to the old industrial areas of Scotland, Wales and northern England (see Chapter 3). The result of the 1997 election was perhaps the delayed, but logical, outcome of those policies – a final unwelcome present from Thatcher to Major. The Conservatives also polled nearly 5 million fewer votes than Labour.[15] The mood of early May 1997 was one of huge relief at the ending of an ineffective and discredited government but also of hope for a new dawn.

THATCHER AND THE RISE OF NEW LABOUR

But did New Labour offer a new dawn, or were its emphases and values more Thatcherite than is usually recognised? Did Margaret Thatcher, even as her health began to fade, continue to exercise huge influence over British politics into the twenty-first century? These questions have attracted much recent debate. One leading sociologist argued that the strong political position that Blair assumed after the 1997 general election gave 'New Labour' a genuine choice. It could either adopt 'an alternative radical strategy to Thatcherism' with bold thinking and emphasis on a clear new direction or it could 'adapt to Thatcherite, neo-liberal terrain'.[16] In embracing both the language and the methods of 'modernisation', in its obeisance to private sector as efficient and wealth creating, and in its determination to work with the grain of free market economics, rather than against it, this commentator concluded that the similarities between New Labour and Thatcherism were far more important than the differences. It has chosen what he calls a 'grim alignment with corporate capital and power' and has turned its back on old Labour traditions. As the political editor of *The Spectator* put it in 2002, on the occasion of her medically enforced removal from political life: 'Make no mistake: Margaret Thatcher begat Tony Blair'.[17]

This interpretation has some force. One of Thatcher's major objectives was to destroy socialism as a potent political force in Britain. Although other reasons help to explain its demise, her success cannot be denied. Her triumph needs, however, to be set in the context of Labour politics. The Labour Party was the only significant political organisation in Britain remotely interested during the twentieth century in promoting socialist policies although, for the most part, its leaders have avoided them like the plague. They were able to do this because the trade unions, which paid most of Labour's bills, were also usually led from the centre, rather than the socialist left. Trade union barons were no more natural socialists than was Labour's predominantly upper middle-class leadership. We might, therefore, legitimately wonder whether Thatcher's anti-socialist crusade was against a real, or an imaginary, dragon. On this view, Blair's success in persuading Labour to drop the famous 'socialist' Clause 4 from its Constitution in 1995 – traumatic although it was for many 'Old Labour' faithful – was little more than window dressing.

The Labour Party that emerged from its splits and ideological traumas of the early 1980s was a distinctively different beast from the tormented animal with which Thatcher toyed in her prime. Both Neil Kinnock's attacks on 'Old Labour' shibboleths, such as socialist sloganising and crude trade union power, and his attempts to modernise his party during his time as leader from 1983 to 1992 owed much to Thatcher's expert attacks in the mid-1980s. His only plausible assault on power at the 1992 general election foundered on the dual rocks of an implacably populist right-wing press and a more shrewdly defensive Conservative campaign than most commentators had believed possible (see above).

The Conservatives were also helped by two other important factors.

First, Kinnock himself was voluble enough to be unfairly but damagingly dismissed as 'a Welsh windbag' who tried to turn a large political meeting in Sheffield at the height of the campaign into a premature victory rally.[18] Second, he was opposed by a shrewdly personable Prime Minister in John Major rather than by the shrill, obstinate termagant that Margaret Thatcher had become by 1990. Although the Conservatives had an overall majority of only twenty-one seats, they claimed had a very substantial lead (7.6 per cent) over Labour in the popular vote.[19]

The 'New Labour' project, which came to dominate British politics from the mid-1990s, had its origins in the heyday of Thatcher. Her successes strongly suggested that 'Old Labour' had become unelectable. In the approach to the 1997 general election, the few remaining real socialists, to use a term much favoured by Thatcher, either put up or shut up. Meanwhile, Labour leaders and spin doctors either expunged the 'S' word from their political vocabulary or, if they used it, talked about 'ethical socialism'. This piece of political fudge was meant to square internal political circles; it was not for consumption by the electorate, who were steered very clear of any kind of socialist message. The phrase was rarely heard on the lips of Blair's ministers after 1997. Perhaps one of Thatcher's most unlikely achievements is one about which she was ambivalent: she helped to make Labour electable again – albeit an overtly non-socialist Labour Party and at the safe distance of almost seven years from her own political demise.

Thatcher might even have argued herself into the quixotic position that a Labour victory might offer more long-term sustenance to the causes dearest to her heart than a second election victory for John Major. Her friends heard her express the view that 'New Labour' under Tony Blair was a safe, capitalist enterprise perhaps closer to the Democrats in the United States than to any British party. All taint of socialism had been expunged. While the Democrats were less desirable allies for Thatcher than the Republicans, who had been led by her great friend Ronald Reagan, they were certainly 'safe' and a healthy democracy required a change of governing party. Of course, she went through the loyal Conservative motions during the election campaign of 1997, but her heart was clearly not in it. Her natural supporters in the shires would not flock to the polls to keep her successor in office. It is significant that the turnout, at 71.5 per cent, was the lowest in any general election since the Second World War, although some of the lowest turnouts were encountered in very solidly Labour- rather than Conservative-held seats.[20,21]

The 1997 election provided ample evidence that Tony Blair could 'win big'. Although the 2001 election result was less impressive, especially in terms of Labour's popular vote, which fell by almost 3 million, an overall majority of 167 confirmed that Blair was even more capable than Thatcher had been at winning huge majorities.[22] It is worth noting that the big election victories of 1983, 1987, 1997 and 2001 were won by party leaders who, although they had contrasting personalities, experienced similar relations with their parties. Both were outsiders; both considered old party loyalties and values as a drag on progress and momentum. Both also had limited use for established constitutional forms. Thatcher did not see her Cabinet as a forum for rational debate, rather than as a rubber stamp for decisions taken elsewhere – not infrequently just by her and a small number of advisers. Blair continued this process. Cabinets met rather less frequently and for a far shorter time.[23] Both Blair and Gordon Brown brought in their own political advisers, often seeking to sideline official civil service procedures. One political commentator argued that the Blair regime accelerated the process, developed during the Thatcher era, of increasing political centralisation – but always with an eye on electoral advantage.

> [The Blair government] is marinated in clichés about One Nation, Third Way, social inclusion and aspirational society. But its appeal is…to offer a rigidly controlled state sector to the tax conscious floating voters of middle England.[24]

Thatcher's initial problems with an established Conservative Party hierarchy have been noticed elsewhere (see Chapter 4). Tony Blair came from a quintessentially Conservative background. His father was a successful businessman and a Tory councillor who educated his son at a leading Scottish public school. Blair never imbibed the 'beer-and-sandwiches' culture of Labour activism and took far less interest than most party leaders in cultivating deep roots in the party. Like Thatcher, he intended to stand or fall on his direct appeal to the British people. Like Thatcher, also, he stressed the key role of business: 'In the end there is no escaping from the fact that businesses run business. And the best thing government can do is set a framework within which business has the stability to plan and invest in the future'.[25]

The weapons that Thatcher and Blair used were often different, but in their willingness to challenge party custom and tradition the two leaders were remarkably similar. As one commentator put it, 'In the view of Blair and his fellow modernisers, the Labour Party was an ingrown and backward-looking organisation locked into an outdated set of dogmas related to a new and rapidly changing cultural and global conditions'.[26] To bringing those changing conditions about, Thatcher had contributed much.

Similarities have also been detected in the way the two leaders used the press. In a sense, management was easier for Thatcher, who usually faced a sympathetic right-wing press anyway. At times of high diplomatic or foreign policy drama, the decisive and populist Thatcher could be guaranteed strong support. Nevertheless, Thatcher, while less directly concerned about personal press comment, was always careful to ensure that her relations with the press barons, and especially Rupert Murdoch, were cordial. Blair and his entourage were well aware that the press was rarely sympathetic to Labour and that, even as he tried to pull the party around, Neil Kinnock's media relations 'were essentially a permanent exercise in damage limitation'.[27] Blair learned much from this experience. He was keen to project himself as a strong leader, in control of his party, particularly as Major was demonstrably not in control of his. With his key advisers on media affairs, Alastair Campbell and Peter Mandelson, he ensured that Labour was able to 'ride the tiger' of media influence and manipulate it, perhaps for the first time, to the party's advantage.[28] In doing this, Blair also adopted a populist style. Just as Thatcher had no compunction about appealing over the heads of the Conservative Party to connect with 'her' people, so Blair's discourse was replete with references to 'the people'. In discussing the National Lottery while still in opposition, he asserted that he 'wanted the people's money to go on the people's priorities'.[29] The British people should not have been surprised, although many fastidious stomachs turned, when Blair immediately massaged what had been the highly ambiguous reputation of the recently deceased Diana into populist canonisation when he dubbed her 'the people's princess'.

Blair's critics would say that the downside of media manipulation – brain-deadened 'on message' statements from Labour MPs, the closing down of vigorous political debate and the insidious, pervasive culture of 'spin' – was further evidence of his indebtedness to the legacy of Thatcher. Although Campbell and Mandelson took this to much more extreme lengths than Ingham in the Thatcher era, New Labour's recognition that it was almost impossible for a party to survive in the face of sustained hostile press coverage owed much to past Labour experience and to their understanding of the reasons for the contrasting political fortunes of Thatcher and Major. Not surprisingly, obsession with news management has attracted vigorous criticism from senior Labour politicians resistant to the blandishments of Tony Blair's big political tent. For Roy Hattersley, for example,

> The abiding tragedy of Blairism is its absolute obsession with appearances. What New Labour looks like is more important than

what New Labour does. Presentation, which ought to be employed to promote policy, often dictates what policy shall be. That produces the worst sort of short-termism, for it focuses even the most important decisions on tomorrow's headlines.[30]

In foreign affairs, also, Blair's leadership shows elements of Thatcherite priorities. The events of 2002–3, culminating in the allied US–UK attack on Iraq, have dominated public perception. These appear to indicate that, when the chips are down, British foreign policy falls meekly in behind an agenda set by the United States. The war with Iraq might be seen as the continuation of George Bush Jr's crusade against terrorism in the wake of the attack on the twin towers in September 2001. On this analysis, when Bush whistled, Blair obediently came to heel. Blair might thus be seen as following Thatcher in sacrificing other considerations for the so-called 'special relationship' (see Chapter 8).

It is important, however, not to judge Blair's foreign policy purely in the context of the Iraq war. Compared with Thatcher, New Labour foreign policy attempted much greater inclusiveness. The attempt to define what Blair's first foreign secretary Robin Cook called an 'ethical foreign policy' ran into difficulties and attracted substantial criticism when highflown principle bowed to pragmatic considerations. Nevertheless, it is impossible to imagine Margaret Thatcher asserting, as Cook did in 2000, 'we have put human rights at the heart of foreign policy'.[31] Similarly, Tony Blair's Chicago speech in April 1999 asserted a distinctively new role for the international community by emphasising that intervention 'in other people's conflicts' might be morally justified.[32] This speech was far more than an *ex post facto* rationalisation for intervention in Kosovo. Ironically, in the light of the heavy criticism which the Iraq War of 2003 provoked within the international community, it was an attempt to claim British moral leadership in support of international efforts to halt genocide and to curb threats to international security while these were still containable. It is difficult to imagine Thatcher acknowledging that international activity should ever take priority over national self-interest.

In Europe, too, Blair's government has taken a distinctly non-Thatcherite line. Her legacy of division on Europe did, of course, continue. Blair was well aware of the divisiveness of any decision to join the European single currency and thus (as many in the press characterised it) to 'sacrifice the pound'. The issue was endlessly delayed while he said that he was waiting for spurious 'economic tests' to be met, whereas he was waiting either for something to turn up or for the heat to go out of the issue. Overall, though, Blair proved much more pro-European than Thatcher. He rebuilt bridges that Thatcher contemptuously demolished in the 1980s (see Chapter 7) and which Major had feared to approach in the 1990s. Unlike Thatcher, he was happy to speak French. He supported the expansion of the EU and he promoted initiatives designed to achieve common EU foreign and security policies. Blair is, without question, much more of an internationalist than Thatcher. European policy is the area in which he has most decisively turned his back on the Thatcher legacy.

Blair's determination to promote New Labour as a non-socialist enterprise explicitly recognised the importance of the Thatcher legacy. As part of a deliberate assertion of his power over his party, which retained a visceral hatred for Thatcher, he went out of his way to state that she 'had got certain things right' and he approved of aspects of her modernisation programme against 'vested interests'.[33] He kept to the key element of her taxation policy, instructing his Chancellor of the Exchequer, Gordon Brown, much against his better judgement not to raise either the standard or the higher rate of taxation. His government has also continued with a raft of Thatcherite policies and attitudes. Some changed rhetoric aside, New Labour works much more readily with the grain of private- than public-sector initiatives. It has absorbed and extended the ugly, windy rhetoric of managerialism. It sets targets, measures outcomes and venerates 'performance indicators'. It also manipulates figures with the best of them so that they can be spun to indicate 'progress' and 'achievement'.

The importance of the Thatcher legacy for Blair is undeniable but it should not be overdone. What became known as the Blairite 'Third Way' – driven neither by capitalist imperatives nor by socialist certainties – *was* not only distinctively different from Thatcherism. In important areas, it directly refuted it. Thatcher was hostile to all forms of devolution. The creation of Scottish and Welsh assemblies was one of the earliest initiatives of the Blair government. Referenda over devolution were held in Scotland and Wales in September 1997. The first elections for the devolved assemblies were held in both countries in 1999. Constitutional reform also encompassed the creation of the role of elected Mayor of London in 1998 and protracted discussions about House of Lords reform began to bear fruit from 2000. None of these initiatives would have come about under Thatcher.

Although the relationship was never cosy, the relationship between government and trade unions became far less hostile under Blair. An initiative blocked by successive Conservative governments, signing up to the so-called 'Social Chapter' of the EU, happened under Blair within a month of his coming into office. A White Paper, *Fairness at Work*, promised workers new safeguards, although some proposals were later watered down under pressure from employers.[34] Another of Thatcher's aversions – the minimum hourly wage – was introduced in April 1999, albeit at a far lower level than had been wanted by the trade unions. Nevertheless, the era of malicious union bashing had clearly come to an end.

Perhaps the most anti-Thatcherite policies pursued by the Blair government, however, were those directed towards the redistribution of wealth, and these were championed both fearlessly and cunningly by Gordon Brown. Thatcher believed that this was not government business. Labour thinkers in opposition frequently drew attention to the appearance of a substantial underclass and believed this to be one of the most malign legacies of Thatcherism. It manifested itself most obviously, perhaps, in greatly increased levels in street begging from the later 1980s, but far more who did not beg were in permanent, grinding poverty, often for no other reason than that they were old. New Labour social policy was directed at directing resources disproportionately towards the losers of the Thatcherite revolution. This meant making hard choices, not least refusing to tie state pensions to earnings levels and rejecting uniform levels of welfare provision. New Labour thinking was that rising levels of overall prosperity had produced large numbers of people who had little or no need of state support. Thus, policy was directed at those in most need – increasing means-tested income support for old people and using a complex system of tax credits and benefits to support the children of lone-parent and out-of-work families. Blair's objective was 'to abolish child poverty in a generation'.[35]

The point of all this is not whether the policies succeeded. The Blair government's objective of what one commentator has called 'selective universalism' – pay lip service to a universal system of health and education but be much more directive about where the bulk of state aid goes – had at least as many successes as failures. It has failed to assuage the resentment felt by those who are – just – able to help themselves, thus falling just outside government-defined safety nets. The widespread feeling among this large group in the lower middle classes that those who have been less prudent and less organised are baled out by unearned 'state-handouts' has potentially serious repercussions. Nevertheless, the assault on child poverty has had some dramatic successes. Whereas 41 per cent of children in out-of-work families were defined as being in severe need in 1999, by 2001 this proportion had dropped to 28 per cent.[36]

New Labour was prepared to use overtly redistributive policies to tackle social problems whereas Thatcher was not. The so-called Blairite 'Third Way' has come in for some severe criticism, largely on the basis of its intellectual plasticity. 'Third Way-ism' may not represent a cogent intellectual strategy but its objectives are distinctly different from those of a government controlled by supply side economics and in thrall to market forces. As we have seen, many similarities may be drawn between Thatcher and Blair. Her legacy was undoubtedly a major influence on his attitudes and his policy formulations. Ultimately, though, he was less 'ideological' than her and much more willing to put social need near to the heart of government strategy.

12 The legacy II

Economy, society and ethos

ECONOMY AND SOCIETY

It was argued in the previous chapter that Margaret Thatcher exercised substantial influence over British politics in the decade after she reluctantly relinquished office. Her political legacy over a weak, if protracted, Major government is understandable. What was not so anticipatory, and certainly not widely anticipated in 1997 when Blair's 'New Labour' government took office and also, coincidentally, when the first edition of this book was published, was the longer-term political legacy. From the perspective of the first years of the twenty-first century, it might be plausibly argued that Thatcher's long administration had effected a longer-term change in the political weather. To what extent, however, did the Thatcher years produce longer-term influence on what the French might call the *mentalité* of British society in the late twentieth and early twenty-first centuries?

Thatcher was uncomfortable with intellectual abstractions, her instinct being to doubt their relevance and utility. Thus, the very idea of 'society' – the living laboratory of social scientists, a key professional group for whom she had little time – worried her. In 1987, she was famously reported in the popular magazine *Women's Own* as holding the view that there was 'no such thing as society'. Her later memoirs attempted to clarify her meaning that:

> ... there are individual men and women and there are families. And no government can do anything except through people, and people must look to themselves first. It's our first duty to look after ourselves first and then to look after our neighbour.[1]

However, even the clarification suggested a clear order of priority and the 'society statement' was frequently quoted as evidence of her selfishness and heartlessness. Abundant evidence exists of her personal kindnesses but there is little doubt of her beliefs both that charity began at home and that people were, to a very large extent, masters of their own fate. As she acidly remarked: 'When I heard people complain that "society"' should not permit some particular misfortune, I would retort, "And what are you doing about it, then?" '. Her perception of society was competitive, not collaborative. It was held more from prejudice tempered by personal experience and it did immense damage, largely because, unlike most other powerfully simple statements which issue from the mouths of politicians, she actually – indeed, fervently – believed in it.

Thatcher's economic legacy is mixed. One central objective of Thatcherism was to reduce the burden of taxation. This failed. At the end of 1996, taxation accounted for 37.2 per cent of a taxpayer's annual income; in 1979 it had been only 31.1 per cent.[2] Characteristically, though, this strategic failure was masked by tactically significant political success for Thatcher the politician. The burden of *direct* taxation in the same period went down from 19.9 per cent to 17.7 per cent and the Labour Party was unable, at least until 1997, to shed its unwelcome image as the party of high taxation. Thatcher well knew that the public perceive taxation as being those amounts that are taken directly from pay packets in Pay As You Earn (PAYE). They do not think of the high levels of tax that they pay every time they buy a gallon of petrol or eat a meal in a restaurant.

The long-term success of Thatcher's policies in this year can be gauged by the fact that the Labour Chancellor of the Exchequer, Gordon Brown, refused to countenance increases in direct taxation – even for the wealthy – during the government of 1997–2001. Since that government wished to spend more on various social policies, these had to be funded by a range of ingenious, but cumulatively mendacious 'stealth taxes', of which hefty increases in National Insurance contributions were the most straightforward.[3] The Thatcher legacy was to confirm for New Labour that a political party could not thrive in the United Kingdom if saddled with the reputation for 'taxing and spending'.

Britain's relative economic decline has not been halted since 1979, although the extent of that decline in the second half of the twentieth century should not be exaggerated. It needs to be set against demonstrable improvements in living standards and economic security for the great majority of British people in the second half of the twentieth century.[4] It is true that annual growth rates in the years 1979–88 and 1988–97, at 1.9 per cent and 1.5 per cent respectively, were considerably higher than those achieved in the period 1973–9. However, these successes stand out as relative failures in comparison with other developed economies, especially those of Germany, Japan and the United States. Also, growth rates in the hated years of 'Butskellite Consensus' were much higher than in the Thatcher years. Again, however, strategic failure needs to be set against some high-profile tactical successes. The British inflation rate, which stood at 22 per cent at the end of Thatcher's first year, came down dramatically during most of the Thatcher years. The early 1980s and early 1990s were periods of spectacular falls and over the last decade the British inflation rate, a crucial blip in 1990 apart, kept in reasonable balance with those of the other main industrialised countries.[5] In all years but two, however – 1984 and 1995 – the British inflation rate has been higher than those of these G7 comparator countries.

By design, Britain became a more unequal society under Thatcher. Incentives for high-earning risk takers were supposed to help them create more jobs, thus increasing overall national prosperity. As we have seen, tax cuts for the better off were real and the Lawson boom (see Chapter 3) did bring widespread economic benefits. General consumption levels increased sharply during the decade 1978–88. For example, the proportion of families with telephones increased from 62 per cent to 85 per cent, and the proportion with central heating increased from 54 per cent to 77 per cent.[6] Those at the bottom of society, however, failed to benefit. If an unofficial 'poverty line' is drawn at one-half of the average national income, the numbers in poverty increased from 5 million in 1979 to 14.1 million in 1992.

The changing balance of work also disadvantaged the poor. Opportunities for women in both part-time and full-time employment increased substantially from the mid-1980s. New levels of prosperity were available to young married couples – the so-called 'dinkies' (dual income, no kids). While the proportion of families in which both adults worked rose during Thatcher's term of office, the proportion of families with no full-time worker also rose – from 29 per cent to 37 per cent. This was only partially due to the increased number of pensioners in an ageing society. Inequality was the inevitable result, with the sharpest anomalies at both the top and bottom of the scale. Thatcherite Toryism brought overall prosperity. After deducting costs of housing, the average real income of British families rose by between 1979 and 1992 by 37 per cent. However, the real incomes of the poorest 10 per cent declined by 18 per cent, while those of the richest 10 per cent increased by 61 per cent. In 1979, the richest 10 per cent of the population held 20.6 per cent of the nation's wealth and the poorest 10 per cent held 4.3 per cent. In 1991, the proportions were 26.1 per cent and 2.9 per cent respectively.[7]

Thatcher's personal success is beyond dispute. Thatcherism also had more substantial successes than its detractors like to pretend, and those successes were presented in an extremely favourable light by a generally sympathetic press. Thatcher's image, except with relatively small minorities – including the highly educated professional middle classes and left-wing political activists – remains that of a strong, successful leader who 'turned Britain around'. Perhaps, in a depressingly post-modernist age, the fact that she did not matters less than the fact that she is widely perceived to have done so. She did, however, bring about substantial changes. Britain was indoctrinated to consider material success the main, if not the only, goal and to embrace the so-called 'enterprise culture'.

LEARNING AND THE ARTS

The contempt with which Thatcherism is regarded by many in the intellectual élite and by the professional classes is understandable, even if their manner of expressing it is not. Intellectuals and creative artists derided the economics of the corner shop and discerned in Thatcher the cultural sensitivity of a Philistine with learning difficulties. Intellectuals were also profoundly uncomfortable with someone who did not experience the exquisite mental stimulation afforded by either doubt or alternative views. The language used about her by the rationalists was quite irrationally intemperate, owing at least as much to social and intellectual snobbery as to political antagonism. Perhaps the most comprehensive, even cosmic, *bien-pensant* denunciation came from Will Hutton, the economist, journalist and best-selling author of *The State We're In*:

> How much better a place Britain would have been had Baroness Thatcher never existed. Its politics would be less disfigured, its society less unequal, its public services less run down and its Conservative media less rabid. It would be more at peace with Europe and with itself. She was the high priestess of prejudice, breaking the back of her own party and the principles of the Labour party alike.[8]

Baroness Warnock, incongruously for a philosopher, found much to criticise in her dress sense: 'packaged together in a way that's not exactly vulgar, just *low*'.[9] Dr Jonathan Miller, polymathic intellectual and aesthete rolled into one (and satirised by *Private Eye* as the Dr Samuel Johnson *de nos jours* for his pains), deplored her 'odious suburban gentility and sentimental, saccharine patriotism, catering for the worst elements of consumer idiocy'. He found her 'loathsome, repulsive in every way'.

Intriguingly, however, Miller's productions for English National

Opera during the 'powerhouse years' of the 1980s contributed much to the substantial creative renaissance that took place there under the direction of the Earl of Harewood (the Queen's cousin) while state funding for the arts was being cut back. Harewood's boys offered to a predominantly young, and growing, audience experimental and challenging music theatre. Inevitably, some productions offered only silly and self-indulgent examples of 'producer-licence'. One such, *Orpheus in the Underworld*, guyed Thatcher as a morally censorious 'Public Opinion'. More, however, used art creatively to illuminate and examine life. There was no cause-and-effect relationship between state parsimony and artistic creativity, although much high-quality art was fuelled by anger and frustration. British opera and British film were two cultural forms that attracted worldwide critical admiration in the 1980s. Artistic managers discovered unsuspected entrepreneurial and marketing talents as they attracted sponsorship from private industry, especially during the Lawson boom. Meanwhile, Andrew Lloyd Webber's apparently limitless supply of saccharine melodies allied to the talents of managers like Cameron Mackintosh attracted unprecedentedly large numbers to the commercial musical theatre. Tourism boomed in Thatcher's Britain, and *The Phantom of the Opera* was one of the things the tourists came to see. Out of its profits, and those of the musical clones, Lloyd Webber, a man of considerable cultural sensitivity, accumulated one of the most impressive private art collections in the world.

Universities, almost all of which were more than 80 per cent government funded, were likewise unfamiliar with the disciplines of the market place. Most initially derided these as uncertain guides to quantity and utterly irrelevant to their over-riding concern for quality. Academic tenure encourages a critical independence of view, which short-term contracts do not. It is not surprising that tenured professors should use their independence, while it survived, to lambast a Prime Minister who rejected their values and who, in 1981, instituted an 18 per cent cut in higher education funding over three years.[10] Famously, Oxford University refused her an honorary degree in 1985, arguing that her education policies were doing 'deep and systematic damage to the whole public education system in Britain'. Right-wing supporters of Thatcher the universities did produce, if in small numbers. Ironically, if their expertise lay in economics or business, they tended to be scooped up to work in government 'think tanks' or as special advisers to the Prime Minister. Some, such as Patrick Minford and Alan Walters, on occasion exercised greater influence even than Cabinet ministers (see above).

Were the academics right to be so censorious? Thatcher presided over a substantial expansion in higher education. Student numbers increased from 535,000 to 710,000 during the 1980s, leading to even more rapid expansion to 1.3 million by the early 1990s and more than 2 million by the time Major's government left office. At the same time, both the Thatcher and the Major governments maintained ferociously tight controls over education spending. Expenditure utterly failed to keep pace with expansion. Higher education suffered a 25 per cent per head cut in the decade 1989–99.[11]

The consequences were predictable enough. Universities became more productive but hardly *better*. Students were taught in larger classes and scrabbled for library books whose number did not increase pro rata; they had less personal contact with tutors whose research and administrative performance, as well as their teaching skills, were now being measured. Universities successfully defended the concept of peer, rather than outsider, review in these, but the criteria handed down to the academic peers required quantitative as well as qualitative measurement. The need to ensure that public money was being properly spent was entirely laudable, and should have been instituted long before. The *means* of measurement, however, were bureaucratic, labour intensive and contentious. The resources channelled to those institutions that showed themselves most adept at form-filling, self-promotion and presentation were inadequate to sustain the quality they claimed. All too often, inappropriate 'performance indicators' were instituted to gauge success against value-for-money criteria. Too many either failed to work at all or measured the wrong things. More, but not necessarily better, research papers and books were written to meet the requirements of regular 'research assessment exercises'. A distressingly frequent ailment in the academic world of the 1990s was premature publication.

Research assessment exercises survived the change of government in 1997 and some in universities grew to love them. Their validity, however, remained open to challenge. By 2001, a combination of bureaucratic gigantism and 'game-playing' by many institutions produced expensively generated, if in many cases implausible, indicators of the 'international excellence' of academic research in the United Kingdom. Whether the universities themselves believed the outcomes is unclear, as they have a vested interest in asserting that they do when they appear to tell a good tale. That the government had no intention of funding the ever-inflating grades that all league table activities engender sooner or later is certain. For many observers, one of Thatcher's key performance indicators of higher education quality lacked credibility.

Thatcher bamboozled those on the intellectual left as much as she antagonised them. Academic Marxists in particular, always a more numerous group than any other kind, thrashed about trying to explain why simplification, homily, insistence and repetition delivered in a curious, synthetic voice should have so much more persuasive power over working people than their own intricately argued hypotheses about consciousness, solidarity, hegemony and the rest. Some grudgingly conceded the attractions of what was dubbed her 'authoritarian populism'.[12] Language was one thing, of course. Even allowing for the wide disparity in relative resources, Thatcher was far more effective than the intellectual left at getting her message across. Unless most of them, she paid attention to effective, accessible communication.

Patriotism, however, was more important. Most people, although perhaps not most intellectuals, love their country. They respond to assertions about, and some promise of, national revival. They tend, as Margaret Thatcher told them in 1982 they should, to 'rejoice' at victory. Too many intellectuals forgot the vigorous patriotic tradition that characterised radical politics in the later eighteenth and nineteenth centuries. Reformist radicals identified with their country against their government in a pre-democratic age.[13] This lost tradition has weakened the left. Patriotism became appropriated by the right-wing of the political spectrum during the imperialist expansion of the late nineteenth century. In the 1980s, a populist of genius drew upon it to devastating effect. For some left-wing intellectuals, it was the last straw. Unhinged from the old certainties, they sank without trace – although not without noise – into that huge, relativist black hole of intellectual vacuity known as postmodernism. Margaret Thatcher did not notice their passing.

IMAGES AND VALUES

The unintended by-products of Thatcherism defined late twentieth-century British society unflatteringly. As it became more diverse and less anchored in traditional structures such as the nuclear family, it became less tolerant, more greedy and far less humane. It elided the socially critical distinction between selfishness and self-interest. Three dominant symbols of materialist Britain in the late 1980s and early 1990s stand out. Harry Enfield's brilliant comic parody 'Loadsamoney' offered a coarse stereotype of 'wad-wielding' vulgarity, judging everything in terms of immediate material gain. Striped-shirt yuppies, the complacent beneficiaries of deregulated, booming finance capitalism, noisily swigged lunchtime champagne in City wine bars just before the Stock Exchange crash of 1987. Privatisation also produced spectacular winners, with rewards out of all proportion to both their efforts and their entrepreneurial talents: chief executives of recently privatised utilities, like Cedric Brown of British Gas, who used what remained monopoly positions to award themselves huge salaries supplemented by share options, and outgoing directors of state-owned companies who saw privatisation through and who collectively pocketed almost 27 million as compensation.[14] The Blair government, complicit in the Thatcherite culture of greed and grab, did nothing to curb the excesses of executive reward, even during the huge stock market falls of 2001–3 when the 'kings of business' could not begin to argue that they had added value to their companies.

In the wake of these excesses, it is almost too painful to recall Thatcher's stated objective to recover what she variously called 'Victorian virtues' and 'Victorian values'. Her own narrow conception of these tells us much:

> The Victorians . . . had a way of talking which also summed up what we were now rediscovering – they distinguished between the 'deserving' and the 'undeserving poor'. Both groups should be given help: but it must be help of very different kinds if public spending is not just going to reinforce the dependency culture . . . The purpose of help must not be to allow people merely to live a half-life, but rather to restore their self-discipline and their self-esteem.[15]

Here we encounter the cultural essence of Thatcherism: make people stand on their own feet and replace a dependency with an enterprise culture. Her analysis presents two problems. First, it rests on a spectacularly narrow, and atypical, perception of what these values actually were. Second, it distorted both policy and public attitudes. Thatcher's briskly confident assertions on subjects about which she knows little – and nineteenth-century British history certainly falls into that category – were surprisingly often not made for political effect but as statements of deeply-held belief.

In reality, although the Victorians distinguished between the deserving and the undeserving poor, they did so within a clear *social* context. Those same Victorians who believed in *laissez-faire* as a guiding principle of economic policy also produced substantial amounts of state intervention, in the form of Factory, Mines and Employment legislation and of government agencies to administer poor law and education. These were – in some senses – the precursors of the welfare legislation of the twentieth century. They believed such 'social legislation' to be an essential element in an emerging ethic of public service rooted in social, as well as individual, improvement.[16] The Victorians also had a developed civic ideal, manifested in the promotion of local government to administer a wide range of services. Administrative experts in Victorian Britain – men such as Edwin Chadwick in public health or James Kay-Shuttleworth in education, for example – would have described policy making on the basis of inadequate knowledge as government rooted in prejudice rather than principle. For these reasons, it is difficult to accept the judgement of one political scientist that Thatcherism can be explained 'as a reassertion of nineteenth-century liberalism'.[17] Another, David Marquand, was much nearer the mark when he pointed out that the 'vigorous virtues' of the nineteenth-century market economy were themselves nourished by 'a stock of moral capital accumulated over long generations to which the norms of the market place were at best alien and at worst anathema'.[18]

THE A-HISTORICAL PRIME MINISTER

A major defect of Thatcher's view of the world, in short, was that it lacked historical sense and perspective. This had important political and moral consequences. It was an entirely unintended malevolence of Thatcherism that it saw Britain became more corrupt and its political leaders less accountable as, intentionally, it became ever more centralised. The drive against the local authorities, which mostly rejected the Thatcherite message, concentrated power in Whitehall. One distinguished commentator believed that political centralisation 'has so strained the conventional limits of the British constitution that the constitution became a part of party politics, rather than a set of rules set above conventional party-political conflict'.[19]

Perhaps the greatest paradox of the 1980s is that a regime which came to power vowing to get the state off people's backs ended up substantially increasing the power of central government. Its enthusiastic henchmen were highly politicised 'political advisers', chairmen of quangos appointed on grounds of political sympathies rather than administrative abilities, and a civil service whose political neutrality was tested to destruction by managerialist ministers. Some civil servants, like Clive Ponting (see Chapter 8), responded by leaking government secrets. One distinguished journalist noted the changing culture:

Until Mrs Thatcher took the stage, leaks from career civil servants (as opposed to so-called ministerial 'advisers' from outside Whitehall) weren't just rare; they were almost unthinkable. So why the change? One reason is the sheer shabbiness of what . . . government is doing under the cloak of confidentiality. Another is the steady and intentional mix of politicisation and deliberate destabilisation which has been government policy ever since 1979.[20]

Another political commentator asserted that 'officials' role as givers of objective advice and askers of inconvenient questions has been battered into submission. In its place has grown a system and practice of surrender to ministerial imperatives'.[21] Too many MPs, especially but by no means exclusively on the Conservative side, cut corners (see also Chapter 11).

Thatcher's policies were driven by conviction rather than insight. They were pursued with courage yet sustained against both common sense and the conclusion of rational debate. Thatcherism at the end of the twentieth century was, in its way, as insensitive and 'driven' an ideology as Bolshevism had been at its beginning. Despite its political successes, the overall impressions left by the turbulent Thatcher decade are negative. True, Thatcherism believed in the beneficence of market forces, using these, in some inchoate way, to 'turn Britain around' and re-establish an era of national greatness. But not in much else. The list of those things Thatcherism attacked or demeaned is far longer: welfare, the power of the state to improve people's lives, the professional ethic of service, local government, trade unions, the notion of community, Europe. Margaret Thatcher's 'conviction politics' led her more readily to destroy than to create and her abiding narrowness of vision prevented her from seeing the likely medium- and long-term consequences of her policies. She entirely failed to notice, for example, that what might be termed the long century of growing state responsibility, dating roughly from 1830 to 1970, was fuelled in significant part by the need to control and moderate brute capitalism which, for all its wealth-creating potential, contained what Bernard Porter termed 'inexorable . . . self-destructive tendencies'.[22] In using the power of the state negatively – to resurrect as much unbridled capitalism as a decade of power in an elective dictatorship could encompass – Thatcherism morally impoverished and desensitised a nation.

Ideology is a reasonable servant for politicians but a disastrously bad master. Too much of Margaret Thatcher's regime vindicates the rhyming couplets written 250 years earlier, during the tenure of another long-serving Prime Minister, Robert Walpole:

> For forms of government let fools contest;
> Whate'er is best administered, is best:
> For modes of faith, let graceless zealots fight;
> His can't be wrong whose life is in the right:
> In faith and hope the world will disagree,
> But all mankind's concern is charity.[23]

That Margaret Thatcher's regime placed too much emphasis on forms and faiths – supply side economics, monetarism, privatisation and the rest – and too little on charity is perhaps its greatest indictment. Despite, or perhaps because of, the extraordinary political triumphs of Margaret Thatcher, Britain by the late 1980s had become a more grasping, greedy, mendacious and mean-spirited society and so it has remained. The regimes of first Major and then Blair have signally failed to alter the tone. Britain in the early twenty-first century remains a country too ready to equate achievement with merely monetary reward. It values fame and celebrity over solid indicators of worth and achievement. In the first edition of this book, the present author underestimated both the pervasiveness and the longevity of Thatcher's influence. The intervening years, however, have done nothing to alter the overall conclusion. Thatcher's remains a legacy to live down.

Notes

1 THE 1970s: EXPLANATIONS AND ORIGINS

1 Patrick Cosgrave, *Thatcher: The First Term* (Bodley Head, London, 1985), pp. 26–7.
2 Margaret Thatcher, *The Downing Street Years* (HarperCollins, London, 1993), p. 38.
3 J. Bulpitt, 'The Discipline of the New Democracy: Mrs Thatcher's Domestic Statecraft', *Political Studies*, 34 (1986); *Daily Telegraph*, 23 November 1990, quoted in J. Charmley, *A History of Conservative Politics, 1900–96* (Macmillan, London, 1996), p. 236; S. Letwin, *The Anatomy of Thatcherism* (Fontana, London, 1992). A useful summary of the arguments about Thatcherism as an ideology can be found in B. Evans and A. Taylor, 'The Debate about Thatcherism' in *From Salisbury to Major: Continuity and Change in Conservative Politics* (Manchester University Press, Manchester, 1996), pp. 219–40.
4 I. Gilmour, *Dancing with Dogma* (Simon & Schuster, Edinburgh, 1993); Francis Pym, *The Politics of Consent* (Hamish Hamilton, London, 1994).
5 This is a line that initiates will recognise as deriving from Gramsci and is reliably rendered in S. Hall, *The Hard Road to Renewal: Thatcherism and the Crisis of the Left* (Verso Books, London, 1988).
6 Quoted in P. Riddell, *The Thatcher Government* (Blackwell, 1985 edn, Oxford), p. 7.
7 For information about Thatcher's father, see John Campbell, *Margaret Thatcher: the Grocer's Daughter* (Jonathan Cape, London, 2000), especially pp. 8–13.
8 Quoted in K. Harris, *Thatcher* (Fontana, London, 1989), p. 250.
9 C. Cook and J. Stevenson (eds), *Britain since 1945* (2nd edn, Pearson Education, Harlow, 2000), pp. 55–60.
10 Ibid.
11 R. Skidelsky (ed.), *Thatcherism* (Blackwell, Oxford, 1989), p. 14.
12 The ideas of Friedman and Hayek were not identical. Friedman was a more thoroughgoing monetarist, whereas Hayek placed greater stress upon the supremacy of markets over all other kinds of organisation, political and social. See F. A. Hayek, *Denationalisation of Money* (Institute of Economic Affairs, London, 1978), Milton Friedman, *Inflation and Unemployment*

(IEA, London, 1977), and Norman Barry, *Hayek's Social and Economic Philosophy* (Macmillan, London, 1979). Monetarism and the new right in the 1970s are accessibly discussed in A. Gamble, *The Free Economy and the Strong State* (Macmillan, London, 1988), pp. 27–60.

13 International Monetary Fund statistics, quoted in http://www.clev.frb.org/research.
14 A. Gamble, *Britain in Decline* (Macmillan, Basingstoke, 1985), pp. 13–15; J. F. Wright, *Britain in the Age of Economic Management* (Oxford University Press, 1979), p. 21.
15 A. Gamble, op. cit., p. 16; S. Pollard, *The Wasting of the British Economy* (Croom Helm, Beckenham, 1982), p. 11.
16 Keith Robbins, *The Eclipse of a Great Power: Modern Britain, 1870–1992* (Addison Wesley Longman, London, 1994), p. 429.
17 Bernard Porter, *Britannia's Burden: The Political Evolution of Modern Britain, 1851–1990* (Arnold, London, 1994), p. 343.
18 P. Cosgrave, op. cit., p. 42.
19 A. Gamble, op. cit., pp. 90–5.
20 M. Pugh, *State and Society: British Political and Social History 1870–1992* (Arnold, London, 1994), p. 298.

2 ELECTION AND DEPRESSION, 1979–81

1 Margaret Thatcher, *The Downing Street Years* (HarperCollins, London, 1993), pp. 4–5.
2 Kenneth Harris, *Margaret Thatcher* (Weidenfeld & Nicholson, London, 1988), p. 71.
3 Quoted in Andrew Gamble, *The Free Economy and the Strong State: The Politics of Thatcherism* (Macmillan, London, 1988), p. 140.
4 Ian Gilmour, *Inside Right* (Hutchinson, London, 1977), pp. 96 and 121.
5 Kenneth Harris, *Thatcher* (Weidenfeld & Nicolson, London, 1988), p. 82.
6 Quoted in S. Edgell and V. Duke, *A Measure of Thatcherism* (HarperCollins, London, 1991), p. 3.
7 Cited in A. Gamble, op. cit., p. v.
8 D. Kavanagh (ed.), *The Politics of the Labour Party* (Allen & Unwin, London, 1982), pp. 9–45.
9 For development of this point see E. J. Evans, *The Forging of the Modern State: Early Industrial Britain, 1783–1870* (Longman, London, 2nd edn, 1996), pp. 261–2 and 367–70, and Martin Pugh, *The Making of Modern British Politics, 1867–1939* (2nd edn, Blackwell, Oxford, 1993).
10 Peter Jenkins, *Mrs Thatcher's Revolution: the ending of the Socialist era* (Jonathan Cape, London, 1987), p. 95. For a detailed analysis of the 1979 election see D. Butler and D. Kavanagh, *The British General Election of 1979* (Macmillan, London, 1980).
11 Margaret Thatcher, op. cit. p. 43.
12 Martin Holmes, *The First Thatcher Government, 1979–1983* (Harvester, Brighton, 1985), p. 133.
13 P. Cosgrave, *Thatcher: The First Term* (Bodley Head, London, 1985), p. 94.

14   Quoted in Kenneth Harris, op. cit., p. 103.
15   P. Riddell, *The Thatcher Government* (Blackwell, Oxford, 1985), pp. 64–8; Will Hutton, *The State We're In* (Vintage edn, 1996), p. 70; Martin Pugh, *State and Society: British Political and Social History* (Arnold, London, 1994), p. 304.
16   M. Thatcher, op. cit., pp. 144–5.
17   K. Harris, op. cit., p. 109.

3   THATCHER TRIUMPHANT, 1982–8

1   Calculations from Bryan Cribble, 'Candidates' in D. Butler and D. Kavanagh, *The British General Election of 1987* (Macmillan, London, 1987), pp. 197–205. See also D. Butler, *British General Elections since 1945* (2nd edn, Blackwell, Oxford, 1985), pp. 81–4.
2   Emma Nicholson, *Secret Society: Inside and Outside the Conservative Party* (Indigo Books, London, 1996), pp. 89 and 96.
3   The core reference points for British general elections since 1951 are the studies by the psephologist David Butler. Those that cover the Thatcher period are D. Butler and D. Kavanagh, *The British General Election of 1979* (Macmillan, London, 1980), *The British General Election of 1983* (Macmillan, London, 1984) and *The British General Election of 1987* (Macmillan, London, 1988).
4   Margaret Thatcher, *The Downing Street Years* (HarperCollins, London, 1993), p. 339.
5   Ivor Crewe, 'Has the Electorate become Thatcherite?' in R. Skidelsky (ed.), *Thatcherism* (Blackwell, Oxford, 1988), p. 32.
6   Peter Jenkins, *Mrs. Thatcher's Revolution* (Jonathan Cape, London, 1987), p. 166.
7   Ibid., p. 169.
8   S. Hall and M. Jacques (eds), *The Politics of Thatcherism* (Lawrence & Wishart, London, 1983), p. 30.
9   Patrick Minford, 'Mrs Thatcher's Economic Reform Programme' in R. Skidelsky (ed.), *Thatcherism* (Blackwell, Oxford, 1989), p. 96.
10   Cited in M. Holmes, *The First Thatcher Government, 1979–83* (Wheatsheaf, Brighton, 1985), p. 67.
11   Figures from HMSO *Economic Trends* and OECD *Labour Force Statistics* and collected in L. Hannah, 'Crisis and Turnaround? 1973–1993' in Paul Johnson (ed.), *20th Century Britain* (Addison Wesley Longman, London, 1994), p. 347. For changes in unemployment calculations, see the *Guardian*, 22 October 1996.
12   Harold Perkin, *The Third Revolution: Professional Elites in the Modern World* (Routledge, London, 1996), p. 59.
13   M. Thatcher, op. cit., p. 308.
14   Leslie Hannah, 'Mrs Thatcher, Capital Basher?' in D. Kavanagh and A. Seldon (eds), *The Thatcher Effect* (Oxford University Press, Oxford, 1989), p. 39.
15   Lesley Hannah, 'Crisis and Turnaround? 1973–1993' in Paul Johnson (ed.),

Britain in the Twentieth Century (Addison Wesley Longman, London, 1994), p. 345.

16 Samuel Brittan, 'The Government's Economic Policy' in D. Kavanagh and A. Seldon, op. cit., p. 13.

17 Martin Holmes, op. cit., p. 68.

18 M. Dunn and S. Smith, 'Economic Policy and Privatisation' in S. P. Savage and Lynton Robins (eds), *Public Policy under Thatcher* (Macmillan, London, 1990), p. 34.

19 S. Edgell and V. Duke, *A Measure of Thatcherism* (HarperCollins, London, 1991), p. 140.

20 Ivor Crewe, 'The Values that Failed' in D. Kavanagh and A. Seldon, op. cit., pp. 248–9.

21 Figures quoted in M. Holmes, *Thatcherism: Scope and Limits, 1983–87* (Macmillan, London, 1989), p. 60.

22 Quoted in M. Holmes, *Thatcherism*, p. 61.

23 Margaret Thatcher, *The Downing Street Years* (HarperCollins, London, 1993), p. 676.

24 'Famous' quotations are often attributed to politicians, rather than to the news editors who 'translated' them from the politicians' first thoughts in order to fit on the tabloid page. I am grateful to Alan Watkins, *A Conservative Coup* (2nd edn, Duckworth, London, 1992), pp. 105–6, for going back to the original text of Macmillan's speech.

25 ProShare statistical information, quoted in the *Observer*, 13 October 1996.

26 Harold Perkin, op. cit., p. 69.

27 On trade union law in the 1980s, see D. Farnham, 'Trade Union Policy' in S. P. Savage and L. Robins, op. cit., pp. 60–74.

28 K.O. Morgan, *The People's Peace: British History, 1945–90* (Oxford University Press, Oxford, 1990), p. 472.

29 M. Thatcher, op. cit., p. 342.

30 Ibid., p. 377.

31 C. Cook and J. Stevenson, *The Longman Companion to Britain since 1945* (2nd edn, Pearson Education, Harlow, 2000), pp. 110–11.

4   THATCHERISM AND THE CONSERVATIVE PARTY

1 A. Sked and C. Cook, *Post-war Britain: A Political History* (2nd edn, Penguin, London, 1984), p. 329.

2 For the Conservative Party in the nineteenth century, see R. Stewart, *The Foundation of the Conservative Party, 1830–67* (Longman, London, 1978). A useful brief assessment is found in B. I. Coleman, *Conservatism and the Conservative Party in Nineteenth-century Britain* (Arnold, London, 1988). See also R. Blake, *The Conservative Party from Peel to Thatcher* (Fontana, London, 1985).

3 John Ramsden, *The Age of Balfour and Baldwin, 1902–40* (Longman, London, 1978), and Anthony Seldon, 'Conservative Century' in A. Seldon and S. Ball (eds), *Conservative Century* (Oxford University Press, Oxford, 1994), pp. 17–65. For a briefer account of early twentieth-century

Conservatism, see Stuart Ball, *The Conservative Party and British Politics, 1902–51* (Longman, London, 1995).

4   D. Kavanagh, *Thatcherism and British Politics* (Oxford University Press, Oxford, 1987), p. 183.

5   Powell put a distinctive gloss on his own contribution to the conversion of the party to monetarism in 'The Conservative Party' in D. Kavanagh and A. Seldon (eds), *The Thatcher Effect* (Oxford University Press, Oxford, 1989), pp. 80–88. See also R. Shepherd, *Enoch Powell* (Hutchinson, London, 1996).

6   Andrew Gamble, *The Free Economy and the Strong State: The Politics of Thatcherism* (Macmillan, London, 1988), p. 150.

7   Quoted in Hugo Young, *One of Us* (Pan Books, London, 1990 edn), p. 127.

8   Jim Prior, *Balance of Power* (Hamish Hamilton, London, 1986), p. 117.

9   Hugo Young, op. cit., p. 331.

10   Alan Clark, *Diaries* (Weidenfeld & Nicholson, London, 1993), p. 215.

11   George R. Urban, *Diplomacy and Disillusion at the Court of Margaret Thatcher* (I. B. Tauris, London, 1996), pp. 17 and 183.

12   Jim Prior, op. cit., p. 119.

13   Quoted in Kenneth Harris, *Thatcher* (Weidenfeld & Nicolson, London, 1988), p. 109.

14   Quotations from *Inside Right* in Peter Jenkins, *Mrs Thatcher's Revolution* (Jonathan Cape, London, 1987), p. 97, and A. Sked and C. Cook (eds), op. cit., p. 330.

15   Martin Holmes, *The First Thatcher Government, 1979–83* (Harvester, Brighton, 1985), p. 74.

16   Hugo Young, op. cit., p. 205.

17   Op. cit., p. 207.

18   This point is developed by Vernon Bogdanor in D. Kavanagh and A. Seldon (eds), *The Thatcher Effect* (Oxford University Press, Oxford, 1989).

19   For a more charitable view, see R. N. Kelly, *Conservative Party Conferences* (Manchester University Press, Manchester, 1989).

20   Richard Kelly, 'The Party Conference' in A. Seldon and S. Ball (eds), *Conservative Century* (Oxford University Press, Oxford, 1994), p. 251.

21   On grass-roots Conservative Party support, see P. Whiteley, P. Seyd and J. Richardson (eds), *True Blues: The Politics of Conservative Party Membership* (Clarendon, Oxford, 1994), especially pp. 150–60, where it is argued that Thatcher assimilated and reflected existing grass-roots attitudes at least as much as she pulled the party to the right, especially on social issues.

22   For this section, see Anthony Adonis, 'The Transformation of the Conservative Party in the 1980s' in A. Adonis and T. Hames (eds), *A Conservative Revolution: The Thatcher–Reagan Decade in Perspective* (Manchester University Press, Manchester, 1994), pp. 159–65.

23   P. Whiteley, P. Seyd and J. Richardson (eds), op. cit., pp. 231–3.

24   An opinion poll held in the autumn of 1996 discovered that two-thirds of respondents believed that corruption was endemic among politicians of all parties, the *Guardian*, 19 October 1996.

5 THE ATTACK ON THE GOVERNMENT ETHIC

1 Margaret Thatcher, *The Downing Street Years* (HarperCollins, London, 1993), pp. 45–6.
2 K. Theakston and G. Fry, 'The Party and the Civil Service' in A. Seldon and S. Ball (eds), *Conservative Century* (Oxford University Press, Oxford, 1994), pp. 394–5.
3 P. Hennessy, 'The Civil Service' in D. Kavanagh and A. Seldon (eds), *The Thatcher Effect* (Oxford University Press, Oxford, 1989), p. 115. See also his more extended study, *Whitehall* (Free Press, London, 1989).
4 Quoted in P. Jenkins, *Mrs. Thatcher's Revolution* (Jonathan Cape, London, 1987), p. 261.
5 M. Thatcher, op. cit., p. 30.
6 P. Hennessy in (eds) D. Kavanagh and A. Seldon, op. cit., p. 117.
7 C. Cook and J. Stevenson, *The Longman Companion to Britain since 1945* (Addison Wesley Longman, London, 1996), p. 87.
8 Hugo Young, *One of Us* (Pan Books, London, 1989), pp. 230–2 and 336–8.
9 M. Heseltine, *Where There's a Will* (Hutchinson, London, 1987), p. 21.
10 See, for example, Clive Ponting, *Whitehall: Tragedy and Farce* (Sphere, London, 1986). The extent of change is debated in R. Atkinson, 'Government during the Thatcher Years' in S. P. Savage and L. Robins (eds), *Public Policy under Thatcher* (Macmillan, London, 1990), pp. 8–16 and K. Theakston and G. Fry 'The Party and the Civil Service', loc. cit., pp. 398–9.
11 K. Theakston and G. Fry, loc. cit., pp. 399–400.
12 E. J. Evans, *The Forging of the Modern State: Early Industrial Britain, 1783–1870* (3rd edn, Pearson Education, Harlow, 2001), pp. 360–1.
13 Quoted in Peter Jenkins, *Mrs. Thatcher's Revolution* (Jonathan Cape, London, 1987), p. 178.
14 Sylvia Horton, 'Local Government 1979–89: A Decade of Change' in S. P. Savage and L. Robins (eds), *Public Policy under Thatcher* (Macmillan, London, 1990), pp. 172–86.
15 Kenneth Baker, *The Turbulent Years* (Faber & Faber, London, 1993), p. 112.
16 H. Butcher, I. Law, R. Leach and M. Mullard, *Local Government and Thatcherism* (Routledge, London, 1990) p. 64.
17 G. Stoker, *The Politics of Local Government* (2nd edn, Macmillan, Basingstoke, 1991), p. 13.
18 Rate-capping was the term used to describe the powers taken by central government to limit the revenue that local authorities could raise from the rates. It was introduced in Scotland in 1982 and in England and Wales by the Rates Act of 1984.
19 Quoted in H. Butcher, I. Law and M. Mullard (eds), op. cit., p. 71.
20 G. Stoker, op. cit., pp. 169–74. See also M. Goldsmith (ed.), *New Research in Central–Local Relations* (Gower Press, Aldershot, 1986).
21 On Liverpool in the context of broader local government concerns, see G. Stoker, op. cit., pp. 45, 102 and 135. For a sympathetic appraisal of

Liverpool's position, see M. Parkinson, *Liverpool on the Brink* (Policy Journals, Hermitage, Berkshire, 1985), and for the Militant defence, see P. Taafe and A. Mulhearn, *Liverpool: A City that Dared to Fight* (Fortress Books, London, 1988).

22   G. Stoker, op. cit., pp. 216–19.

23   From *Good Council Guide: Wandsworth, 1982–87* and quoted in J. A. Chandler, *Local Government Today* (2nd edn, Manchester University Press, Manchester, 1996), p. 235.

24   The *Guardian*, 18 July 1990, quoted in G. Stoker, op. cit., p. 221.

25   Margaret Thatcher, op. cit., p. 645.

6   THE ATTACK ON THE PROFESSIONAL ETHIC

1   HMSO, *Social Trends, 1992* (HMSO, London, 1993), Table 1.5.

2   P. Riddell, *The Thatcher Government* (Blackwell, Oxford, 1985 edn), p. 134.

3   P. Riddell, op. cit., p. 137.

4   Charles Webster, 'The Health Service' in D. Kavanagh and A. Seldon (eds), *The Thatcher Effect* (Oxford University Press, Oxford, 1989), p. 171. The NHS share of public expenditure increased from 12 per cent to 15 per cent in the years 1979–96, the *Guardian*, 4 November 1996.

5   Margaret Thatcher, *The Downing Street Years* (HarperCollins, London, 1993), p. 607.

6   Ian Kendall and Graham Moon, 'Health Policy' in S. P. Savage and L. Robins (eds), *Public Policy under Thatcher* (Macmillan, London, 1990), p. 112.

7   Thatcher, op. cit., p. 615.

8   Thatcher, op. cit., p. 607.

9   Interview in the *Guardian*, 21 January 1995.

10   Interview in *The Sunday Times*, 26 June 1994.

11   Quoted in the *Guardian*, 6 February 1995.

12   The phrase is Ian Hargreaves', in a review of Simon Jenkins, *Accountable to None: The Tory Nationalisation of Britain* (Hamish Hamilton, London, 1995). Jenkins's book discusses the paradox of the Thatcher revolution. Pledged to liberate the individual from the burden of the state, it produced a central government exercising greater powers than any before it.

13   John Gray, 'The reinventing of the NHS', *Guardian*, 3 January 1995.

14   Information from report in the *Independent*, 4 November 1996.

15   M Thatcher, op. cit., p. 590.

16   The literature on this subject is vast. For a brief selection, see M. J. Wiener, *Industrialism*, M. Sanderson, *Educational Opportunity and Social Change in England* (Faber, London, 1987) and A. P. Summerfield and E. J. Evans (eds), *Technical Education and the State* (Manchester University Press, Manchester, 1990).

17   Quoted in Kenneth Baker, *The Turbulent Years* (Faber & Faber, London, 1993), p. 161.

18   Malcolm McVicar, 'Education Policy' in S. P. Savage and L. Robins (eds), *Public Policy under Thatcher* (Macmillan, London, 1990), p. 133.

19   K. Baker, op. cit., p. 189.

20   M. Thatcher, op. cit., pp. 595–6.

21   K. Baker, op. cit., p. 206.

22   Means of quantifying attainment in higher education also became fashionable in the later stages of the Thatcher era. See Chapter 12.

23   D. Downes and R. Morgan, 'Hostages to Fortune? The Politics of Law and Order in Post-War Britain' in M. Maguire, R. Morgan and R. Reiner (eds), *The Oxford Handbook of Criminology* (Clarendon Press, Oxford, 1994), pp. 183–232. For criminal statistics, see M. Maguire, loc. cit., pp. 233–91. On notifiable offences, see C. Cook and J. Stevenson (eds), *Britain since 1945* (Addison Wesley Longman, London, 1996), p. 140.

24   Stephen P. Savage, 'A War on Crime? Law and Order Policies in the 1980s' in S. P. Savage and Lynton Robins (eds), *Public Policy under Thatcher* (Macmillan, London, 1990), pp. 89–102.

25   R. M. Evans, 'Situational Crime Prevention In late Twentieth-century Britain – A Critique', BA Dissertation, Department of Criminology, University of Hull, 1996, p. 8.

26   P. Riddell, *The Thatcher Government* (Blackwell, Oxford, 1985 edn), pp. 196–7.

27   On situational crime prevention (SCP), see R. M. Evans, op. cit. The protagonist of SCP was R. V. G. Clark, 'Situational Crime Prevention: Theory and Practice', *British Journal of Criminology* (1980), pp. 136–47. Patten's advice is quoted in S. P. Savage, loc. cit., p. 98.

28   G. Laycock and K. Heal, 'Crime Prevention: The British Experience' in D. J. Evans and D. T. Herbert (eds), *The Geography of Crime* (Routledge, London, 1989); M. Maguire, 'Crime Statistics' in R. Morgan, M. Maguire and R. Reiner (eds), op. cit., pp. 251–62.

29   Margaret Thatcher, *The Downing Street Years* (HarperCollins, London, 1993), p. 143.

30   M. Maguire, loc. cit., p. 206.

7   THATCHER ABROAD I: EUROPE

1   Quoted in A. May, *Britain and Europe since 1945* (Addison Wesley Longman, Seminar Studies, London, 1999), p. 103.

2   D. Reynolds, 'Britain and the World since 1945: Narratives of Decline or Transformation', in K. Burke (ed.), *Britain since 1945* (Oxford University Press, Oxford, 2003), pp. 161–2.

3   Reginald Maudling, *Memoirs* (Sidgwick and Jackson, London, 1978), p. 225.

4   Hugo Young, *One of Us* (Pan revised edn, London, 1990), p. 557.

5   Hugo Young, op. cit., pp. 551–2. Extracts from the Bruges speech can be found in M. Thatcher, op. cit. pp. 744–5.

6   Quoted in Kenneth Harris, *Thatcher* (Weidenfeld & Nicolson, London, 1988), p. 99. For the Carrington incident, see Margaret Thatcher, *The Downing Street Years* (HarperCollins, London, 1993), p. 86.

7   Hugo Young, *One of Us* (Macmillan, London, 1989), p. 121.

8   M. Thatcher, op. cit., pp. 60–1.
9   Quoted in Patrick Cosgrave, *Thatcher: The First Term* (Bodley Head, London, 1985), p. 86.
10 David Willets, *Modern Conservatism* (Penguin Books, London, 1992), pp. 168–9.
11 M. Thatcher, op cit., p. 743.
12 Lord Carrington, *Reflect on Things Past* (Collins, London, 1988), p. 319.
13 M. Thatcher, op. cit., pp. 62, 313 and 733.
14 M. Holmes, op. cit., p. 77.
15 Keith Robbins, *The Eclipse of a Great Power: Modern Britain, 1870–1992* (2nd edn, Addison Wesley Longman, London, 1994), pp. 381–2.
16 John Turner, *The Tories and Europe* (Manchester University Press, Manchester, 2000), p. 99.
17 M. Thatcher, op. cit., p. 742.
18 M. Thatcher, op. cit., pp. 741–6 and 759.
19 M. Thatcher, op. cit., p. 722.
20 Bruce Arnold, *Margaret Thatcher: A Study in Government* (Hamish Hamilton, London, 1984), pp. 200–1.
21 Quoted in Martin Holmes, *Thatcherism: Scope and Limits, 1983–87* (Macmillan, London, 1989), pp. 75–6.
22 M. Thatcher, op. cit., p. 745.
23 S. Glynn and A. Booth, *Modern Britain: An Economic and Social History* (Routledge, London, 1996), p. 240.

8   THATCHER ABROAD II: DEFENCE AND THE AMERICAS

1   From a speech made in New York in August 1991. Quoted in Tim Hames 'The Special Relationship' in A. Adonis and T. Hames (eds), *A Counter-Revolution? The Thatcher–Reagan Decade in Perspective* (Manchester University Press, 1994), p. 114.
2   Quoted in Hugo Young, *One of Us* (Pan Books, London, 1990 edn), p. 396.
3   Margaret Thatcher, *The Downing Street Years* (HarperCollins, London, 1993), p. 157.
4   Ronald Reagan, 'Margaret Thatcher and the Revival of the West', *National Review*, 19 May 1989. The article is reprinted in the Margaret Thatcher Foundation Archives: http://www.margaretthatcher.org.
5   Speech in Washington, 29 September 1983. Reproduced in Margaret Thatcher, *In Defence of Freedom: Speeches on Britain's relations with the World, 1976–1986* (Aurum Press, London, 1986), pp. 89–95. The extract quoted is found on p. 91.
6   Tim Hames, 'The Special Relationship', loc. cit., p. 128. For Thatcher's account of the negotiations, see M. Thatcher, op. cit., pp. 244–8.
7   Fergus Carr 'Foreign and Defence Policy' in (eds) S. P. Savage and L. P. Robins, *Public Policy under Thatcher* (Macmillan, London, 1990), p. 236.

8   Speech to the United States Congress, 20 February 1985, reproduced in M. Thatcher, *In Defence of Freedom*, p. 107.

9   Ibid.

10 Quoted in Martin Holmes, *Thatcherism: Scope and Limitations, 1983–87* (Macmillan, London, 1989), p. 80.

11 M. Holmes, op. cit., p. 85.

12 B. Pimlott, *The Queen: A Biography of Elizabeth II* (HarperCollins, London, 1996), p. 497.

13 Private communication from Reagan to Thatcher, 24 October 1983, from the Reagan Library and reproduced in the Margaret Thatcher Foundation Archive, loc. cit.

14 M. Thatcher, op. cit., p. 331.

15 M. Thatcher, ibid. For an alternative account of the Prime Minister's incandescent rage over the Grenada incident, see H. Young, op. cit., pp. 345–8.

16 *The Spectator*, 29 October 1983, quoted in Bruce Arnold, *Margaret Thatcher: A Study in Power* (Hamish Hamilton, London, 1984), p. 255.

17 Quoted in Roy Hattersley, *Fifty Years On: a prejudiced history of Britain since the Second World War* (Little, Brown and Company, London, 1997), p. 287.

18 M. Thatcher, op. cit., p. 235, and quoted in Eric Hobsbawm, 'Falklands Fallout' in S. Hall (ed), *The Politics of Thatcherism* (Lawrence and Wishart, London, 1983), p. 260.

19 Jim Prior, *A Balance of Power* (Hamish Hamilton, London, 1986), p. 148.

20 M. Thatcher, op. cit., p. 174.

21 Alexander Haig, *Caveat*, quoted in Peter Jenkins, *Mrs. Thatcher's Revolution* (Jonathan Cape, London, 1987), p. 161.

22 Lord Carrington, *Reflect on Things Past* (Collins, London, 1988), p. 370.

23 Alan Bennett, *Writing Home* (Faber & Faber, London, 1994), p. 123.

24 M. Thatcher, op. cit., p. 215–16.

25 David Hooper, *Official Secrets: The Use and Abuse of the Act* (London, 1987). The specific incident is discussed in Bernard Porter, *Plots and Paranoia: A History of Political Espionage in Britain, 1790–1988* (Routledge, London, 1992 edn), p. 215. Ponting's own defence is told in his two books: *The Right to Know* (Sphere, London, 1985) and *Whitehall: Tragedy and Farce* (Sphere, London, 1986).

9   THATCHER ABROAD III: THE BRINGER OF FREEDOM? PRINCIPLE, PRAGMATISM AND THE LIMITS OF POWER

1   Helmut Kohl's view of Thatcher's diplomatic methods, quoted in the *Independent*, 5 October 1996.

2   Lord Carrington, *Reflect on Things Past* (Collins, London, 1988), p. 290.

3   *Hansard*, 4 March 1980, cols. 234–41.

4   Speech at a lunch at No. 10 Downing Street for Robert Mugabe, 19 May 1982. Reproduced in Margaret Thatcher Foundation archive, http://www.margaretthatcher.org.

5   Margaret Thatcher, *The Downing Street Years* (HarperCollins, London, 1993), pp. 73 and 78.

6   Thatcher's speech signing the Joint Declaration on Hong Kong, 19 December 1994, and reproduced in the Thatcher Foundation Archive, loc. cit.

7   For Thatcher's own account of the discussions in 1982 and the 1984 agreement, see M. Thatcher, op. cit., pp. 259–62 and 487–95. See also Hugo Young, *One of Us* (Pan edn, London, 1990), pp. 397–8, and B. Porter, *Britannia's Burden* (Arnold, London, 1991), p. 376.

8   Alan Clark, *Diaries* (Phoenix Books, London, 1994), p. 160.

9   George R. Urban, *Diplomacy and Disillusion at the Court of Margaret Thatcher* (I. B. Tauris, London, 1996), p. 167.

10   M. Thatcher, op. cit., pp. 454–8 and 808–9.

11   M. Thatcher, op. cit., p. 779.

12   Margaret Thatcher: remarks at a joint press conference with Jozsef Antall, Prime Minister of Hungary, in Budapest, 19 September 1990. Reproduced in Margaret Thatcher Foundation Archive, loc. cit.

13   Margaret Thatcher: speech to the Czechoslovak Federal Assembly, 18 September 1990, loc. cit.

14   Hugo Young, *One of Us* (Macmillan revised edn, London, 1983), p. 385.

15   Tim Hames, 'The Special Relationship' in A. Adonis and T. Hames (eds), *A Special Relationship? The Thatcher–Reagan Decade in Perspective* (Manchester University Press, Manchester, 1994), pp. 133–4.

16   Press conference after NATO Summit in Brussels, 17 February 1988, reproduced in Margaret Thatcher Foundation Archive, loc. cit.

17   G. Urban, *op. cit.*, p. 131.

18   Roy Denman, *Missed Chances: Britain and Europe in the Twentieth Century* (Cassell, London, 1996), p. 259. Quoted also in A. May, *Britain and Europe since 1945* (Seminar Studies in History, Addison Wesley Longman, London, 1999), p. 77.

19   M. Thatcher, op. cit., p. 791.

20   Television interview, 17 December 1984 and reproduced in the Margaret Thatcher Foundation Archive, loc. cit.

21   H. Young, op. cit., p. 514.

22   M. Thatcher, op. cit., pp. 478–85.

23   Interview in *The Sunday Times*, 21 February 1990 and reproduced in the Margaret Thatcher Foundation Archive, loc. cit.

24   R. Crampton, *Eastern Europe in the Twentieth Century* (Routledge, London, 1994), pp. 410–15.

10 THE FALL

1   Margaret Thatcher, *The Downing Street Years* (HarperCollins, London, 1993), p. 435.

2   The Westland affair is discussed in detail in Peter Jenkins, *Mrs. Thatcher's Revolution* (Jonathan Cape, London, 1987), pp. 185–204 and Hugo Young, *One of Us* (Pan Books, London, 1990), pp. 435–57.

3   M. Thatcher, op. cit., 587.
4   H. Young, *One of Us* (Pan Books, London, 1990 edn), pp. 508–12.
5   Alan Watkins, *A Conservative Coup* (2nd edn, Duckworth, London, 1992), pp. 108–23. The contrasting accounts by the protagonists of Lawson's departure can be found in M. Thatcher, *op. cit.*, pp. 713–18 and N. Lawson, *The View from Number 11: Memoirs of a Tory Radical* (Corgi, London, 1993), pp. 960–8.
6   As quoted in Nigel Lawson, *The View from Number 11: Memoirs of a Tory Radical* (Transworld Publishers, London, 1992), p. 470.
7   Interview for the television programme, The Fall of Mrs Thatcher, broadcast on BBC4 on 11 August 2003.
8   M. Thatcher, op. cit., 661.
9   The interview appeared in *The Spectator* on 13 July 1990.
10 Alan Clark, *Diaries* (Phoenix Books, London, 1993), p. 341.
11 Howe's speech can be savoured in full in *Hansard*, vol. 180, for 13 November 1990. Extracts are widely quoted in recent political studies. See, for example, Alan Watkins, *A Conservative Coup* (2nd edn, Duckworth, London, 1992), pp. 152–4.
12 Nigel Lawson, op. cit., p. 1001.
13 Hansard, 22 November 1990.
14 M. Thatcher, op. cit., p. 855.
15 Sarah Curtis (ed.), *The Journals of Woodrow Wyatt* (two volumes, Macmillan, Basingstoke, 1999), ii, pp. 397–400.
16 Ingham's views were given in an interview on the television programme *Thatcher and the Poll Tax*, broadcast on BBC4 on 11 August 2003.
17 M. Thatcher, op. cit., p. 860.

11 THE LEGACY I: POLITICS – THATCHERISM AFTER THATCHER

1   Alan Watkins, the *Observer*, 7 April 1991, quoted in Peter Hennessy, *The Prime Ministers: The Office and its Holders since 1945* (Penguin Books, London, 2001 edn), p. 399.
2   C. Cook and J. Stevenson, *The Longman Companion to Britain since 1945* (2nd edn, Pearson Education, Harlow, 2000), p. 179.
3   C. Cook and J. Stevenson, op. cit., pp. 60–2.
4   D. Butler and D. Kavanagh, *The British General Election of 1992* (Macmillan, Basingstoke, 1992), p. 283.
5   Peter Hennessy, op. cit., p. 454. Thatcher refers to the phrase herself with the comment: 'It was, unfortunately, the shape of things to come', Margaret Thatcher, *The Downing Street Years* (HarperCollins, London, 1993), p. 861.
6   C. Cook and J. Stevenson, op. cit., p. 177.
7   K. Burke (ed.), *The British Isles since 1945* (Oxford University Press, Oxford, 2003), p. 67.
8   Margaret Thatcher, *The Path to Power* (HarperCollins, London, 1995), pp. 474–5.

9   Quoted in John Turner, *The Tories and Europe* (Manchester University Press, Manchester, 2000), p. 161.

10 On the Tory travails over Europe in the Major years, see John Turner, op. cit., pp. 142–80, and A. May, *Britain and Europe since 1945* (Addison Wesley Longman, Harlow, Seminar Studies, 1999), pp. 79–86.

11 John Major, *The Autobiography* (HarperCollins, London, 1991), p. 351.

12 John Major, op. cit., p. 613.

13 John Major, op. cit., pp. 644–5.

14 Ibid.

15 C. Cook and J. Stevenson, *Britain since 1945* (2nd edn, Pearson Education, Harlow, 2000), pp. 62–3. See also D. Butler and D. Kavanagh, *The British General Election of 1997* (Palgrave Macmillan, London, 1997).

16 Stuart Hall, 'New Labour has Picked up Where Thatcherism Left Off', *Guardian*, 6 August 2003.

17 Peter Oborne, writing in the *Observer*, 24 March 2002, p. 17.

18 For discussion of the impact of the rally, see D. Butler and D. Kavanagh, op. cit., pp. 124–6.

19 Ibid., p. 269.

20 C. Cook and J. Stevenson, op. cit., 53.

21 D. Butler and D. Kavanagh, op. cit., pp. 299–300.

22 D. Butler and D. Kavanagh, *The British General Election of 2001* (Palgrave, Basingstoke, 2002), pp. 260–2.

23 For further development of the constitutional issues involved, see Michael Foley, *The British Presidency* (Manchester University Press, Manchester, 2000), and Peter Hennessy, op. cit., pp. 478–82.

24 Simon Jenkins, *The Times*, 27 January 1999, quoted in Michael Foley, op. cit., p. 272.

25 Quoted in Michael Foley, op. cit., p. 96.

26 Michael Foley, op. cit., p.91.

27 Margaret Scammell, 'Media and media management' in A. Seldon (ed.), *The Blair Effect* (Little, Brown and Company, London, 2001), p. 513.

28 Peter Hennessy, *The Prime Ministers* (Penguin Books, London, 2000), pp. 471–2.

29 Michael Foley, op. cit., p. 97.

30 Roy Hattersley, 'Keeping Up Appearances', *Guardian*, 27 August, 2003, p. 19.

31 Christopher Hill, 'Foreign Policy' in A. Seldon (ed.), op. cit., p. 332.

32 Loc. cit., p. 341.

33 Michael Foley, op. cit., p. 99.

34 Robert Taylor, 'Employment Relations Policy' in A. Seldon (ed.), op. cit., pp. 256–7.

35 For fuller discussion on this, see Howard Glenerster, 'Social Policy' in A. Seldon (ed.), op. cit., pp. 383–403.

36 Figures calculated by Professor Alan Marsh and published in the *Guardian*, 5 August 2003.

12 THE LEGACY II: ECONOMY, SOCIETY AND ETHOS

1 *Woman's Own*, 31 October 1987; Margaret Thatcher, op. cit., p. 626.
2 House of Commons Library Research Paper, quoted in the *Independent on Sunday*, 6 October 1996.
3 Howard Glennerster, 'Social Policy' in Anthony Seldon (ed.), *The Blair Effect: the Blair Government 1997–2001* (Little, Brown and Company, London, 2001), pp. 383–403.
4 For a useful analysis both of Britain's economy and its relative performance against other countries since 1945, see R. Middleton, *The British Economy since 1945: Engaging with the Debate* ('British History in Perspective', Macmillan, Basingstoke, 2000).
5 OECD Economic Outlook Statistics, July 1996.
6 HMSO, *Social Trends* (HMSO, London, 1988).
7 Material compiled from HMSO, Households below Average Income (London, 1996) and government statistics in Charles Leadbeater 'How Fat Cats Rock the Boat', *Independent on Sunday*, 3 November 1996.
8 Will Hutton, writing in the *Observer*, 24 October 2002, the weekend after she announced her full retirement from public life.
9 Quoted in Hugo Young, *One of Us* (Macmillan, London, 1989), p. 411.
10 H. Young, op. cit., p. 414. See also M. Holmes, *Thatcherism* (Macmillan, London, 1989), pp. 122–37, and Kenneth Minogue, 'The Emergence of the New Right' in R. Skidelsky (ed.), *Thatcherism* (Blackwell, Oxford, 1988), pp. 125–42.
11 Alan Smithers, 'Education Policy' in A. Seldon (ed.), *The Blair Effect* (Little, Brown and Company, London, 2001), p. 421.
12 The phrase is Stuart Hall's. The debate may be followed in Bob Jessop, Kevin Bonnett, Simon Bromley and Tom Ling (eds), *Thatcherism: A Tale of Two Nations* (Polity Press, Oxford, 1988), especially pp. 57–124. See also S. Hall, 'Popular-democratic versus authoritarian populism' in Alan Hunt (ed.), *Marxism and Democracy* (Lawrence & Wishart, London, 1980), and S. Hall and M. Jacques, *The Politics of Thatcherism* (Lawrence & Wishart, London, 1983).
13 E. J. Evans, 'Englishness and Britishness, c. 1790–1870' in Alexander Grant and Keith J. Stringer (eds), *Uniting the Kingdom? The Making of British History* (Routledge, London, 1995), pp. 223–43. See also R. Samuel (ed.), *Patriotism: The Making and Unmaking of British National Identity* (two vols, Routledge, London, 1989), H. Cunningham, 'The Language of Patriotism, 1750–1914', *History Workshop Journal*, xii (1981), and E. J. Hobsbawm, *Nations and Nationalism since 1780: Programme, Myth and Reality* (2nd edn, Cambridge University Press, Cambridge, 1992).
14 Accounts of privatised utilities recorded with Companies House in 1996 and reported in 'The Power Game Millionaires', *Guardian*, 15 November 1996.
15 Margaret Thatcher, *The Downing Street Years* (HarperCollins, London, 1993), p. 627.
16 For further development of this point, see Eric J. Evans, *Social Policy, 1830–1914* (Routledge, London, 1978), pp. 1–18 and 110–36, and Harold

Perkin, *The Third Revolution: Political Elites in the Modern World* (Routledge, London, 1996), pp. 70–1.

17   M. Garnett, *Principles & Politics in Contemporary Britain* (Addison Wesley Longman, London, 1996), p. 95.

18   D. Marquand, 'Moralists and Hedonists' in D. Marquand and A. Seldon (eds), *The Ideas that Shaped Post-War Britain* (Fontana, London, 1996), pp. 25–6.

19   V. Bogdanor, in D. Kavanagh and A. Seldon (eds), *The Thatcher Effect* (Oxford University Press, Oxford, 1989), p. 142.

20   Ian Aitken, 'Civil Service leaks lead to corrosion', *Guardian*, 21 November 1996.

21   Hugo Young, 'RIP – an inconvenient Civil Service', *Guardian*, 14 November 1996.

22   Bernard Porter, 'Thatcher and History', *The Durham University Journal*, l: xxxvi (1994), pp. 1–12.

23   Alexander Pope, Epistle No. 3.

Guide to further reading

PRELIMINARY NOTE

A detailed archival study of the Thatcher years will not be possible until the release of key government sources, which will not become available for the whole period until 2020 at the earliest. The student is, therefore, largely dependent upon material published either at the time or soon afterwards. Much of it comes from politicians themselves and, vital although they are, all such evidence needs to be treated with caution. Most politicians, especially if they remain active in public life, are desperate to have their actions viewed in a favourable light and are keen to ensure that the policies for which they were responsible are understood from their own perspective. Thatcher herself is no exception to this.

Much of the largest collection of Thatcher material has been brought together by the Margaret Thatcher Foundation and is available for consultation on the web: http://www.margaretthatcher.org. Inevitably, such an organisation does not set out to represent all views equally and the brief biographical introduction is hardly a dispassionate assessment. However, the site is well worth exploring. As it claims, it 'offers thousands of documents touching on the career of Margaret Thatcher and the events of the last quarter century, to inform and advance understanding of the period'. It is a most valuable archive, not least for the access it provides to recently released or declassified documents from the United States, especially from the Reagan Archive. It includes manuscript as well as printed material.

The available published literature on Thatcher and Thatcherism is huge. It is of very variable quality, and not all of it takes the story down to 1990. Many works that are cited in the footnotes do not appear here. What follows represents a selective, but not – the author hopes – arbitrary, guide to the most useful, and most accessible, works written by politicians, historians, political scientists, economists and sociologists.

GENERAL HISTORIES

Kathleen Burke (ed.)	*The British Isles since 1945* (Oxford University Press, Oxford 2003) – a useful brief overview, which puts the Thatcher period in context.
J. Charmley	*A History of Conservative Politics, 1900–96* (Macmillan, London, 1996) – generally sympathetic but well aware of the diversities that characterise twentieth-century Conservatism.
P. Clarke	*Hope and Glory: Britain, 1900–1990* (Allen Lane, London, 1996) – a useful account, which puts Thatcher into the overall perspective of Britain's decline.
B. Harrison	*The Transformation of British Politics, 1860–1995* (Oxford University Press, Oxford, 1996) – a distinguished study that offers valuable insights on 'Victorian values'.
K. O. Morgan	*The People's Peace: British History, 1945–90* (Oxford University Press, Oxford, 1990) – an authoritative account.
B. Porter	*Britannia's Burden: The Political Evolution of Modern Britain, 1851–1990* (Arnold, London, 1990) – a much longer perspective, but very good, if waspish, on Thatcher.
A. Seldon and S. Ball (eds)	*Conservative Century* (Oxford University Press, Oxford, 1994) – massive collection of authoritaive essays on twentieth-century Conservatism, with useful comment on Thatcherism.

BIOGRAPHIES AND STUDIES OF THE THATCHER GOVERNMENTS

Bruce Arnold	*Margaret Thatcher* (Hamish Hamilton, London, 1984) – a highly critical view of Thatcher's 'totalitarian' methods. Deals with the first government only.
Patrick Cosgrave	*Thatcher: The First Term* (Bodley Head, London, 1983) – Cosgrave was one of Thatcher's political advisers and provides some significant 'insider comment'.

S. Edgell and V. Duke (eds)	*A Measure of Thatcherism* (HarperCollins, London, 1991) – strongly sociological perspective in a disparate collection of essays.
Brendan Evans	*Thatcherism and British Politics, 1975–1997* (Sutton Publishing, Stroud, 2000) – a workmanlike account, which has the advantage of taking the story forward into the Major years.
Kenneth Harris	*Thatcher* (Weidenfeld & Nicholson, London, 1988) – accurate and well organised but lacking a cutting edge.
Martin Holmes	*The First Thatcher Government, 1979–83: Contemporary Conservatism and Economic Change* (Wheatsheaf, London, 1985) – a sympathetic assessment.
Martin Holmes	*Thatcher and Thatcherism: Scope and Limitations, 1983–87* (Macmillan, London, 1989) – in essence a sequel to the volume cited above.
Peter Jenkins	*Mrs Thatcher's Revolution: The Ending of the Socialist Era* (Jonathan Cape, London, 1987) – well written and adopts a stance broadly critical of Thatcher.
K. Minogue and M. Biddiss (eds)	*Thatcherism: Personality and Politics* (Macmillan, London, 1987).
Dennis Kavanagh	*Thatcherism and British Politics: The End of Consensus?* (Oxford University Press, Oxford, 1987).
D. Kavanagh and A. Seldon (eds)	*The Thatcher Effect* (Oxford University Press, Oxford, 1989) – a very variable collection of brief essays; the best are excellent.
Peter Riddell	*The Thatcher Government* (2nd edn, Blackwell, Oxford, 1985) – another high-class journalistic study of the first government.
Peter Riddell	*The Thatcher Decade* (Blackwell, Oxford, 1989).
Peter Riddell	*The Thatcher Era and its Legacy* (Blackwell, Oxford, 1991).
S. P. Savage and L. Robbins (eds)	*Public Policy under Thatcher* (Macmillan, London, 1990) – useful collection of essays on the implications of specific policies.

Anthony Seldon and Daniel Collings	*Britain under Thatcher* (Longman, Seminar Studies in History, London, 2000) – a useful introduction to the period, with a range of brief contemporary sources.
R. Skidelsky (ed.)	*Thatcherism* (Chatto & Windus, London, 1988) – an eclectic set of essays with a cerebral introduction by the editor.
Alan Watkins	*A Conservative Coup: The Fall of Margaret Thatcher* (2nd edn, Duckworth, London, 1992) – the title is somewhat misleading. The focus is on why, and how, she went but there are many longer-term references. Particularly strong on political gossip and sharp, precise constitutional references.
Hugo Young	*One of Us: A Biography of Margaret Thatcher* (Pan Books, London, 1990) – a long, but consistently engaging, read from a distinguished journalist. Especially strong on how the specific details illuminate the overall picture.

MAINLY POLITICAL, ECONOMIC AND THEORETICAL ANALYSES

Andrew Adonis and Tim Hames (eds)	*A Conservative Revolution: The Thatcher–Reagan Decade* (Manchester University Press, Manchester, 1994) – brings a useful comparative perspective and attempts to show why right-wing ideas were dominant in the West throughout the 1980s.
Michael Foley	*The British Presidency* (Manchester University Press, Manchester, 2000) – basically a study of Blair's exercise of power but considers the Thatcher period as a 'precedent'. Sees Thatcher provocatively as a 'populist insurgent'.
Andrew Gamble	*The Free Economy and the Strong State* (2nd edn, Macmillan, London, 1994).
Mark Garnett	*Principles & Politics in Contemporary Britain* (Addison Wesley Longman, 1996) – useful brief introduction to the main issues.
S. Hall and NM. Jacques (eds)	*The Politics of Thatcherism* (Lawrence & Wishart, London, 1983) – another collection of essays from the left, some of them theoretical.

Peter Hennessy	*Whitehall* (Fontana, London, 1990) – unrivalled study by a Professor of Contemporary History of how the government machine actually works. Draws heavily on the experience of the Thatcher years.
Peter Hennessy	*The Prime Minister: The Office and its Holders since 1945* (Penguin, London, 2001) – asserts himself 'protective of the lady's significance', while strongly aware of her faults. Scholars will be disconcerted at the number of footnotes that read, mysteriously, 'private information'. Rightly, they do not like not being able to check references, and harsh critics might argue that their frequency impugns the academic integrity of a fascinating book. Why does so much of it rely on insider gossip?
Will Hutton	*The State We're In* (Vintage edn, London, 1996) – deservedly a bestseller. Accessibly written, but a tough-minded Keynesian critique of monetarist theory and its political practitioners.
Will Hutton	*The World We're In* (Time Warner Books, London, 2002) – a more global perspective, which revisits some of the themes that made Hutton such a cogent critic of Thatcher's economic policy.
David Marquand	*The Unprincipled Society: New Demands and Old Politics* (Fontana, London, 1988) – another attack on Thatcherism, from a political scientist with a social democratic, ethical perspective.
Harold Perkin	*The Third Revolution: Political Elites in the Modern World* (Routledge, London, 1996) – written by a social historian, the title notwithstanding. Lucid and vigorous, with a trenchant line on Thatcher's attack on the professionals.
Bob Jessop, K. Bonnett, S. Bromley and T. Ling (eds)	*Thatcherism: A Tale of Two Nations* (Polity Press, Oxford, 1988) – another tendentious title that betrays its political provenance. The unwieldy practice of the editorial 'collective' is a strong clue.
Christopher Johnson	*The Economy under Mrs Thatcher, 1979–90* (Penguin, London, 1991).

Roger Middleton   *The British Economy since 1945* (Macmillan, Basingstoke, 2000) – broadly critical of Thatcher's 'modest' economic success in halting long-term economic decline when set against the inegalitarian consequences of Thatcherite economic policy, including and the social costs of high unemployment.

G. Stoker   *The Politics of Local Government* (2nd edn, Macmillan, London, 1991) – a very valuable introduction to the often complex – and during the Thatcher years immensely controversial – world of local government responsibility.

Alan Walters   *Britain's Economic Renaissance: Mrs. Thatcher's Reforms, 1979–84* (Oxford University Press, Oxford, 1986) – the tendentious title betrays the book's origins. Walters was a key economic adviser to Thatcher. The book is skilfully argued.

David Willetts   *Modern Conservatism* (Penguin, Harmondsworth, 1992) – a thoughtful interpretation from a Tory politician arguing, not always convincingly, the case for continuity in Conservative principles from Disraeli through to Thatcher and Major.

AUTOBIOGRAPHIES AND STUDIES BY PRACTISING AND RECENT POLITICIANS

Kenneth Baker   *The Turbulent Years* (Faber & Faber, London, 1993) – anodyne in places but useful as the memoirs of a wet who – as Chairman of the party – was one of Thatcher's most loyal Cabinet supporters at the end.

Alan Clark   *Diaries* (Phoenix, London, 1993) – Clark was not an important politician, although would have desperately liked to be one. He rates a single entry in the index of Thatcher's big book. However, he was close to many people who *were* politically important and writes about them in a wonderfully uninhibited manner. Much the best diary of the Thatcher years and one of the best of the 'political' contributions.

Ian Gilmour — *Dancing with Dogma: Britain under Thatcherism* (Simon & Schuster, London, 1992) – a graceful attack by Thatcher's ablest 'wet' opponent in Cabinet. Also brings a useful wider perspective to bear. One of very few of Thatcher's ministers (Baker, Carrington and Hurd are the others) with a well-developed historical awareness.

Roy Hattersley — *Fifty Years on: A Prejudiced History of Britain since the Second World War* (Little, Brown and Company, London, 1997) – an underused and well-written account by someone who was deputy leader of the Labour Party in the Kinnock period and who saw the Thatcher years at close hand.

Nigel Lawson — *The View from Number 11* (London, 1993) – equals Thatcher's books in length and in its penchant for self-justification; comfortably exceeds them in style and readability. Lawson was a journalist as well as a politician. The book of a strong-minded man only rarely visited by doubt.

John Major — *John Major: The Autobiography* (HarperCollins, London, 1999). Contains a number of interesting and perceptive insights, not least on the circumstances that brought about the fall. The book offers more reservations about Thatcher's leadership than her successor ever felt it appropriate to voice at the time.

James Prior — *Balance of Power* (Hamish Hamilton, London, 1986) – a reasonably frank account of the difficulties of a left-wing Conservative in a right-wing government.

Norman Tebbit — *Upwardly Mobile* (Futura, London, 1989) – a visceral right-winger who was close to the centre of power in the middle years of Thatcher's ascendancy. His view would have been more enlightening if it had been as indiscreet as Clark's.

Margaret Thatcher — *The Downing Street Years* (HarperCollins, London, 1993) – absolutely essential, not because it is a brief – or a specially good – read. Thatcher, to be blunt, is a pedestrian writer.

However, her account contains so many insights into both government and the workings of a highly political mind. Many of the insights are unintentional, which adds to the book's value.

Margaret Thatcher   *The Path to Power* (HarperCollins, London, 1995) – 'prequel' to the above and written in a very similar style. Entirely outside the chronology covered by the rest of the book, it contains a self-justificatory epilogue, which argues, rightly, that the lady's contribution made a huge difference to the world in which she operated.

Margaret Thatcher   *Statecraft* (HarperCollins, London, 2002) – a characteristically trenchant and frequently unsubtle *tour d'horizon*, replete with minatory comments on the limitations of international organisations and the necessity of *realpolitik* in international relations. Informed by substantial direct experience of world politics and, as usual with Thatcher's writings, unintentionally revealing about aspects of her character.

Index